Book A

SPANISH IS FUN

Lively Lessons for Beginners

Second Edition

Heywood Wald, PhD

Formerly of Martin Van Buren High School
New York City

AMSCO SCHOOL PUBLICATIONS, INC.
315 Hudson Street New York, N.Y. 10013

Cassettes

The cassette program comprises four two-sided cassettes. The voices are those of native speakers of Spanish from Spanish-American countries.

Each of the twenty-one lessons in the book includes the following cassette materials:

Oral exercises in four-phased sequences: cue—pause for student response—correct response by native speaker—pause for student repetition.

The narrative or playlet at normal listening speed.

Questions or completions based on the narrative or playlet in four-phased sequences.

The conversation, first at normal listening speed, then by phrases with pauses for student repetition.

The Cassettes (ordering code N 529 C), with accompanying script, are available separately from the publisher.

Photo credits

Introduction
p.1, Comstock photos: Caribbean Island / Macchu Picchu / Spain-Madrid (Alcalá Arch Gate) / Puerto Rico-El Morro

Part Opening Photos
p. 21,   PART I / Comstock Photo (Family Group)
p. 131, PART II / Comstock Photo (Wind Surfer)
p. 227, PART III / Comstock Photo (Clock)
p. 329, PART IV / The Stock Market (Thermogram)
p. 427, PART V / The Stock Market (Food)

Cultural Page Photos
p. 265, Comstock Photo / New York-Spanish Harlem
p. 284, Comstock Photo / Miami-Cuban section
p. 398, The Stock Market / Los Angeles-Olivero street
p. 497, Image Bank / El Yunque-Puerto Rico (Rain forest)
p. 515, Image Bank / Galapagos Islands-Ecuador

When ordering this book, please specify:

R 529 S *or* SPANISH IS FUN, BOOK A, 2ND ED., SOFTBOUND
or
R 529 H *or* SPANISH IS FUN, BOOK A, 2ND ED., HARDBOUND

Cover and text design by Merrill Haber.
Illustrations and electronic composition by Initial Graphic Systems, Inc.

ISBN   0-87720-140-4 (Softbound edition)
ISBN   0-87720-141-2 (Hardbound edition)

Preface

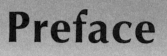

SPANISH IS FUN, BOOK A offers an introductory program that makes communication in Spanish a natural, personalized, enjoyable, and rewarding experience. The book provides all the elements for an introductory-level course.

SPANISH IS FUN, BOOK A helps students learn communicative skills through simple materials in visually focused contexts. Students can easily relate these contexts to their own experiences. Easy-to-answer questions require students to speak about their daily lives, express their opinions, and supply real information. Topic-based lessons dealing with functional situations are designed to develop proficiency in listening, speaking, reading, and writing. Cultural connections are built into the various lesson components.

This SECOND EDITION, while retaining the proven organization and successful program of the original edition, has been strengthened in several ways:

1. A new design including completely new illustrations.
2. A new introductory section acquainting students with Spain and the Spanish-speaking world. Short quizzes and suggestions for projects and activities are also included.
3. A new lesson on Spanish names and greeting expressions.
4. New vocabulary and structure exercises presented in a communicative framework, with greater emphasis on personalized communication.
5. New illustrated playlets or narratives and personalized dialogue exercises.
6. Additional games and puzzles.
7. A vocabulary list at the end of each lesson summarizes words to know and useful expressions.
8. **¿Sabías que... ?**, a new cultural section after each lesson, offers varied and fun views of the Spanish-speaking world, its people, and culture. Culture quizzes and suggested projects and activities are also provided.

9. A new, separate CUADERNO DE EJERCICIOS provides additional written practice.
10. An expanded TEACHER'S MANUAL includes Answer Keys for all exercises and two Achievement Tests.
11. A new CASSETTE program to supplement the SECOND EDITION is also available separately.

SPANISH IS FUN, BOOK A consists of five parts. Each part is followed by a **Repaso**, in which vocabulary and structure are recapitulated and practiced through a variety of **Actividades** that include games and puzzles, as well as more conventional types of exercises.

Each lesson includes a step-by-step sequence of student-directed elements designed to make the materials immediately accessible, encourage communication and self-expression, and give students the feeling that they can have fun learning Spanish.

Vocabulary

Each lesson begins with topically related sets of drawings that convey the meanings of new words in Spanish without recourse to English. This device enables students to make a direct and vivid association between the Spanish terms and their meanings. The vocabulary sets are followed by **Actividades** that also use picture stimuli to practice and review Spanish words and expressions. The vocabulary list at the end of each lesson serves to organize and summarize the new vocabulary recently acquired by the student.

To facilitate comprehension, the book uses cognates of English words wherever suitable, especially in Lesson 1, which is based entirely on Spanish words that are identical to or closely resemble their English equivalents. Beginning the course in this way shows students that Spanish is not so "foreign" after all and helps them overcome any fears that they may have about learning a foreign language.

Structures

SPANISH IS FUN, BOOK A uses a simple, straightforward presentation of new structural elements. These elements are introduced in small learning components—one at a time—and are directly followed by appropriate **Actividades**, many of them visually cued and personalized. The text guides students into making their own discoveries and formulating their own conclusions about structures. Thus, students gain a feeling of accomplishment and success.

Reading

Each lesson contains short, entertaining narratives or playlets that feature the new vocabulary and structural elements and reinforce previously learned expressions and grammar. These passages deal with topics that are related to the everyday experiences of today's student generation. Cognates and near-cognates are used extensively.

Conversation

Short situation-dialogs—sometimes practical, sometimes humorous—provide models for meaningful communication in all lessons beginning with Lesson 2. All conversations are illustrated to provide a sense of realism. They are accompanied by illustrated dialog exercises that serve as springboards for personalized conversation. The section **Vamos a conversar** allows the student to practice performing oral tasks, as required in oral-proficiency tests.

Culture

The section headed **¿Sabías que... ?** provides the student with information in English concerning the language, customs, and history of the Spanish-speaking people. Each short, lively theme is intended to pique the student's interest. The suggested activities in the "Let's Find Out More" section encourage the student to learn more about Spain and Spanish America by further investigating each topic.

TEACHER'S MANUAL WITH ANSWERS

A separate TEACHER'S MANUAL AND KEY, available from the publisher, provides suggestions for teaching all elements in SPANISH IS FUN, BOOK A, additional practice, a complete Key to all exercises and puzzles, and two Achievement Tests designed to give ALL students a sense of accomplishment. The tests use a variety of techniques through which comprehension of structure and vocabulary, as well as situation skills, may be evaluated. Teachers may use the Achievement Tests as they appear in the book or modify them to fit particular needs.

Thanks are due to the consultants, especially Wigberto Rivera and José Antonio Méndez, who reviewed a substantial part of the manuscript and made valuable suggestions.

The Author

Contents

CUARTA PARTE

QUINTA PARTE

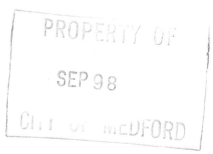

El mundo de habla hispana
A Trip Around the Spanish-Speaking World

Suppose someone offered you a free ticket that would allow you to travel to wonderful lands hundreds or even thousands of miles away. Some of these lands would be tropical islands with white, sandy beaches and swaying palm trees surrounded by crystal clear waters. Others would be mountainous lands with towering peaks reaching into the clouds, and cities so high that their climate is an eternal springtime. Still others would be modern industrial countries with factories, bustling seaports, and cities teeming with millions of people. Of course, anyone with a spirit of adventure would be overjoyed at taking such a thrilling voyage.

These countries are not fantasies; they do exist. They are in our own backyard. They are our neighbors: countries in Central and South America, the Caribbean, and our immediate neighbor to the South, Mexico.

1

THE HISPANIC WORLD

These are the countries of the Hispanic world, which, of course, also include Spain. There are nineteen Spanish-speaking countries and the Commonwealth of Puerto Rico. All together they contain a population of over 300 million people and cover approximately one sixth of the land surface of the earth. Spanish is the third most widely spoken language in the world today and one of the six official languages of the United Nations.

Some day, many of you will probably visit one or more of these places, and your trip promises to be a wonderful experience.

But why wait? Let's get a bird's-eye view right now of all the marvelous Spanish-speaking countries.

Where shall we begin? Well, what better place than where it all began: Spain, the motherland—**España, la madre patria.**

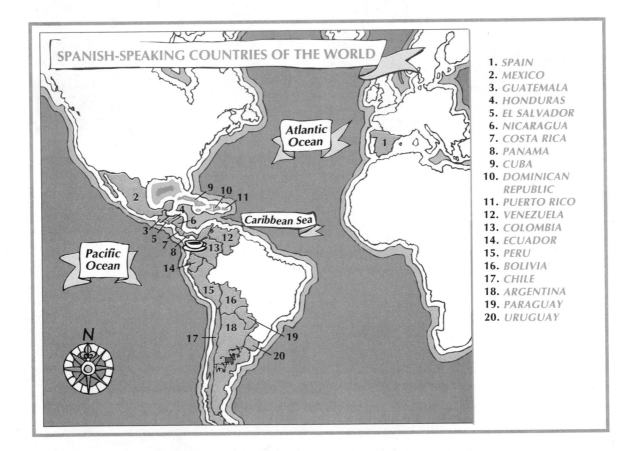

SPANISH-SPEAKING COUNTRIES OF THE WORLD

1. SPAIN
2. MEXICO
3. GUATEMALA
4. HONDURAS
5. EL SALVADOR
6. NICARAGUA
7. COSTA RICA
8. PANAMA
9. CUBA
10. DOMINICAN REPUBLIC
11. PUERTO RICO
12. VENEZUELA
13. COLOMBIA
14. ECUADOR
15. PERU
16. BOLIVIA
17. CHILE
18. ARGENTINA
19. PARAGUAY
20. URUGUAY

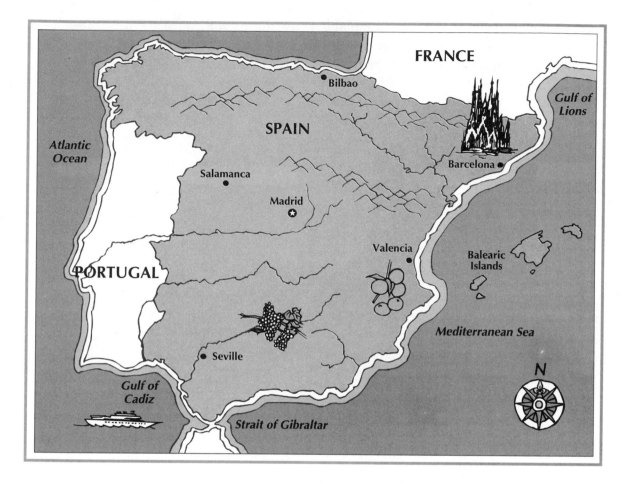

Spain

Spain has a land area of almost 200,000 square miles and is the second-largest country in Western Europe after France. Located at the very tip of the continent, it occupies, with Portugal, the Iberian Peninsula. Most of the country is surrounded by water—the Mediterranean Sea to the East and the Atlantic Ocean to the West. To the South, across the narrow Strait of Gibraltar, lies Africa, only eight miles away.

Spain is separated from France and the rest of the European continent by the mighty, snow-capped Pyrenee Mountains (**Los Pirineos**)—a range higher than the Alps.

Spain is also, after Switzerland, the most mountainous country in Europe. Its rugged mountain ranges, however, are only part of its varied landscape. Spain is a sunny land of plains and valleys, with terraces of grapevines and olive groves, quaint fishing villages, ancient walled cities, Gothic cathedrals, Roman ruins, great art treasures, and more than 1,400 medieval castles and palaces. Spain's 1,697-mile coastline contains over 2,000 beaches. To spend just one day on each of Spain's beaches would take a person six years!

No wonder Spain is the world's number one tourist attraction. About fifty million tourists—ten million more than Spain's entire population—visit Spain each year.

In addition to its own coastline, Spain's Balearic Islands in the Mediterranean Sea and the Canary Islands in the Atlantic Ocean are also great tourist spots.

It would take a volume to describe all of Spain's major cities. And so, we will concentrate on two of them: Madrid and Barcelona. Madrid, Spain's capital and largest city, is a huge metropolis of over four million people located in the exact geographic center of the country. This beautiful city, with its broad avenues, stately buildings, theaters, department stores, spacious public squares, parks and fountains, covers an area of over 300 square miles.

Barcelona, a busy port city of about two million inhabitants, is the country's richest commercial city, with the highest standard of living in Spain. Its most famous street, **Las Ramblas**—a broad pedestrian avenue lined with flower stands, bird vendors, street cafés, and book stalls—is the center of social life for the whole city. There are many other major Spanish cities: Valencia, Seville (**Sevilla**), Cordova (**Córdoba**), Granada, Málaga, Bilbao, Toledo, Segovia, Salamanca, Cádiz, Zaragosa (**Zaragoza**)—each one very Spanish and yet unique in its own way. These great urban centers, together with the tiny towns and villages, make up the fascinating country that is Spain.

Quick Quiz

1. There are _____ Spanish-speaking countries in the world.

2. The number of Spanish-speaking people is over _____ million.

3. Spanish is the _____ most-spoken language in the world.

4. The words **la madre patria** mean _____.

5. Spain shares the Iberian Peninsula with the country of _____.

6. The _____ Mountains separate Spain from the rest of Europe.

7. Spain is the world's number one country for attracting _____.

8. The _____ Islands in the Mediterranean Sea are part of Spain.

9. The capital of Spain is _____.

10. Spain's second-largest city is the seaport of _____.

Let's Find Out More

1. Make a geographical map of Spain. Indicate the major rivers, mountains, and cities.

2. Draw a map showing Spain's most famous beaches such as Costa del Sol, Costa Brava, and the like.

3. If there is a Spanish Tourist Office where you live, get materials such as brochures and posters to bring to class.

4. Find out more about the Spanish tourist industry—its size and its importance, the reasons of its success, and so on.

THE SPANISH HERITAGE

The Spaniards are descended from many peoples. These peoples conquered and lived in Spain, contributing to its traditions and customs. For over 3,000 years, Spain was invaded by the Phoenicians, the Carthaginians, the Romans, various Germanic tribes, and finally the Moors of North Africa. After the Spaniards reconquered Spain from the Moors in 1492, Christopher Columbus, sailing in Spanish ships, arrived in America and claimed it for Spain. Spanish explorers and troops extended the Spanish language throughout the world—Vasco Núñez de Balboa to the Pacific Ocean, Juan Ponce de León to Puerto

Rico and Florida, Francisco Pizarro to Peru, Hernán Cortés to Mexico. Spain created one of the greatest empires in history and was called "the mistress of the world and the queen of the ocean."

Spain's language and culture were spread throughout a large part of the New World. Today, after more than 500 years, the Spanish Empire is no more. In its place are independent countries. And within them lives the heritage of Spain.

Let's now recross the Atlantic Ocean, returning to the New World to revisit these Spanish-speaking lands.

The Islands of the Caribbean

The Caribbean Sea is a vast area of the Atlantic Ocean, 1,700 miles from west to east and between 500 to 800 miles from north to south. It contains hundreds of islands large and small. The largest of the islands are called the Greater Antilles. Three of them are Spanish-speaking: Cuba, the Dominican Republic, and Puerto Rico. Cuba, with an area of 44,218 square miles, is the largest of the Greater Antilles. It lies about ninety-miles south of Key West, Florida. Called "the pearl of the Antilles," Cuba has a population of eleven million, of which two million reside in the capital city of Havana (**La Habana**).

The Dominican Republic (**República Dominicana**) is the oldest nation in the Caribbean. It's located on the island of Hispaniola, which it shares with the French-speaking Republic of Haiti. The Dominican Republic has an area of 18,704 square miles and contains the highest mountains in the Caribbean, rising more than 10,000 feet. In the capital city of Santo Domingo is the oldest university in the New World: the University of Santo Domingo, founded in 1538.

Puerto Rico, called "the enchanted isle" (**La isla del encanto**), is one hundred miles long and thirty-five miles wide (an area of 3,492 square miles). This island—2 hours by airplane from Miami and $3\frac{1}{2}$ hours from New York—has become America's vacation paradise. Puerto Rico is a blend of the old and the new, with centuries-old Spanish fortresses and modern, glamorous resort hotels. Puerto Rico is neither an independent country nor a state; it's a commonwealth, a self-governing part of the United States. Puerto Ricans were granted U.S. citizenship in 1917.

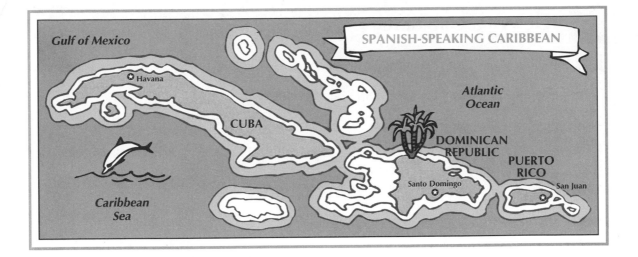

Quick Quiz

1. The Spanish explorer Balboa discovered the _____ Ocean.

2. The Caribbean Sea is an area of the _____ Ocean.

3. The Greater Antilles are a group of _____.

4. The largest island in the Caribbean Sea is _____.

5. Cuba is only _____ miles from the United States.

6. The two countries that share the island of Hispaniola are _____ and

   _____.

7. The capital of the Dominican Republic is _____.

8. Puerto Rico is a _____ of the United States.

9. The people of Puerto Rico are citizens of _____.

10. The island of Puerto Rico is _____ miles long.

Let's Find Out More

1. Who were the original inhabitants of the Caribbean islands?

2. What is the racial background of the people today?

3. When were people of African descent introduced to the New World?

4. Research and discuss the influence of African culture in the Spanish-speaking countries of the Caribbean. Focus on their music, customs, food, and so forth.

Mexico

Next, we travel across the blue-green waters of the Caribbean to the United States of Mexico (**Estados Unidos Mexicanos**), a land of beauty and excitement. With an area of over 750,000 square miles, Mexico is the second largest Spanish-speaking country in the world. Separated from the United States of America by the Rio Grande (**Río Bravo**), Mexico is a land of towering mountain ranges, broad plateaus, dry deserts, and tropical jungles. Mountains cover two thirds of the country. (Twenty-two of Mexico's mountain peaks are more than two miles high!)

You can see modern cities, snow-capped volcanoes, and beautiful beaches with over 6,000 miles of coastline on three different seas. No other country in the world offers such a variety of beaches and resorts. The beach resorts of Acapulco and Puerto Vallarta on the Pacific Ocean and Cancún and Cozumel on the Caribbean Sea are tourist playgrounds of worldwide fame.

Mexico is the land of the ancient Maya and Aztec civilizations. Today, the very ancient and the very modern exist side by side. You can see the temples and pyramids of civilizations long gone, along with ultramodern skyscrapers, elegant hotels, and magnificent restaurants. Indians dressed in traditional costumes walk past shop windows displaying the latest European fashions.

The capital of Mexico, Mexico City (**el Distrito Federal**), is the largest city in the world, with a growing population of over twenty million people. Built on the site of an ancient Aztec city, Mexico City is 7,800 feet above sea level, making it the highest major city in the world.

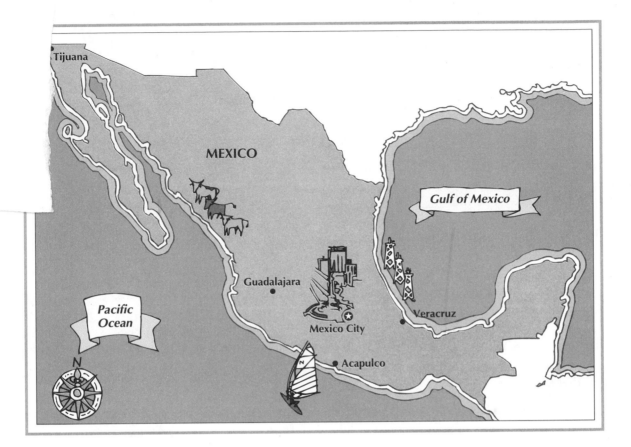

There are many other important Mexican cities, including Guadalajara, the country's second-largest; Veracruz, one of Mexico's main ports; Cuernavaca, the city of eternal springtime; and Taxco, with its many silver shops.

Quick Quiz

1. Mexico is the _____ largest Spanish-speaking country in land area.

2. The _____ separates Mexico from the United States.

3. Mexico has over 6,000 miles of _____.

4. Acapulco and Cancún are resorts famous for their _____.

5. Two ancient civilizations of Mexico are the _____ and the

    _____.

   ᵕdences of ancient civilizations are the temples and the _____.

      ₚital of Mexico is _____.

   ᵕ. Mexico City has a population of over _____ people.

9. Mexico City is the _____ city in the world.

10. Mexico's second-largest city is _____.

Let's Find Out More

1. Find out what are some of the problems of a major metropolitan area such as Mexico City and how these problems compare to the ones existing in the city where you live. Propose some solutions.

2. Find out about Mexican artists and muralists, such as Diego Rivera, José Clemente Orozco, and David Alfaro Siqueiros. Discuss how their works help explain Mexican history.

3. A large percentage of Mexicans are **mestizos**. Explain what that word means.

Central America

Now it's time to proceed south into the Spanish-speaking countries of Central America—the narrow bridge of land that connects the continents of North and South America. Central America covers an area of over 200,000 square miles (about the size of Texas), ranging in width from 30 to 300 miles and stretching more than 1,100 miles between Mexico and Colombia, with a combined Pacific Ocean and Caribbean Sea coastline of 3,465 miles.

Central America contains six Spanish-speaking countries: Guatemala, Honduras, El Salvador, Nicaragua, Costa Rica, and Panama (**Panamá**). Guatemala has the largest population and Nicaragua has the largest land area. The Panama Canal connects the Atlantic and Pacific Oceans. All but the largest ships can pass through its locks and waterways.

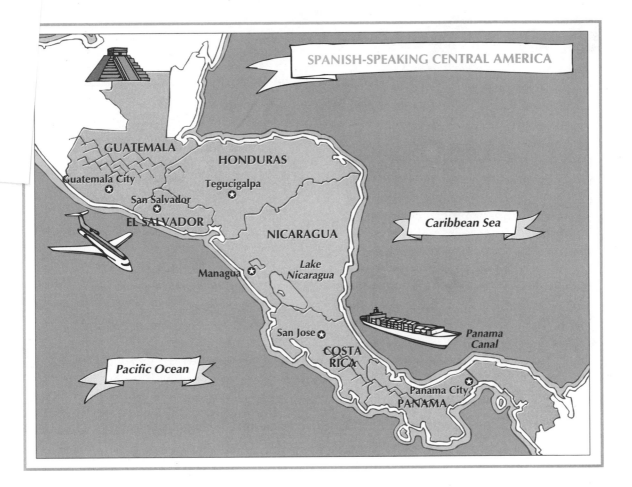

Central America consists of a wide range of environments. Jungles on the Caribbean coast slope upward to towering mountains in the central highlands. Small rivers and lakes dot the landscape, including the largest lake in Central America, Lake Nicaragua, covering an area of 3,000 square miles. (It even has fresh-water sharks.) Nearly all of Central America's twenty million people have Indian, Spanish, or mixed Indian and Spanish ancestry.

Central America was the home of the Mayas, one of the earliest and most advanced civilizations of the New World. They built large cities, temples, pyramids, and other major structures and acquired considerable knowledge of astronomy, mathematics, and farming.

Today, the countries of Central America produce much of the world's coffee, bananas, cocoa, rubber, coconuts, and chicle (the main ingredient in chewing gum).

Quick Quiz

1. Central America is a narrow land bridge connecting _____

   and _____.

2. Central America is more than _____ miles long.

3. There are _____ Spanish-speaking countries in Central America.

4. The Central-American country with the largest population is _____.

5. The Central-American country with the largest land area is _____.

6. The country with a canal connecting the Atlantic and Pacific Oceans is _____.

7. Many of the people in Central America have mixed _____

   and _____ ancestry.

8. Central America was the home of the _____ Indians.

9. Three important products coming from Central America are _____,

   _____, and _____.

10. **Chicle** is the main ingredient in _____.

Let's Find Out More

1. Research the history of the Panama Canal. Make a model of the canal and explain its importance to the United States and to the world.

2. Find out more about the Mayas. Name some of their accomplishments. Mention the modern countries whose territories made up the Mayan empire originally.

South America

Now it's time to finish our journey. We're going to South America. The world's fourth-largest continent, South America covers an area of approximately seven million square miles—almost twice as large as the United States and about one eighth of the world's land surface. Except where it

...rica by a narrow strip of land—the Isthmus of
...a is surrounded by water.

...etches from the warm tropical waters of the Caribbean
...to the icy waters near the Antarctic Circle, where the
...fic Oceans join.

...e a backbone through the continent—from the Caribbean to
...nmost tip of land at Cape Horn—are the high, cold Andes
...as. They form the longest mountain range in the world, and only
the Himalaya Mountains in Asia are higher. More than 4,000 miles long
and sometimes 500 miles wide, the Andes Mountains have thirty-two
peaks over 20,000 feet (more than $3\frac{1}{2}$ miles high).

South America contains nine Spanish-speaking countries: Argentina,
Bolivia, Colombia, Chile, Ecuador, Paraguay, Peru (**Perú**), Uruguay, and
Venezuela. The largest among them is Argentina, with over one million
square miles of territory. On the vast grasslands, known as **pampas**, where
the cowboys (**gauchos**) ride, there are many cattle ranches larger than one
hundred thousand acres, while some sheep ranches cover more than one
million acres!

Argentina's capital, Buenos Aires, with ten million residents, has the
second-largest population in South America. A modern sophisticated
metropolis with wide boulevards—the largest one, the Ninth of July
Avenue, is one city block wide—lined with elegant shops, theaters, and
restaurants, Buenos Aires is known as "the Paris of the Americas."

Argentina's neighbor to the west, Chile, is one of the strangest-shaped
countries in the world. Long and skinny like a chile pepper, it's almost
3,000 miles long but in some places less than 50 miles wide. Chile extends
from the blazing-hot Atacama Desert in the north, one of the driest spots in
the world—in some areas no rainfall has ever been recorded!—to the freez-
ing waters of the Antarctic. With its spotlessly clean cities, sparkling mountain lakes, and world-famous ski areas, Chile is often compared to
Switzerland.

To the east of Argentina, separated by a river called **Río de la Plata**, is
South America's smallest Spanish-speaking country, Uruguay. Although
not as large as its neighbors, Uruguay enjoys one of the highest living and
educational standards in the continent. Its rolling pasture lands support a

flourishing sheep and cattle industry. The beautiful capital of Montevideo has some of South America's most popular beaches. Uruguay's most elegant beach resort, **Punta del Este,** is often called "the Riviera of South America."

Venezuela and Colombia are the two northernmost countries of South America. Venezuela is one of the major producers of oil in the world. Forty percent of its land is rain forest. Venezuela's capital, Caracas, is a prosperous and dynamic metropolis with the highest standard of living of any Spanish American city.

West of Venezuela is the neighboring country of Colombia—the second-largest coffee producer in the world and a major source of emeralds. Colombia's capital, **Bogotá**, is located at an altitude of more than $1\frac{1}{2}$ miles above sea level; consequently, the city has a pleasant climate throughout the year, despite its close location to the Equator. The Spanish spoken in Colombia is said to be the purest in Spanish America.

South of Colombia is the country of Ecuador. In Spanish, **ecuador** means equator, the imaginary line that divides the earth in two hemispheres and runs right through the country of Ecuador. Belonging to Ecuador are the famous Galápagos Islands, a nature reserve containing unique animal life, such as huge turtles (**galápagos**) weighing more than a quarter of a ton, and giant lizards called **iguanas**, which can grow up to four feet long!

South of Ecuador is Peru (**Perú**), the land of the ancient Incas. The capital of Peru, Lima, is called "the city of kings" and is one of the most modern cities in South America. The shining jewel of Peru is Macchu Picchu, known as "the lost city of the Incas." Hidden within the Andes Mountains is a remarkably preserved ancient Inca city. To get there on foot, many people take the "Inca Trail," a three-to five-day trip!

Bolivia and Paraguay are the only two countries of South America without sea coasts. La Paz, Bolivia's capital, is the highest capital city in the world, located more than $2\frac{1}{2}$ miles above sea level. Although it has no access to the ocean, it borders Lake Titicaca, the highest navigable lake in the world. On this huge 3,500-square-mile inland sea—180 miles long and 50 miles wide—modern speedboats share the waters with Indian rafts made of reeds. Sleek hydrofoils carry passengers across the deep blue waters to the shores of neighboring Peru.

Paraguay is the other nation without a sea coast. Many Paraguayans are Guarani Indians. Since both Spanish and Guarani are the official languages of the country, most Paraguayans are bilingual. Ninety-five percent of the population is mestizo.

We have finished our journey. Now, it's time to return home.

Quick Quiz

1. Running through the continent of South America is the longest mountain range in the world, the _____ Mountains.

2. The largest Spanish-speaking country is _____. Its capital is _____.

3. The longest and skinniest country in South America is _____.

4. Montevideo is the capital of South America's smallest Spanish-speaking country, _____.

5. Caracas is the capital of _____, one of the world's major oil producer.

6. The capital of Colombia is _____.

7. The Spanish word for equator gives _____ its name.

8. The land of the ancient Incas is the modern day country of _____.

9. La Paz, the highest capital city in the world, is the capital of _____.

10. The two South-American countries without a coast are _____ and _____.

Let's Find Out More

1. Study the history of Argentina. Who are the gauchos? Discuss their customs and practices. Compare them to the cowboys of our country. Discuss the "pampas" and their importance to cattle raising. Read about modern Argentina. Can you name a popular dance from Argentina?

2. What is Venezuela's most important export? Why is it important to the United States?

3. Find out more about the great civilizations that existed before Columbus's arrival. For example, what was the Inca Empire and where was it located?

SPAIN COMES TO THE NEW WORLD

Even as we return to the United States of America, we never really leave the Spanish-speaking world completely. The United States today has the fifth largest Spanish-speaking population in the world, after Mexico, Spain, Colombia, and Argentina.

There are more than twenty-five million Americans of Hispanic origin in the United States—one out of every ten inhabitants of the country. The majority of the Hispanic population consists of Mexican Americans, Puerto Ricans, and Cuban Americans.

Today there are almost as many Puerto Ricans on the mainland of the United States as there are on the entire island of Puerto Rico. There are about three quarters of a million Cubans in Miami, Florida—half the total population of the city. Almost two million Mexican Americans live in Los Angeles, making it the city with the second-largest Mexican population in the world after Mexico City.

Large parts of our country were settled by Spanish-speaking people a century before the arrival of the Pilgrims, the first English-speaking settlers to come to the New World. St. Augustine, Florida, for example, was founded by the Spaniards in 1565.

The states of Texas, New Mexico, Arizona, California and Colorado, as well as parts of Utah and Nevada were originally Mexican territory and part of the Spanish Empire. Spaniards explored and settled in these southwestern territories before there was a country called the United States. Even after Mexico became independent, these lands remained part of that country.

Many of the people living there today are descendants of these early Spaniards and Mexicans.

What's the name of the town or city in which you live? Did you ever wonder where it got its name? Many of our states and cities, particularly those in the southwestern part of the United States have the Spanish names that the early Spanish explorers gave them. Many of them begin with San or Santa (Saint, Holy). A look at the following map shows how much our country is part of the Spanish world.

SPANISH	ENGLISH	SPANISH	ENGLISH
Amarillo	Yellow	Montana	Mountain
Boca Raton	Mouse Mouth	Nevada	Snowy
Colorado	Red	San Antonio	Saint Anthony
El Paso	The Pass	San Diego	Saint James
Florida	Flowery	San Francisco	Saint Francis
Las Vegas	The Plains, Flatlands	Santa Barbara	Saint Barbara
Los Alamos	The Poplar Trees	Santa Cruz	Holy Cross
Los Angeles	The Angels	Santa Fe	Holy Faith

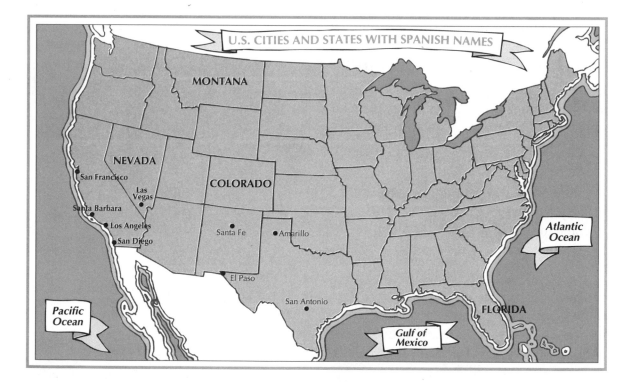

Spain's influence can also be seen in the many words that have come into the English language. The American cowboy of the Southwest borrowed many terms from his Mexican neighbors. Some terms were incorporated into English without any change.

burro	fiesta	rodeo
chocolate	mesa	sierra
corral	patio	vista
coyote	plaza	

Others (sometimes with Indian origins) had only slight spelling changes.

SPANISH	ENGLISH	SPANISH	ENGLISH
cañón	canyon	patata	potato
cucaracha	cockroach	rancho	ranch
desesperado	desperado	¿sabe?	savvy?
huracán	hurricane	tomate	tomato
lazo	lasso	vamos	vamoose

Quick Quiz

1. There are approximately _____ million Americans of Hispanic origin in the U.S.

2. One out of every _____ Americans is of Hispanic origin.

3. Cuban-Americans make up half the total population of the city of _____.

4. The American city with the second-largest Mexican population in the world is

   _____.

5. One hundred years before the arrival of the Pilgrims, Spaniards settled the city of

   _____, Florida.

6. Texas and California were originally part of _____.

7. Three American cities beginning with San or Santa are _____,

   _____, _____.

8. **Amarillo** is the color _____ in Spanish; _____ is the color red.

9. Three Spanish words incorporated into English are _____,

   _____, and _____.

10. The cowboy words *vamoose* and *savvy* come from Spanish _____

    and _____.

Let's Find Out More

1. Look at a map of the United States. Examine closely the Southwest and Florida. Pick out the Spanish place-names and find out what they mean in English. Indicate on the map the areas with the greatest concentrations of Spanish-speaking people.

2. Look for other Spanish words that come from Indian languages, like **chocolate, tomate, huracán, canoa**, and so forth.

3. Look for other foreign words and phrases found in the English language.

PRIMERA
Parte

Tu primera lección

Pronunciation of Vowels (**a, e, i, o, u**);
Words that Are the Same or Similar
in Spanish and English;
How to Say *the* in Spanish

We have just taken a trip through the Spanish-speaking countries. If you really want to communicate with the people, you will have to learn Spanish. But don't worry! Learning Spanish won't be hard at all. In fact, you're going to have a terrific time doing it, and this book will help you along. As you go through the lessons and learn the new material, you will soon be able to use common expressions, recognize the names of different foods, ask for directions, use numbers, tell time, give and receive information, go shopping, and, in general, get along in Spanish.

Each lesson contains lots of useful words and loads of activities that are different, exciting, and fun. There are hundreds of colorful pictures that will help you think in Spanish without having to go back to English.

Well, what are we waiting for? Let's begin! First, we have to learn some basic pronunciation. Some of the most important sounds of the Spanish language are the sounds of its vowels (**a, e, i, o, u**).

Repeat these sounds after your teacher. Practice them by always saying them the same way each time. Let's begin with the Spanish vowel **a**.

Dígalo bien

■ In Spanish, the letter **a** is pronounced like *ah*, as when the doctor tells you to say *auah*.

¡caramba!	**dama**	**papá**
cama	**mamá**	**pasta**
Carlos	**nacho**	**patata**
casa	**Pablo**	**San Juan**

*A*na, p*a*sa la ban*a*na.
H*a*sta m*a*ñana, Ju*a*na.
¿Qué t*a*l, P*a*co? D*a*me un t*a*co.

■ The letter **e** is pronounced like *e* in *café* or *Diego*.

bueno	**mesa**	**presente**
cero	**¡Olé!**	**¡Qué pena!**
Eva	**papel**	**tarde**
leche	**peseta**	**Teresa**

Jos*é*, ¿hay caf*é*? No s*é*.
¿Y *e*l qu*e*so? Tr*e*s p*e*sos.

■ The letter **i** is pronounced like *i* in *machine* or *Rita*. (The letter **y** is pronounced like **i** when it appears at the end of a word or alone.)

ch*i*le	**Mar*í*a**	**r*i*co**
ha*y*	**med*i*c*i*na**	**señor*i*ta**
L*i*ma	**n*i*ño**	**s*í***
L*i*sa	**p*i*pa**	**y**

An*i*ta es una ch*i*ca bon*i*ta de Costa R*i*ca.
El poll*i*to d*i*ce p*í*o, p*í*o, p*í*o.

■ The letter **o** is pronounced like *o* in *roll*.

coca cola	gota	ropa
coco	hotel	tonto
costa	Lola	tostada
foto	nota	voto

Hola, Manolo. ¿Estás solo? No.
¿Estás loco? Un poco.

■ The letter **u** is pronounced like *u* in *Rudolph* or *ruler*.

cura	lunes	puro
fruta	octubre	ruso
julio	Perú	tú
junio	pregunta	Uruguay

Hay mucha luz en Veracruz.
¿Le gusta la música de Cuba?

2 LET'S SPEAK SPANISH! There are many words that are written the same way in Spanish and in English. Try to pronounce them in Spanish. Repeat after your teacher.

el actor	el doctor	popular
el animal	el general	el taxi
el auto	el hospital	terrible
el cereal	el hotel	la televisión
el chocolate	horrible	tropical
el color	el piano	

Some Spanish words look just a little different from English. Repeat them after your teacher.

americano	la familia	inteligente
el apartamento	famoso	la medicina
el barbero	fantástico	la música
la bicicleta	la fruta	rápido
el calendario	importante	la rosa
el diccionario	el insecto	

Other Spanish words are different from English, but they can still be recognized. Try to figure out their meaning as you repeat them after your teacher.

el aeropuerto	**el estudiante**	**la lámpara**
el banco	**la fiesta**	**el parque**
el café	**la flor**	**el teatro**
el cine	**el gigante**	**el tren**

Finally, there are Spanish words that do not look at all like English. Try to figure out what they mean by using the pictures.

el hombre   **la mujer**   **el padre**

la madre   **el niño**   **la niña**

el amigo

la amiga

la señorita

el gato

el perro

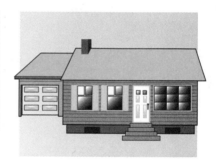

la casa

la puerta

la ventana

la escuela

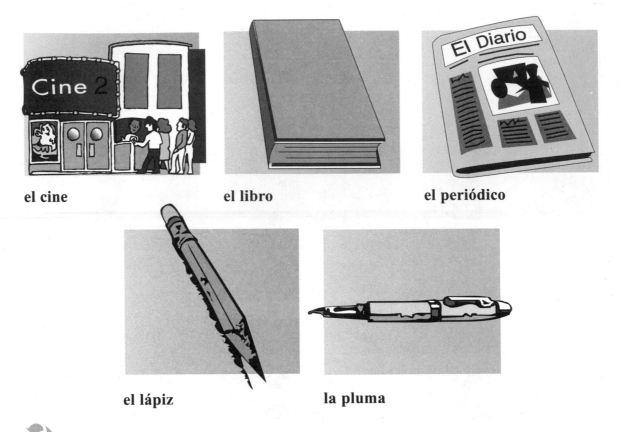

el cine

el libro

el periódico

el lápiz

la pluma

Let's look at another difference between Spanish and English. Did you notice the words **el** and **la** before all of the nouns? These two words are Spanish for "the." That's right. Spanish has two words for "the" in the singular: **el** and **la**. The word **el** is used before masculine nouns and **la** is used before feminine nouns.

How do we know which words are masculine and which are feminine? With some words, it's easy. Obviously, **madre** (mother), **niña** (girl), and **mujer** (woman) are feminine, while **padre** (father), **niño** (boy), and **hombre** (man) are masculine. But why is **cine** masculine and **lámpara** feminine? There really is no logical reason. So, the easiest way to learn Spanish vocabulary is to memorize the noun together with its corresponding word for "the." You don't memorize **fruta**, for instance, but **la fruta**, not **piano**, but **el piano**.

Here's a helpful hint: most nouns ending in **-o** are masculine (**el piano, el libro, el disco**), and those ending in **-a** are generally feminine (**la sopa, la gasolina, la fiesta**). With nouns ending in other letters, just memorize the article (the word for "the") along with the word: **el cine, la clase**, and so on.

Actividad

A
_____

Couple each word below with a related word from the following list.

EXAMPLE: el padre y la madre

el amigo   el lápiz   el perro
la escuela   la madre   el piano
el hombre   la niña   la ventana

1. la música _____   **2.** la puerta _____

3. el niño _____   **4.** la amiga _____

5. la mujer _____   **6.** el estudiante _____

7. la pluma _____   **8.** el gato _____

Now that you have learned some Spanish words and grammar, try to figure out the meaning of these ten sentences. Repeat them aloud after your teacher.

1. El hotel es moderno.

2. La doctora es importante.

3. El presidente es popular.

4. El actor es famoso.

5. La fruta es tropical.

6. El dragón es horrible.

**7. El chocolate es
delicioso.**

**8. La televisión es
interesante.**

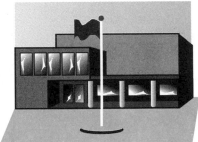

**9. La escuela es
necesaria.**

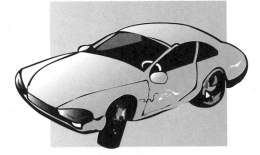

10. El auto es americano.

Actividad

B

Miss López made some Spanish flash cards for her class, but someone mixed them up. Help her by matching the following labels with the correct pictures.

el barbero	la escuela	el insecto
la bicicleta	el gato	el periódico
el cine	el hotel	la rosa
el dragón		

1. _____

2. _____

3. _____

4. _____

5. _____

6. _____

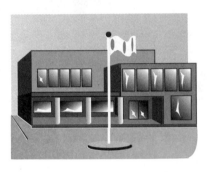

7. _____

8. _____

9. _____

10. _____

Actividad

Your assignment is to make a picture dictionary of basic vocabulary. Label the following pictures. Make sure to use **el** or **la**.

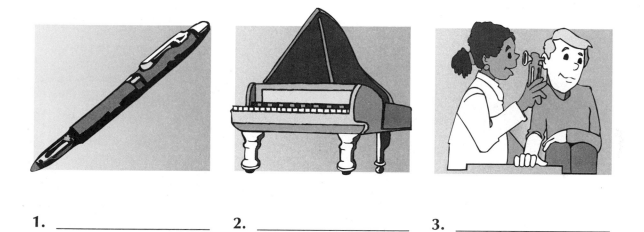

1. _____ 2. _____ 3. _____

4. _____ 5. _____ 6. _____

7. _____

8. _____

9. _____

10. _____

11. _____

12. _____

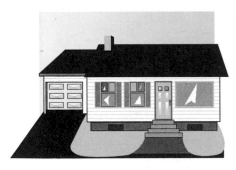

13. _____

14. _____

15. _____

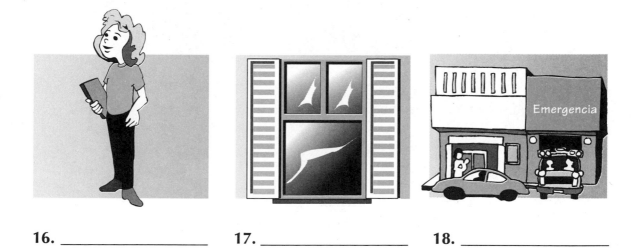

16. _____ 17. _____ 18. _____

Actividad

D

Work with a partner. Take turns reading words from the following list and repeating them with the correct article (**el** or **la**). Then write the correct article in the space provided.

1. _____ fiesta   2. _____ tren

3. _____ gasolina   4. _____ animal

5. _____ mosquito   6. _____ mujer

7. _____ hombre   8. _____ niña

9. _____ profesora   10. _____ puerta

11. _____ madre   12. _____ niño

13. _____ profesor   14. _____ clase

15. _____ padre   16. _____ aeropuerto

Actividad

Complete the following sentences, using a word from the list that follows. Note that some words may be used in more than one sentence.

EXAMPLE: **El hotel es famoso.**

americano	inteligente	rápido
delicioso	moderno	terrible
famoso	natural	tropical
importante	popular	

1. El hombre es _____.

2. La flor es _____.

3. El tigre es _____.

4. El café es _____.

5. El auto es _____.

6. El actor es _____.

7. La fruta es _____.

8. El tren es _____.

9. El teléfono es _____.

10. El presidente es _____.

Actividad

F

The school newspaper is running an opinion poll. Say if you agree with the following statements. If the statement is true, write **Sí**. If it's false, write **No**. (Remember—opinions may differ!)

1. El mosquito es popular.   _____

2. La televisión es interesante.   _____

3. La profesora es inteligente.   _____

4. El doctor es necesario.   _____

5. El automóvil es rápido.   _____

Actividad

G

Ms. McCarthy put a vocabulary test on the board, but someone erased all the nouns. Can you complete each sentence with an appropriate noun?

```
1. La          es interesante.
2. El          es romántico.
3. La          es importante.
4. El          es rápido.
5. La          es inteligente.
6. El          es necesario.
7. La          es famosa.
8. El          es moderno.
```

Información personal

You know enough Spanish now to tell the class a little about yourself. Here's a list of words. Pick out all the words that you would use to describe yourself and include them in the sentence **Yo soy...** (I am . . .) Be careful! Your classmates will show whether they agree with you or not by saying **Sí** or **No**.

musical	interesante
horrible	natural
importante	popular
imposible	terrible
inteligente	ignorante

Yo soy _____

_____

Comunicación

Make a list of four things or people you might find in the park. Make sure to use **el** and **la** correctly.

1. _____   2. _____

3. _____   4. _____

OCTOBER 12: *Día de la Raza*

Día de la Raza? Isn't October 12 Columbus Day? Every American student knows that on October 12, 1492, Christopher Columbus and his three ships, the *Santa María*, the *Pinta*, and the *Niña*, landed on the shores of a land until then unknown to the rest of the world. On the first encounter with the native inhabitants, whom he called "Indians," there was a meeting of the races.

Columbus' journey opened the door to a new world where advanced and thriving civilizations lived. Among them were the Aztecs in North America, the Mayas in Central America, and the Incas in South America. The Mayas possessed extraordinary knowledge of mathematics, science, and architecture. They had developed a writing system and a calendar more accurate and sophisticated than any other used in Europe at the time. The Aztecs and the Incas were outstanding astronomers, architects, and craftsmen.

Columbus and the other explorers who followed changed the course of history and set forth the formation of Spanish America. These countries became a cultural and ethnic mix made of the several groups of native inhabitants, the Spanish colonists, the descendants of Africans, and other immigrants for all over the world.

Spanish Americans living in the United States number approximately twenty-five million, almost ten percent of the total population. In general, they tend to live in large urban centers such as New York, Los Angeles, Chicago, Boston, and Miami. Whether they call themselves **hispanos**, **latinos**, **hispanoamericanos**, or Hispanics, they are a varied group: sixty percent are of Mexican heritage, twelve percent are of Puerto Rican heritage, and five percent are of Cuban heritage. Recently, the fastest growing Spanish-American group comes from Central America (El Salvador, Nicaragua, and Guatemala).

Today almost everyone living in a big city in the United States has learned a word or two of Spanish, has heard some Latin rhythms and melodies, or has tasted Spanish or Spanish-American food. Even without going abroad, one can expand one's horizons and enrich one's culture.

And that brings us back to October 12. In Spain, it's called **Día de la Hispanidad**, and in most of Spanish America, **Día de la Raza**. It celebrates cultural, ethnic, and racial diversity but also recognizes the common heritage that unites Hispanic people everywhere.

Quick Quiz

1. Spanish Americans in the United States number about _____ percent of the population.

2. The largest number of Spanish Americans in the United States is of _____ heritage.

3. The _____ were one of the highly advanced civilizations living in the New World before the arrival of Columbus.

4. The three major races that make up the Spanish-American component of our society are

   _____.

5. _____ is the Hispanic holiday that celebrates cultural, ethnic, and racial diversity.

Let's Find Out More

1. Find out how Spanish Americans celebrate **El Día de la Raza** different countries.

2. Draw a map of the neighborhood, town or city where you live, and highlight the areas that have a considerable Spanish-speaking population.

3. Find out what are some of the greatest contributions of Spanish Americans to the culture of the United States. Focus on areas such as music, art, and food.

4. Go to the library and study more about the Aztecs, the Mayas or the Incas. Write an essay discussing their origins, culture, and achievements.

Vocabulario

WORDS TO KNOW

la amiga *(female) friend*
el amigo *(male) friend*
la bicicleta *bicycle*
el café *coffee, cafe*
la casa *house*
el cine *movies, movie theater*
la clase *class*
la escuela *school*
el gato *cat*
el hombre *man*
el lápiz *pencil*
el libro *book*
la madre *mother*

la mujer *woman*
la niña *girl*
el niño *boy*
el padre *father*
el parque *park*
el periódico *newspaper*
el perro *dog*
la pluma *pen*
el profesor *(male) teacher*
la profesora *(female) teacher*
la señorita *young lady*
el tren *train*

EXPRESSIONS

es *is*   **de** *of*   **y** *and*

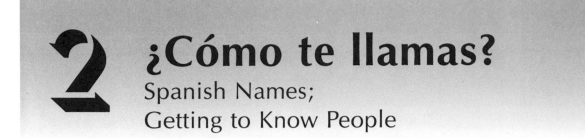

2 ¿Cómo te llamas?

Spanish Names;
Getting to Know People

Now that you have a better idea of what the Spanish language is like, we can learn some common expressions that people use every day like "Hello, what's your name?," "How are you?," "I'm fine," "So long," "See you later," and so on.

When people meet each other, the first thing they usually mention is their name. Here is a list of common Spanish names for girls, followed by a list of common Spanish names for boys. Try to find your name on the list. You will notice that many English names have no exact Spanish equivalents (for example: Gary or Brian), and that some Spanish names have no exact English equivalent. If your name is not on the lists, feel free to "adopt" a Spanish name for yourself and use it in your Spanish class.

Alicia	Estrella
Ana	Francisca
Bárbara	Graciela
Beatriz	Inés
Blanca	Isabel
Carolina	Josefina
Catalina	Juana
Cecilia	Lucía
Clara	Luisa
Cristina	Luz
Diana	Marta
Dolores	Margarita
Elena	María
Elisa	Rosa

Alejandro	Jaime
Andrés	Jorge
Antonio	José
Arturo	Juan
Carlos	Luis
Cristóbal	Marcos
Domingo	Mateo
Eduardo	Miguel
Enrique	Nicolás
Esteban	Pablo
Felipe	Patricio
Francisco	Pedro
Geraldo	Rafael
Guillermo	Roberto

Actividad

Mr. Levine has just met his new class. They all have English first names. Can you help him pick out an equivalent Spanish name for each of his students? Write the names in the space provided.

1. Joan _____

2. Charles _____

3. Ralph _____

4. Catherine _____

5. Stephen _____

6. Anthony _____

7. Joseph _____

8. Elizabeth _____

9. Helen _____

10. James _____

11. Paul _____   **12.** William _____

13. Lucy _____   **14.** Michael _____

Actividad

B

Your homeroom teacher has just received a list of new students. Can you help her determine which names are boy's and which ones are girls'? Write each name in the appropriate column.

NEW STUDENT	MUCHACHAS	MUCHACHOS
1. Luz	_____	_____
2. Sara	_____	_____
3. Lucía	_____	_____
4. Felipe	_____	_____
5. Miguel	_____	_____
6. Jaime	_____	_____
7. Patricio	_____	_____
8. Joaquín	_____	_____

NEW STUDENT	MUCHACHAS	MUCHACHOS
9. Josefina	_____	_____
10. Antonia	_____	_____
11. Luis	_____	_____
12. Dolores	_____	_____
13. Inés	_____	_____
14. Andrés	_____	_____

Dígalo bien

■ In Spanish, the double **l** (**ll**) is pronounced much like *y* in *yes* or *j* in *jet*.

amari*ll*o	ga*ll*o	pae*ll*a
caba*ll*o	*ll*amo	po*ll*o
ca*ll*e	*ll*over	si*ll*a
e*ll*a	mi*ll*ón	torti*ll*a

La si*ll*a amari*ll*a es de Sevi*ll*a.
Me *ll*amo Estre*ll*a.
El po*ll*o amari*ll*o se *ll*ama Gui*ll*ermo.

2

Now let's get into some real conversation in Spanish! In the following situation, two young people get to know each other.

Use these common Spanish expressions when meeting people.

Buenos días. *Good morning.*

¡Hola! *Hi!*

¿Cómo te llamas? *What's your name?*

Me llamo... *My name is . . .*

¿Y tú? *And you?*

Mucho gusto. *It's a pleasure (to meet you).*

Adiós. *Good-bye.*

Hasta mañana. *See you tomorrow.*

¿Comó se llama? *What's his (her) name?*

el muchacho *boy*

él *he*

la muchacha *girl*

ella *she*

Actividad

C
_____

You're now ready to start meeting people in Spanish. Pretend you are in a new class and you want to make friends with your fellow students. Choose a classmate. Say good morning in Spanish and introduce yourself using your Spanish name. Ask your classmate her (his) name. After saying how nice it is to meet her (him), say good-bye and repeat the exercise with other classmates.

Actividad

D
_____

While you're working in the principal's office, a group of new students is waiting to be admitted to school. Can you identify them by looking at their photos?

Luis
Jorge
Maribel
Ana
Luz
Pepe
Principal's Office

1. ¿Cómo se llama la muchacha?

2. ¿Cómo se llama ella?

3. ¿Cómo se llama el muchacho?

4. ¿Cómo se llama él?

5. ¿Cómo se llama ella?

6. ¿Cómo se llama él?

Study the following conversation. It contains a few more expressions that you can use to build up your vocabulary.

CARLOS: **Hola, Clara. ¿Cómo estás?**

CLARA: **Muy bien, gracias. ¿Y tú, Carlos?**

CARLOS: **Bien, gracias. ¿Adónde vas?**

CLARA: **Voy a la escuela. ¿Y tú?**

CARLOS: **Voy a casa. Adiós, Clara. Hasta mañana.**

CLARA: **Hasta la vista, Carlos.**

Here are some more expressions you may use when meeting people.

Hola. *Hello. (Hi.)*

¿Cómo estás? *How are you?*

Muy bien. *Very well.*

Gracias. *Thank you. (Thanks.)*

¿Adónde vas? *Where are you going?*

Voy a casa. *I'm going home.*

Voy a la escuela. *I'm going to school.*

Hasta mañana. *See you tomorrow.*

Hasta la vista. *See you later.*

Actividad

Pepe is talking with Concha. Can you complete the dialogue logically, using the expressions that you have just learned?

Actividad

F

Can you match the Spanish expressions with their equivalent English expressions?

1. **Buenos días.**	——	**a.** What's your name?
		b. And you?
2. **¿Cómo te llamas?**	——	**c.** The pleasure is mine.
		d. See you in the morning.
3. **Me llamo…**	——	**e.** Good morning.
		f. How are you?
4. **¿Y tú?**	——	**g.** My name is . . .
		h. It's a pleasure to meet you.
5. **Mucho gusto.**	——	**i.** Very well, thank you.
		j. Good-bye.
6. **El gusto es mío.**	——	
7. **Adiós.**	——	
8. **Hasta mañana.**	——	
9. **¿Cómo estás?**	——	
10. **Muy bien, gracias.**	——	

Actividad

G

Susan is helping her brother with his Spanish class. She made cards with various words and scrambled them. Help him put the sentences together. Write the sentences in the space provided. Remember: all sentences begin with capital letters.

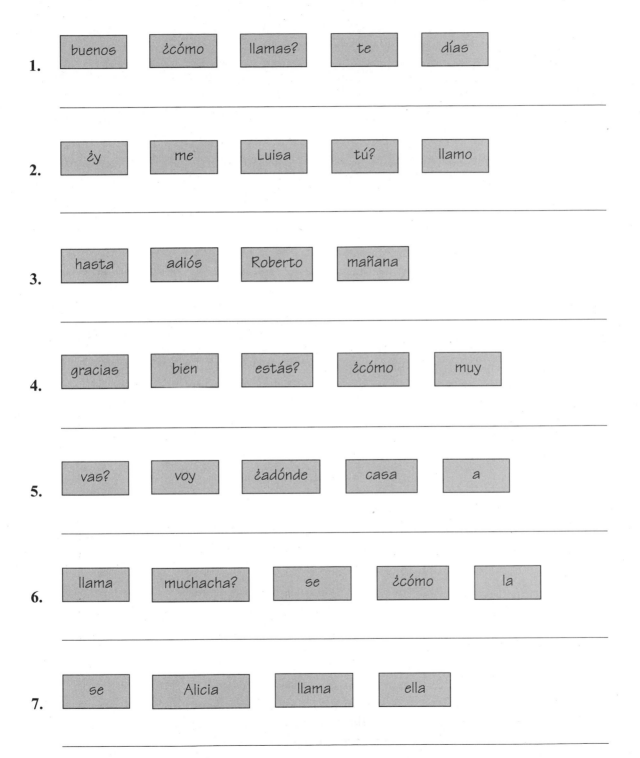

1. | buenos | ¿cómo | llamas? | te | días |

2. | ¿y | me | Luisa | tú? | llamo |

3. | hasta | adiós | Roberto | mañana |

4. | gracias | bien | estás? | ¿cómo | muy |

5. | vas? | voy | ¿adónde | casa | a |

6. | llama | muchacha? | se | ¿cómo | la |

7. | se | Alicia | llama | ella |

Actividad

Francisco and Marta love to construct puzzles. They have made two acrostics using their names. Complete the acrostics by reading the English names and expressions and writing their equivalent in Spanish.

Philip   **F** __ __ __ __ __

Thank you   __ **R** __ __ __ __ __

Where are you going?   **A** __ __ __ __ __ __ __ __

Henry   __ **N** __ __ __ __ __

How are you?   **C** __ __ __ __ __ __ __ __

Well   __ **I** __ __

Young lady, miss   **S** __ __ __ __ __ __ __

What's your name?   **C** __ __ __ __ __ __ __ __ __ __ __

I am going   __ **O** __

Pleased to meet you   **M** __ __ __ __ __ __ __ __

Good-bye   **A** __ __ __ __

Rose   **R** __ __ __

Anthony   __ __ **T** __ __ __ __

Tomorrow   __ **A** __ __ __ __

Conversación

Diálogo

Complete the following conversation. Once you complete it, try it with your class mates.

Comunicación

Write a short note to a new student in your Spanish class whom you would like to
know better. Introduce yourself and ask what is her (his) name. Use any other expressions you have learned in this lesson.

_____

_____

_____

_____

_____

_____

LOS PIROPOS

Boy sees girl. Boy wants to meet girl. Boy starts up a conversation with girl: "Hi. Don't I know you from somewhere?" It's a situation repeated millions of times all over the world every day.

In Spain and in most of the Spanish-speaking world, a very special type of ritual has developed over time: the **piropo.** The **piropo** is a flattering statement that a young man makes to a girl he sees pass by on the street, in the park, or any public place, either when she is alone or with a girlfriend. This traditional custom of complimenting a strange girl on the street is called **echar una flor** or **echar un piropo** (literally, to "throw" a compliment).

This type of flattering remark is not considered rude or offensive in Spanish-speaking countries. On the contrary, many men consider it almost

an obligation to flatter women (thus showing their appreciation of charm and beauty) and have developed the practice to an art form.

Some **piropos** are very simple and straightforward: **Hola, guapa** (Hi, good-looking); **Adiós, preciosa** (See you, precious). Others often try to be poetic or humorous: **¡Eres una muñeca que camina!** (You are a walking doll!).

At times, the **piropos** are truly ingenious: **¡Bendito el árbol de donde sacaron la madera para hacer tu cuna, guapa!** (Blessed be the tree that gave the wood to make your cradle, good-looking!) or **Cuídate de la lluvia, que el azúcar se derrite con el agua** (Be careful when it rains, because sugar melts in water).

And what do women do when showered with these compliments? They may respond: **Gracias por la flor** (Thanks for the compliment) or may just smile. Most often they keep walking, pretending they didn't hear a word.

In recent years, some women have publicly expressed their dissaproval of the **piropos.** They believe this custom is a form of harassment and prefer to walk undisturbed.

Quick Quiz

1. In the Spanish-speaking world, a flattering remark is called a _____.

2. The custom of flattering women is called _____.

3. Women who receive the **piropo** usually walk alone or with _____.

4. Nice flattering remarks are not considered _____.

5. **Hola, guapa** means _____.

6. **Gracias por la flor** means _____.

Let's Find Out More

1. Find out how people from other cultures meet each other. You may ask relatives, friends, and neighbors.

2. Write a composition expressing your opinion about the **piropos**.

Vocabulario

WORDS TO KNOW

¿adónde? *where?*

dice *says*

él *he*

ella *she*

la muchacha *girl*

el muchacho *boy*

vas *you are going*

voy *I am going*

EXPRESSIONS

a casa *at home*

adiós *good-bye*

buenos días *good morning*

¿cómo estás? *how are you?*

¿cómo se llama? *what's his (her) name?*

¿cómo te llamas? *what's your name?*

el gusto es mío *it's my pleasure*

gracias *thank you*

hasta la vista *see you later*

hasta mañana *see you tomorrow*

hola *hello*

me llamo… *my name is . . .*

mucho gusto *glad to meet you*

muy bien *very well*

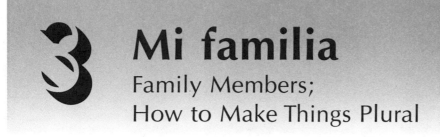

Mi familia

Family Members;
How to Make Things Plural

Here we have one big happy family. Can you tell who all the members are? Let's take a closer look.

el abuelo   **la abuela**

el padre   **la madre**

el hijo

la hija

el hermano   **la hermana**   **el gato**   **el perro**

Now look at this other family. Read the paragraph and see if you can tell who's who.

Los Rodríguez

La familia Rodríguez es grande. El padre de la familia se llama Antonio. La madre se llama Carmen. Carlos y María son los hijos. Carlos y María son hermanos. Alberto y Rosa son los abuelos. Sultán es el perro de la familia y Patitas es el gato. La familia habla español ¿Habla español Patitas? ¿Y Sultán? ¡Sí señor! Patitas dice:—miau, miau. Sultán dice: —guau, guau.

grande *large*

son *are*
hermanos *brothers, siblings* (m. & f.)

dice *says*

Actividad

A

Teresa is putting together a picture album. Help her label the pictures with the words below.

la abuela	la hermana	el padre
el abuelo	el hermano	los padres
los abuelos	la madre	el perro
el gato		

1. _____

2. _____

3. _____

4. _____

5. _____

6. _____

7. _____

8. _____

9. _____

10. _____

Actividad

How good is your memory? Describe each member of the Rodríguez family, using the words below.

la abuela	la hija	el padre
el abuelo	el hijo	el perro
el gato	la madre	

1. Rosa es _____.

2. Carlos es _____.

3. María es _____.

4. Antonio es _____.

5. Patitas es _____.

6. Alberto es _____.

7. Carmen es _____.

8. Sultán es _____.

Actividad

Work with a partner. Take turns reading the statements below. If the statement is true, say **Sí**; if it is false, say **No** and correct it by replacing the word(s) in boldface. Write the answers in the space provided.

1. El perro y el gato son **animales.** _____

2. Carlos y **Rosa** son los hijos. _____

3. Carlos y María son **hermanos**. _____

4. Antonio es **el hijo** de Alberto. _____

5. Sultán es **el padre** de la familia. _____

6. Alberto y Rosa son **los abuelos.** _____

7. El gato se llama **Patitas.** _____

8. El padre de mi madre es mi **abuela.** _____

9. Patitas dice: —guau, guau. _____

Actividad

D

Do you like soap operas? Read the following scene and try to figure out what's happening. Then, choose a partner and play the parts.

(Scene: Nightime. A young man walking in the park. Suddenly, a familiar voice calls him.)

—¡Roberto… Roberto…!

—¿Quién es?

¿Quién? *Who?*

—Roberto, soy yo, tu amigo Juan.

yo *I*
   tu *your* (informal)

—¿Quién? ¿Tú? ¿Es posible? ¿Adónde vas?

tú *you* (informal)

—Sí, voy a tu casa. Deseo hablar con tu hermana Ana.

deseo *I want*
   hablar *to talk*

—¿Mi hermana y tú...?

mi *my* (singular)

—Sí, Roberto...

Actividad

E

Answer the following questions based on the scene above.

1. ¿Cómo se llama el amigo de Roberto?

_____

2. ¿Adónde va el amigo de Roberto?

_____

3. ¿Quién es Ana?

_____

4. ¿Quién es Roberto?

_____

5. ¿Es Ana amiga de Juan?

_____

Dígalo bien

◼ In Spanish, the letter **ñ** is pronounced much like _ni_ in _onion_ or _ny_ in _canyon_.

año	**niña**	**caña**
mañana	**España**	**señor**
señorita	**cumpleaños**	**pequeño**

El señor y la señora van a España.
Mañana es el cumpleaños de la niña.

2 Here's something new. All of the nouns you learned in Lesson 1 were SINGULAR (one object). Now you have also seen nouns that are PLURAL (more than one object). How do we change words from the singular to the plural in Spanish? Read each pair of words carefully.

SINGULAR	PLURAL
el abuelo	los abuelos
la abuela	las abuelas
el padre	los padres
la madre	las madres
el hermano	los hermanos
la hermana	las hermanas
el hijo	los hijos
la hija	las hijas

Let's start by comparing the two groups. Review the nouns in both columns. Now look at them carefully and fill in the rest of the rule:

In Spanish, nouns ending in a vowel (**a, e, i, o, u**) form the plural by adding the letter _____ at the end.

casa → **casas**   **clase** → **clases**   **hijo** → **hijos**

Read these words carefully:

SINGULAR	PLURAL
el doctor	los doctores
el tren	los trenes
la mujer	las mujeres

Do the nouns in the left column end in a vowel? _____

How do they end? _____

What letters do you add to make them plural? _____

Here's the easy rule:

> In Spanish, if a noun ends in a consonant (for example, **l, n,** or **r**), add the letters **es** to the singular form of the noun to make it plural.
>
> **tren** → **tren*es***   **profesor** → **profesor*es***

Now underline all the words that mean *the* on page 66 and complete the following sentences.

> The plural form of **el** is _____ .
> The plural form of **la** is _____ .
> **Los** and **las** mean _____ .

REMEMBER: There are four words for *the* in Spanish: **el, la, los,** and **las.**

Actividad

F

Alicia's class is putting together a Spanish dictionary. Help her choose the appropriate form of *the* for each of the following words. Use **el, la, los,** or **las.**

1. _____ gatos

2. _____ hermano

3. _____ perros

4. _____ niñas

5. _____ familia

6. _____ muchacho

7. _____ padres

8. _____ insecto

9. _____ mujer

10. _____ fiesta

11. _____ hija   12. _____ frutas

13. _____ lámpara   14. _____ puertas

15. _____ bicicletas   16. _____ flor

17. _____ animal   18. _____ hombre

19. _____ clases   20. _____ amiga

Actividad

Work with a partner. One of you reads the singular forms on the left, and the other gives the plural. Switch roles when you get to number 10.

1. el padre _____   **2.** el color _____

3. el tren _____   **4.** la gata _____

5. el auto _____   **6.** la ambulancia _____

7. el tigre _____   **8.** el hombre _____

9. la niña _____   **10.** el profesor _____

11. la hija _____   **12.** el animal _____

13. la clase _____   **14.** la rosa _____

15. el abuelo _____   **16.** la fruta _____

17. la bicicleta _____   **18.** la mujer _____

19. la flor _____   **20.** el doctor _____

Vamos a conversar

Work with a partner. One will read the question, and the other will answer according to the cues in parentheses. Reverse the roles and start again.

—¿Cómo es tu familia?
  (Say that it's big.)
—¿Cómo se llama tu padre (papá)?
  (Say his name.)
—¿Cómo se llama tu madre (mamá)?
  (Say her name.)
—¿Y tu abuela, cómo se llama?
  (Say her name.)

Now look at the following sentences carefully.

Mi hermano se llama Carlos.   Mis hermanos se llaman Carlos y Luis.

Did you notice the differences between both sentences? Did you notice that **Mi** changed to **Mis** and **hermano** changed to **hermanos**?

Mis and **hermanos** are all in the plural form. Like **hermano, mi** adds an **s** in the plural. The same thing happens to the word **tu** (your):

tu hermano   tus hermanos

Did you notice that the action word (the verb **llama**) also changed to the plural? What letter is added to form the plural? If your answer is **n**, you are correct.

Mi hermano se llama Carlos.   Mis hermanos se llaman Carlos y Luis.

Información personal

Work with a partner. One student interviews a classmate about his (her) family, including pets. Make sure you use the proper pronouns.

EXAMPLE: **Mi perro se llama Fifi.   ¿Cómo se llama tu perro?**

WHAT ARE YOUR NAMES?

Many of us are surprised when we learn that people of Spanish heritage use two family names. Not only that, but wives seem to have different last names from their husbands. Is this confusing? Let's see how it works by examining the family in the picture.

First, let's take the father's name: **José Torres López**. **Torres** is not his middle name, but his father's last name; **López** is his mother's maiden name. He should be addressed as "Mr. Torres" or "Mr. Torres-López."

How about José's wife? Her name is **Juana Fonseca de Torres**. **Fonseca** is not her middle name, but her maiden name. How can this be? Isn't she married to Mr. Torres? Yes, but in Spanish-speaking cultures, a married woman keeps her father's name and adds on her husband's preceded by **de** (of). Thus we get **Juana Fonseca** (her maiden name) **de Torres** (her husband's last name).

José Torres López

Maria Torres Fonseca

Luis Torres Fonseca

Juana Fonseca de Torres

Now, what about the children? That's simple. They receive a family name from each parent: the father's last name (**Torres**) followed by their mother's maiden name (**Fonseca**).

Wouldn't it be interesting if we adopted this custom in the United States?

 Quick Quiz

1. Spanish-speaking people have _____ family names.

2. A baby takes its _____ name followed by its _____ name.

3. A woman keeps her _____ name.

4. The husband's name is added to the wife's name preceded by _____ .

5. In the name Gustavo Salinas Ochoa, _____ is the father's name and _____ is the mother's name.

6. If you need to know Gustavo's phone number, you look him up under _____ .

7. If only one last name is used, it is the _____ .

Let's Find Out More

1. What would your name be if written in the Spanish fashion? Find out also your parents and grandparents' names.

2. Ask native Spanish speakers what are the practical reasons for keeping maiden names. Write down their answers and discuss them in class.

3. Ask native Spanish speakers if they use two last names. Find out if that creates any special problems for them.

Vocabulario

WORDS TO KNOW

la abuela *grandmother*

el abuelo *grandfather*

los abuelos *grandparents*

dice *he / she / it says*

la familia *family*

grande *big*

la hermana *sister*

el hermano *brother*

los hermanos *brothers; brother and sister*

la hija *daughter*

el hijo *son*

la mamá *mom*

el papá *dad*

¿quién? *who?*

son *are*

tú *you* (sing. informal)

tu(s) *your* (informal)

usted *you* (sing. formal)

yo *I*

EXPRESSIONS

¿Cómo se llaman? What's their name?

¿Quiénes... ? Who . . . ?

4 La escuela
Classroom Expressions; Indefinite Articles

Here are some useful words related to school and the classroom. Look at the pictures and try to figure out what the words mean.

el señor Valdés

la señora Rojas

la señorita López

el alumno

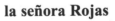

la alumna

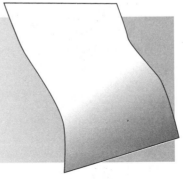

el papel

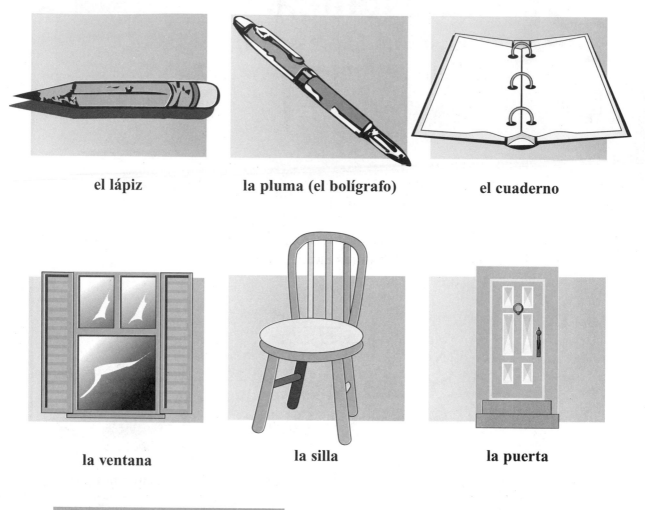

el lápiz

la pluma (el bolígrafo)

el cuaderno

la ventana

la silla

la puerta

la pizarra

el tablón

el escritorio

la mesa

la escuela

el reloj

el borrador

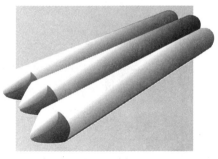

la tiza

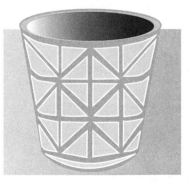

el cesto

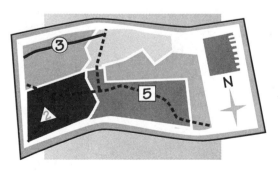

el mapa

Actividad

A

Mr. García-Montero is showing pictures on the overhead projector to test his students on vocabulary. Can you help them write the correct Spanish word for each picture?

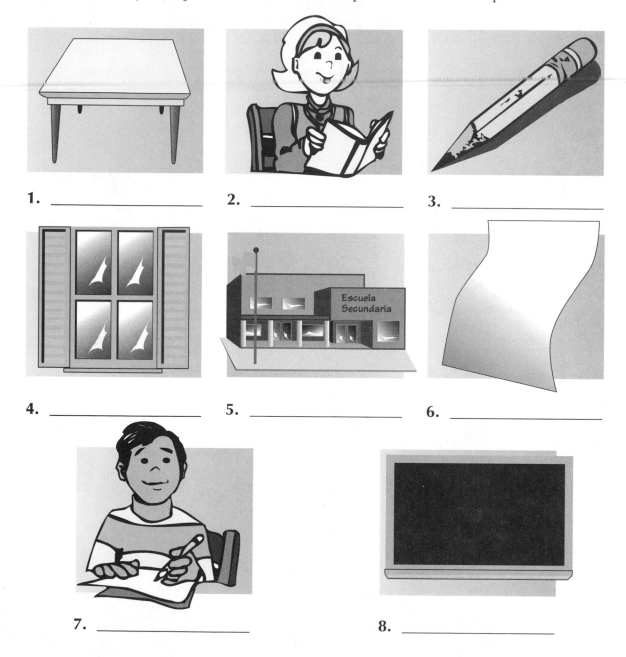

1. _____

2. _____

3. _____

4. _____

5. _____

6. _____

7. _____

8. _____

9. _____

10. _____

11. _____

12. _____

Actividad

B

Jaimito made a list of all the new vocabulary. Then he erased a letter in each word to test your memory. See how many words you can complete correctly.

1. li__ro

2. __scritorio

3. seño__a

4. ces__o

5. lápi__es

6. relo__

7. bo__ígrafo

8. l__piz

9. __apel

10. __illa

11. __orrador

12. tiz__

13. vent__na

14. __apa

15. pl__ma

16. mes__

17. alu__no

18. cuader__o

19. c__ase

20. piz__rra

Dígalo bien

In Spanish, the letter **r** is pronounced like *dd* in *ladder.*

toro	**Mario**	**coro**
hermano	**cero**	**Perú**
dinero	**enero**	**tarea**
para	**señora**	**Mara**

María y Mara son americanas.
Mario está con la señora en Perú.

At the beginning of a word, **r** is pronounced with a double or triple "trill" of the tongue.

ropa	**radio**
Rosa	**Ramón**
rápido	**rico**

Double **r** is also pronounced like the above.

perro	**pizarra**
borrador	**guitarra**
arriba	**horrible**

Serrano borra la pizarra.
Ese perro es horrible.

2

Now that you know the new words, read the following story and see if you can understand it.

El salón de español

El salón de español es grande. Hay muchas ventanas y una puerta. Hay un mapa, una bandera, un reloj y un tablón. Hay también muchos alumnos.

La profesora, la señora Iglesias, es inteligente. Ella va a la pizarra y escribe: «Cómo se dice *pencil*?». Los estudiantes dicen: «lápiz».

La profesora pregunta:—¿Es interesante la clase?—Sí, señorita, muy interesante—dicen los niños.

—¿Y son inteligentes los estudiantes?—pregunta la profesora.

—¡Sí, muy inteligentes!—dicen los niños.

salón *classroom*
  Hay *there is, there are*
un(a) *a, an*
  bandera *flag*
también *also*
  muchos *many*
escribe *writes*
  ¿Cómo se dice…? *How does one say . . . ?*
dicen *they say*
pregunta *asks*

Actividad

C

How well did you understand the story? Read each of the following statements. If the statement is true, write **Sí**; if it is false, write **No** and correct it by replacing the word(s) in boldface.

1. La clase de español es **horrible**. _____

2. Hay muchas **ventanas** en la clase. _____

3. La profesora de la clase es la **señorita López**. _____

4. Hay muchos **estudiantes**. _____

5. **El alumno** va a la pizarra. _____

Actividad

D

Find out which word in each group does not belong. Write the word in the space provided.

1. lápiz, papel, abuelo, escritorio _____

2. borrador, gato, tiza, reloj _____

3. alumna, clase, profesor, casa _____

4. familia, tiza, alumno, borrador _____

5. silla, escritorio, mesa, perro _____

6. pluma, hermana, bolígrafo, lápices _____

7. papel, bolígrafo, tren, cuaderno _____

Actividad

Last week, Lorenzo had to stay home from school. When he returns to school, he finds that the classroom has been rearranged. Can you help him find five missing objects? List them in the space provided.

_____   _____

_____   _____

_____

Actividad

F

Miss Miranda is testing her class on the use of the definite article. See if you can pass her test by filling in the correct definite article **el, la, los,** or **las**.

1. _____ libros   2. _____ escuela

3. _____ lápices   4. _____ mesa

5. _____ papeles   6. _____ ventanas

7. _____ alumnos   8. _____ pluma

9. _____ profesor   10. _____ alumna

When the article **el** is preceded by the preposition **de** to indicate origin or possession, they become **del**. For example:

el libro del (de + el) alumno   *the student's book*
la casa del (de + el) perro   *the dog's house*

REMEMBER: **de + el = del**

3

Lets take another look at the story on page 79. There are two new words that you read several times that are similar. They are **un** and **una**, the Spanish words for *a* or *an*. Can you figure out when to use **un** and when to use **una**? Look carefully.

el **libro**	*un* **libro**
el **lápiz**	*un* **lápiz**
el **muchacho**	*un* **muchacho**
el **doctor**	*un* **doctor**

Let's start by comparing the two groups of nouns. Are the nouns in the left column masculine or feminine? _____ How do you know? _____

What does **el** mean? _____

Now look at the words in the right column. Which word has replaced **el**? _____
What does it mean? _____

Now look at some more examples.

la **clase**	*una* **clase**
la **persona**	*una* **persona**
la **pluma**	*una* **pluma**
la **profesora**	*una* **profesora**

Are the nouns in the left column masculine or feminine? _____ How do
you know?_____ What does **la** mean? _____

Now look at the words in the right column. Which word has replaced **la**? _____
What does it mean? _____

Let's summarize:

Un (a, an) is used before a masculine noun.
Una (a, an) is used before a feminine noun.

You may have noticed that **un** precedes the word **mapa**. Don't let this confuse you: **mapa** ends in **a**, but is a masculine word, that's why we say *un* **mapa**.

Now look at the next two sentences.

La madre de Pedro es profesora.   *Pedro's mother is a teacher.*
El padre de Juana es doctor.   *Juana's father is a doctor.*

Did you notice that the article **a** is not expressed in those Spanish sentences? Here is another example:

El señor Rodríguez es profesor.   *Mr. Rodríguez is a teacher.*

But look at these sentences:

Ella es *una* profesora *mexicana*.   *She is a Mexican teacher.*
Él es *un* doctor *famoso*.   *He is a famous doctor.*

This time around **un (una)** appear in the sentence. How can you know when to use it? It's simple; follow this rule.

In Spanish, the indefinite article **un (una)** IS used to express someone's trade or profession when the trade or profession is followed by an adjective.

Actividad

G

Let's find out how well you understand the use of **un** and **una**. Complete each of the following sentences. Remember that some may not need **un** or **una**.

1. El señor López es _____ doctor.

2. El señor López es _____ doctor mexicano.

3. La señora Rodríguez es _____ profesora.

4. La señora Rodríguez es _____ profesora interesante.

5. Juanito es _____ estudiante inteligente.

6. Juanito es _____ estudiante.

Actividad

Match each of the words below with a corresponding picture. Write the words in the space provided.

un bolígrafo	un lápiz	un reloj
un cesto	un mapa	una silla
un cuaderno	una pizarra	una ventana
un escritorio		

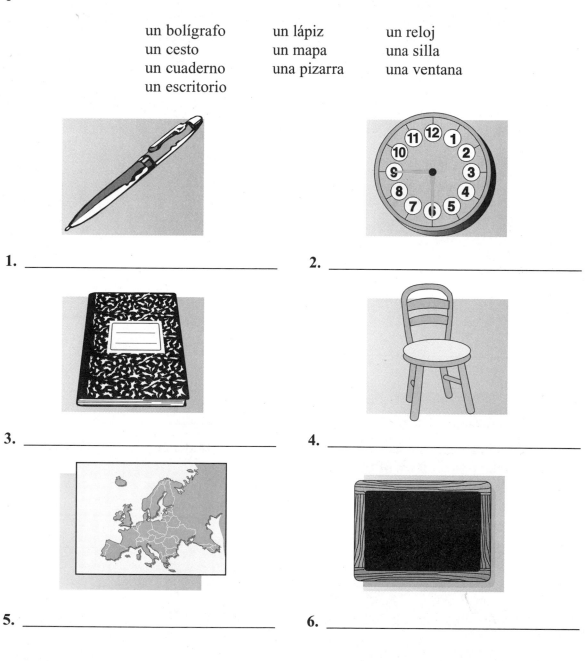

1. _____

2. _____

3. _____

4. _____

5. _____

6. _____

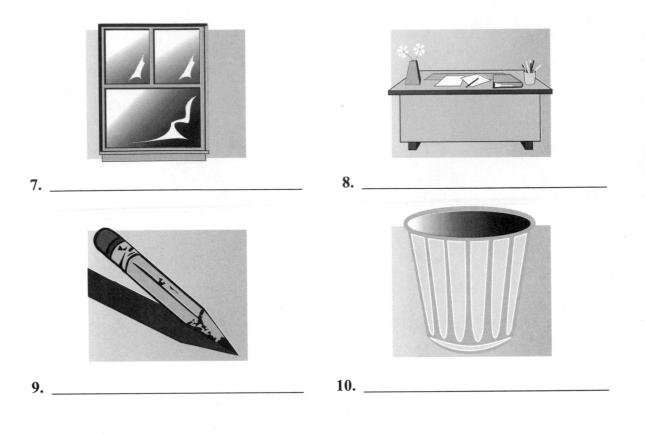

7. _____ 8. _____

9. _____ 10. _____

Actividad

If you can do the next two exercises correctly, you really understood the work. Replace **el** and **la** with the correct form of the indefinite article.

1. la silla _____ **2.** la puerta _____

3. el estudiante _____ **4.** la escuela _____

5. la niña _____ **6.** el reloj _____

7. el profesor _____ **8.** el hijo _____

Actividad

Assign **un** or **una** to each of the following words.

1. _____ silla

2. _____ tiza

3. _____ papel

4. _____ libro

5. _____ lápiz

6. _____ pluma

7. _____ mesa

8. _____ pizarra

9. _____ ventana

10. _____ puerta

11. _____ bandera

12. _____ señorita

13. _____ cuaderno

14. _____ café

15. _____ bicicleta

16. _____ perro

4 Let's have some more fun by reading this short story. See how much you can understand.

¿Dónde está tu libro?

Manuel está en la clase de español. Es una clase grande y hay muchos estudiantes. La profesora de la clase se llama Carmen Ruiz. La señorita Ruiz es una profesora excelente y estricta.

estricta *strict*

—Manuel, ¿dónde está tu libro?

—Está en casa, señorita.

en casa *at home*

—¿En casa? Ay, Manuel, ¿no estás contento en la clase de español?

¿no estás contento? *aren't you happy*

—Oh, sí, señorita. Su clase es interesante y usted es muy inteligente. ¡Mi profesora favorita!

—Muchas gracias, Manuel. ¡Muy generoso! Pero mañana quiero hablar con tu mamá.

quiero *I want*

Actividad

Read each of the following statements. If the statement is true write **Sí**; if it is false, write **No** and correct it by replacing the incorrect information.

1. Manuel es un estudiante excelente. _____

2. El libro de Manuel está en casa. _____

3. La profesora se llama Carmen Pérez. _____

4. Hay muchos estudiantes en la clase. _____

5. La señorita Ruiz es estricta. _____

Conversación

Diálogo

Complete the dialogue using the sentences from the list below:

Mi libro está en la mesa.
Sí, el español es mi clase favorita.
Buenos días, señor González.

Yo me llamo Pilar.
Muy bien. ¿Y usted?
Aquí está mi lápiz.

Preguntas personales

Answer these questions in complete Spanish sentences.

1. ¿Dónde está el profesor/la profesora?

2. ¿Cómo se llama tu profesor/profesora?

_____

3. ¿Dónde está tu pluma?

_____

4. ¿Dónde están tus lápices?

_____

5. ¿Dónde están tus papeles?

_____

 ## Información personal

The school year has just begun, and you are making a shopping list of school supplies that you will need. What would you include in your list? Write at least five items in Spanish:

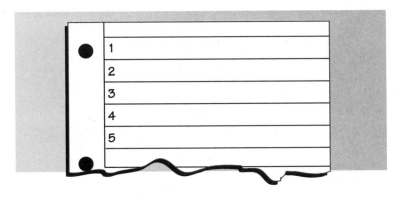

Vamos a conversar

Your little sister is very curious and wants to know everything about your Spanish class. Answer her questions.

TU HERMANA:	¿Cómo es tu clase de español?
TÚ:	(_Tell her it's very interesting_)
TU HERMANA:	¿Cómo se llama tu profesor?
TÚ:	(_Give his/her name_)
TU HERMANA:	¿Qué hay en la clase?
TÚ:	(_Name a few classroom objects_)
TU HERMANA:	¿Hay muchos alumnos?
TÚ:	(_Tell her about size of the class_)

WHAT SHIFT AM I IN?

Enrolling in a new middle school or high school? You may have a few things to consider, like location or type of school. You may also decide to attend—or avoid—the same school as your friends or older brothers or sisters.

Mexican students, however, have another choice to make. Sometimes the school makes the decision for them. In areas like the capital, Mexico City (**el Distrito Federal**), the population is so high that schools cannot accomodate their students all at the same time. When you enroll in a school, you may be placed in the **turno de la mañana** (morning shift), or **turno de la tarde** (afternoon shift). The morning shift starts at 7:00 A.M. and ends at 2:00 P.M. The afternoon shift is from 2:00 P.M. to 8:00 P.M. In many cities, a third school shift is available for adults.

Here is an example of a typical morning schedule of a Mexican middle-school student starting on Monday (**lunes**).

If you ever move to Mexico City and are not very **madrugador** (early bird), here is some advice: Register early for school, or else you might have to wake up at 5:00 or 6:00 A.M. every day.

	LUNES	MARTES	MIÉRCOLES	JUEVES	VIERNES
7:00-7:50	Matemáticas	Historia de México	Biología	Historia Universal	Historia de México
8:00-8:50	Inglés	Matemáticas	Inglés	Química	Biología
9:00-9:50	Física	Leyes	Historia de México	Ciencias Naturales	Leyes
10:00-10:50	Historia Universal	Química	Física	Matemáticas	Física
11:00-11:50	Español	Español	Literatura	Español	Literatura
1:00-2:00	Educación Física	Música	Educación Física	Literatura	Música

Quick Quiz

1. In Mexico City the population is so high that schools have two _____ .

2. In some Mexican schools the morning shift starts at _____ and ends at _____ .

3. The afternoon shift is from _____ to _____ .

4. Students in the morning shift must wake up at _____ .

5. A person who wakes up early in the morning is called _____ .

Let's Find Out More

1. What is the population of Mexico City?

2. Ask someone or consult with books or magazines about the different education systems in Spanish-speaking countries, specially schedules, grading systems, and subjects.

Vocabulario

WORDS TO KNOW

aquí *here*

el bolígrafo *ball-point pen*

el borrador *eraser*

el cesto *basket*

el cuaderno *notebook*

están *are*

el escritorio *desk*

el lápiz (los lápices) *pencil(s)*

el mapa *map*

la mesa *table*

muchos (as) *many*

el papel *paper*

la pizarra *board*

el reloj *watch, clock*

la silla *chair*
el señor *Mr.; gentlemen*
la señora *Mrs.; lady*

el tablón *(bulletin) board*
la tiza *chalk*
un (a) *a*

EXPRESSIONS

en casa *at home*
¿cómo se dice...? *how do you say . . . ?*
¿dónde está...? *where is . . . ?*
¿estás contento(a)? *are you happy?*

hay *there is, there are*
no comprendo *I don't understand*
no sé *I don't know*

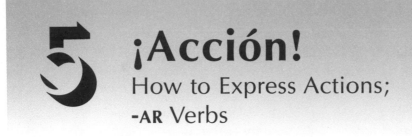

5 ¡Acción!
How to Express Actions;
-AR Verbs

The following words are all action words or verbs. Look at the illustrations and try to guess the meaning of each word.

comprar

entrar

contestar

escuchar

llegar

| visitar | caminar | estudiar |

2

Here are some useful commands you will hear from your teacher for things you do every day in class. You will get used to them with practice.

Expressions For the Classroom

Abre el libro.

Cierra el libro.

Escucha.

Lee.

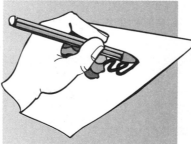

Escribe.

Completa las oraciones.

Saca papel.

Siéntate.

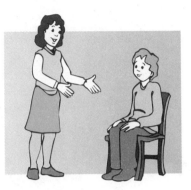

Levántate.

Pasa a la pizarra.

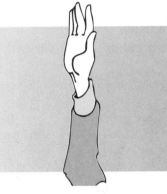

Levanta la mano.

¿Cómo estás?

Dilo en español.

Contesta la pregunta.

No sé.

Here are some more useful expressions that you may use in the classroom:

| **¿Cómo?** | **Mira.** | **No comprendo.** |

Notice that **¿Cómo?** is equivalent to "How was that?"

Actividad

A

Look at each of the following illustrations. Can you tell what command is being given in each case?

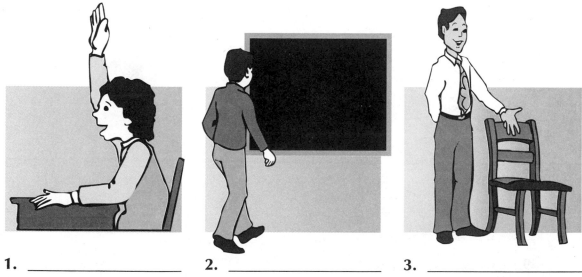

1. _____ 2. _____ 3. _____

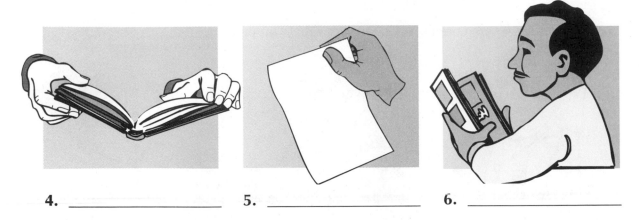

4. _____

5. _____

6. _____

7. _____

8. _____

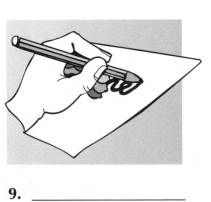

9. _____

10. _____

Actividad

B

Now it's your turn to give orders. Work with a partner. Give a command, for example, **Pasa a la pizarra.** Your classmate will act out the command and, in turn, give you a command to perform.

3

Here are some other useful Spanish verbs. Look at the illustration above each verb and try to guess the verbs' meaning.

cantar   **hablar**   **mirar**

bailar   **trabajar**   **preguntar**

Did you notice that all of these verbs end in **-ar**, like **entrar** (to enter) and **trabajar** (to work)? In Spanish there are groups of verbs that function or "behave" in a similar fashion.

One of these groups is formed by the verbs ending in **-ar**.

But first, let's review the pronouns we already know and learn a few more.

yo *I*

tú *you* (singular)

él *he*

ella *she*

usted *you* (singular)

ustedes *you* (plural)

nosotros *we* (masculine/ masculine and feminine)

nosotras *we* (feminine)

ellos *they* (masculine/ masculine and feminine)

ellas *they* (feminine)

These words are called subject pronouns. Subject pronouns refer to the persons or things doing the action. Did you notice that **tú**, **usted**, and **ustedes** all mean *you*? The following table will help you understand:

tú	is used when you are talking to a close relative, a friend, or a child—someone young or with whom you are familiar.
usted (Ud.)	is used when you are speaking to a stranger, a grown-up, or a person with whom you are or should be formal.
ustedes (Uds.)	is used when you are speaking to two or more persons, whether familiarly or formally.

Note that the subject pronoun *it* has no equivalent in Spanish.

Es moderna. *It is modern.*

Actividad

C

Which subject pronoun would you use to address each of the following people? Use **tú**, **usted**, or **ustedes**, as needed.

1. el profesor _____   **2.** la niña _____

3. el señor Ambert _____

4. Pablo y Concha _____

5. María _____

6. las señoras _____

7. Roberto _____

8. los abuelos _____

Dígalo bien

■ In Spanish, the letter **h** is never pronounced; **h** is always silent.

hablar	*hay*	*ahora*
hola	*hombre*	*hotel*
hermano	*hermosa*	*hasta*
helado	*hamburguesa*	*hoy*

■ Since **h** is silent, it is not necessary to pause before a word beginning with **h**.

■ For example, **el hotel** sounds like "**elotel**," **el hombre** sounds like "**elombre**."

■ Have some fun by reading the following sentences aloud. Read them at normal speed first, then faster and faster.

> *Hola, Héctor. ¿Qué hay hoy?*
> *Hernán hace una hamburguesa ahora.*

4

Now that you are more familiar with the Spanish subject pronouns, you are ready to learn verb forms. Let's see how it works:

Take, for example, the verb **hablar** (to speak). If you want to say *I speak*, take **yo**, remove the ending **-ar** from **hablar**, and add the following endings:

yo habl*o*   *I speak, I am speaking*

tú habl*as*   *you speak, you are speaking* (singular familiar)

usted habl*a*   *you speak, you are speaking* (singular formal)

él habl*a*   *he speaks, he is speaking*

ella habl*a*   *she speaks, she is speaking*

nosotros
nosotras } **habl***amos*   *we speak, we are speaking*

ustedes habl*an*   *you speak* (plural)

ellos
ellas } **habl***an*   *they speak*

Did you notice that there are two possible English meanings for each verb form? **Yo hablo** means *I speak* or *I am speaking*; **tú hablas** means *you speak* or *you are speaking*, and so on.

Actividad

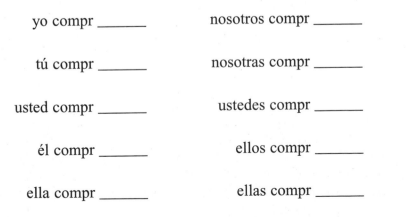

Can you give the appropriate endings for the verb **comprar** (to buy)? Note that the **-ar** ending has already been removed. Just look at the subjects and add the correct endings.

yo compr _____   nosotros compr _____

tú compr _____   nosotras compr _____

usted compr _____   ustedes compr _____

él compr _____   ellos compr _____

ella compr _____   ellas compr _____

Not so difficult, right? What if we use proper names instead of subject pronouns like **yo** and **tú**? Let's take the name "Pedro," for instance. Ask yourself, "Who is Pedro? How could I refer to him? Of course, the answer is "he." And what is the proper verb ending for "*he*" (**él**)? If you said **-a** you are correct.

Pedro = él; if you take the verb **caminar** (to walk), eliminate the **-ar** ending and add **-a**:

> **Pedro camina**   *Pedro walks* or *Pedro is walking*

And which subject pronoun would you use for **María y yo**? Of course, you would use "we." Now, "we" has two forms: **nosotros** (masculine) and **nosotras** (feminine). Which one should you use? It's simple. If both **María** and **yo** are feminine, use **nosotras**. If one of them (in this case **yo**) is masculine, use **nosotros**.

Which Spanish subject pronouns would you use for the following?

los abuelos   _____

el perro   _____

Luis y Ana   _____

Carlos y Roberto   _____

Which form of **caminar** would go with each of the subjects?

los abuelos   _____

el perro   _____

Luis y Ana   _____

Carlos y Roberto   _____

An important point to remember about subject pronouns: In Spanish, they are often omitted if the meaning is clear. The sentence "I speak Spanish" may be either **Yo hablo español** or simply **Hablo español**. The subject pronoun **yo** isn't really necessary except for emphasis. Remember that the **-o** ending in **hablo** already indicates who is speaking. Another example: *We are working* may be **Nosotros (nosotras) trabajamos** or simply **Trabajamos**, since the verb form that ends in **-amos** can be used only with **nosotros**. In fact, any subject pronoun may be omitted if it is not needed for clarity or emphasis:

¿Dónde está Fátima?	*Where is Fátima?*
Está en el mercado.	*She is in the market.*
¿Qué compra?	*What is she buying?*
Compra bananas.	*She is buying bananas.*

In the lessons that follow, we will sometimes omit subject pronouns.

Actividad

E

Look at the following Spanish verbs. Tell who is doing the action by looking carefully at the endings. Write all the subject pronouns that apply.

EXAMPLE: **usted, él, ella** habla

1. _____ contesto
2. _____ compras
3. _____ entro
4. _____ estudian
5. _____ trabaja
6. _____ bailan
7. _____ pregunto
8. _____ cantas

Actividad

F

Write the appropriate verb form for each subject pronoun. Remember to remove the **-ar** ending before adding the new one.

EXAMPLE: hablar: yo **hablo**

1. (*llegar*) yo _____
2. (*trabajar*) tú _____
3. (*contestar*) él _____
4. (*preguntar*) ella _____
5. (*escuchar*) usted _____
6. (*bailar*) nosotras _____
7. (*hablar*) ellos _____
8. (*entrar*) Juan y yo _____

Actividad

G

Everyone, including yourself, is busy. Describe what everyone's doing by completing the Spanish sentences with the correct verb form.

1. (*speak*) Yo_____ español.

2. (*work*) Tú _____ mucho.

3. (*buy*) Nosotros _____ muchos libros.

4. (*enter*) Ellas _____ en la clase.

5. (*study*) Los estudiantes _____ en la escuela.

6. (*walk*) El perro _____ en casa.

7. (*sing*) Yo _____ en el parque.

8. (*listen*) Tú _____ en la clase.

9. (*answer*) Pedro y yo _____ en español.

10. (*look*) Ricardo _____ el diccionario.

5 Let's have fun by reading another story. See how much you understand.

Héctor Hernández estudia en la escuela secundaria. Su hermano Juan estudia ahí también. Ellos estudian muchas cosas: matemáticas, ciencias, música y lenguas. Héctor estudia español, Juan estudia francés. Los hermanos son muy diferentes. Juan es guapo y moreno; Héctor es guapo y rubio. Sus personalidades son diferentes también. Héctor estudia mucho y Juan mira mucha televisión.

—Juan, ¿no estudias?

—No. Miro el béisbol en la televisión.

—¡Buena suerte en el examen mañana!

—¿Examen? ¡Voy a estudiar ahora!

secundaria *secondary*
ahí *there*
  también *also*
cosas *things*
  matemáticas *math*
  ciencias *science*
lenguas *languages*
  francés *French*
guapo *handsome*
moreno *brunette*
  rubio *blond*
  personalidades *personalities*
béisbol *baseball*
¡buena suerte! *good luck*

Actividad

Ｈ

The following statements are based on the story you have just read. If the statement is true, write **Sí**; if it is false, write **No** and replace the words in boldface.

1. Héctor estudia **francés**. _____

2. El hermano de Juan se llama **Héctor**. _____

3. **Héctor** estudia música. _____

4. Juan y Héctor estudian en la escuela **secundaria**. _____

5. **Juan** es guapo. _____

6. Héctor es **moreno**. _____

7. **Juan** estudia mucho. _____

Actividad

Match the descriptions with the correct pictures. Write the sentence below the picture that correctly illustrates the sentence.

Ellos trabajan en un cine.
José mira béisbol en la televisión.
Yo escucho música.

Usted compra una rosa.
Mi abuelo es moreno.
Bailas bien.

1. _____

2. _____

3. _____

4. _____

5. _____

6. _____

Conversación

Vamos a... *Let's . . .*
¡Vamos! *Let's go!*

Diálogo

Fill in the words that are missing in the dialogue. Choose from the following list.

bailar   muy
contestar   rubio
entrar   suerte
guapo   verdad

Información personal

List some of the things you do every day. Complete the following sentences with the correct form of an **-ar** verb. Note that in some cases there may be more than one possible answer.

Yo _____ por teléfono.

_____ muchas cosas.

_____ la televisión.

_____ la radio.

_____ inglés y francés.

_____ en la casa.

_____ en el parque.

Vamos a conversar

You are talking to your friend Marta about your work in school.

MARTA: ¿Qué estudias en la escuela?
TÚ: *(Name some subjects.)*
MARTA: ¿Trabajas mucho?
TÚ: *(Tell her yes, you work a lot.)*
MARTA: ¿Cómo es tu trabajo en la clase?
TÚ: *(Say you answer well in class.)*
MARTA: ¿Miras mucha televisión en casa?
TÚ: *(Tell her no, you don't watch too much TV, you study a lot.)*

¿Sabías que...?

El Béisbol

The two **equipos** (teams) are on the **campo** (field). **El árbitro** (umpire) screams **¡Al bate!** (Batter up!). **El lanzador** or **pícher** (pitcher) throws una **bola rápida** (fast ball). **El bateador** (batter) hits the **pelota** (ball). It looks like a **palomita** (fly ball), but then the announcer says: **"Bésala, que se fue"** (Kiss it, it's gone). It's a **jonrón** (home run). What's going on here? Are they speaking Spanish or English at a baseball game?

Most Americans think of baseball as the truly American pastime. But this sport is in fact the national pastime in many Spanish-speaking countries, particularly in Puerto Rico, Cuba, Mexico, Nicaragua, Panama, Venezuela and the Dominican Republic. The Dominican Republic has given the greatest number of players to American Major-League teams. Of the twenty-six

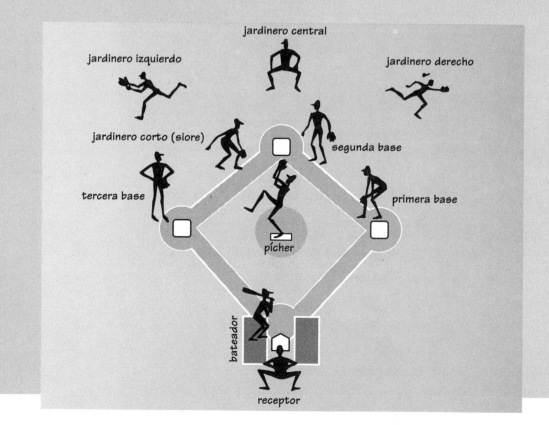

jardinero central

jardinero izquierdo

jardinero derecho

jardinero corto (siore)

segunda base

tercera base

primera base

pícher

primera base

bateador

receptor

116

teams in the majors, seventeen have set up training camps in this small Caribbean country.

Interestingly, Spanish Americans have given the sport their own distinct flavor. In Cuba, "bases loaded" is sometimes referred to as **"cuatro pescados en una sartén"** (four fish in a frying pan), and when a batter strikes out swinging, they say **"abanicó la brisa"** (he fanned the breeze).

Look at **el diamante** (diamond) with all the **peloteros** (ballplayers). See if you recognize the different positions.

Quick Quiz

1. The Spanish word for team is _____.

2. Baseball is the national sport of _____ and _____.

3. The country that has given the U.S. the greatest number of major league players is

   _____.

4. **Abanicó la brisa** (He fanned the breeze) means that the batter _____.

5. **El lanzador** throws the _____.

Let's Find Out More

1. Get a newspaper from a Spanish-speaking country where baseball is played and look up the names of the teams in Spanish, for example:

   los Yanquis
   los Atléticos
   los Medias Rojas

2. Make a survey of the Spanish-American baseball players in the United States. Write down their position and the country they come from.

Vocabulario

WORDS TO KNOW

bailar *to dance*
el béisbol *baseball*
caminar *to walk*
cantar *to sing*
comprar *to buy*
contestar *to answer*
las cosas *things*
ellas *they* (feminine)
ellos *they* (masculine)
entrar *to enter*

escuchar *to listen to*
estudiar *to study*
el francés *French*
guapo *handsome*
hablar *to speak*
el inglés *English*
las matemáticas *math*
mirar *to look at*
moreno *dark, brunette*
a música *music*

nosotras *we*
(feminine)
nosotros *we*
(masculine)

otro(as) *another*
preguntar *to ask*
rubio *blond*
trabajar *to work*
ustedes *you* (plural)

EXPRESSIONS

¡abre el libro! *open the book!*

¡buena suerte! *good luck*

¡cierra el libro! *close the book!*

¡completa las frases! *complete the sentences!*

¡contesta la pregunta! *answer the question!*

¡dilo en español! *say it in Spanish!*

¡escribe! *write!*

¡escucha! *listen!*

¡levanta la mano! *raise your hand!*

¡levántate! *stand up!*

¡lee! *read!*

¡mira! *look!*

¡pasa a la pizarra! *go to the board!*

¡saca papel! *take out paper!*

¡siéntate! *sit down!*

¡vamos! *let's go!*

¡vamos a… ! *let's . . . !*

Repaso I
(Lecciones 1–5)

LECCIÓN 1

a. In Spanish, nouns are either masculine or feminine. Generally, nouns ending in **-o** are masculine, and nouns ending in **-a** are feminine.

niñ*o*   **niñ***a*
gat*o*   **gat***a*

Note that the gender of nouns ending in letters different than **-o** or **-a** must be memorized.

MASCULINE	FEMININE
doctor	**ciudad** (city)
profesor	**actriz** (actress)

b. The definite article (English *the*) used with masculine nouns is **el**; the one used with feminine nouns is **la**.

el **muchacho**   *la* **muchacha**
el **profesor**   *la* **profesora**

LECCIÓN 2

Useful Spanish expressions:

buenos días *good morning*
el señor *sir, gentleman, man, Mr.*
la señora *madam, lady, woman, Mrs.*
la señorita *miss, young lady*

hasta mañana *see you tomorrow*
hola *hello, hi*
¿cómo estás? *how are you?*
(muy) bien *(very) well*

¿cómo te llamas? *what's your name?*	**gracias** *thank you, thanks*
me llamo... *my name is . . .*	**¿adónde vas?** *where are you going?*
¿y tú? *and you?*	**voy a casa** *I'm going home*
mucho gusto *it's a pleasure to meet you*	**voy a la escuela** *I'm going to school*
adiós *good-bye*	**hasta la vista** *see you later*

LECCIÓN 3

a. In Spanish, singular nouns ending in a vowel (**a, e, i, o, u**) form the plural by adding an **-s.** The definite article (English *the*) used with masculine plural nouns is **los**, and the one used before plural nouns **las.**

el **perro**	*los* **perros**
la **doctora**	*las* **doctoras**

b. Singular nouns ending in a consonant form the plural by adding **-es.**

el profesor	**los profesor*es***
la flor	**las flor*es***

LECCIÓN 4

In Spanish, the definite article (English *a* or *an*) has two forms: **un** is used with masculine singular nouns, **una** is used with feminine singular nouns.

un **niño**	*una* **niña**
un **lápiz**	*una* **mesa**

LECCIÓN 5

a. Spanish subject pronouns:

SINGULAR		PLURAL	
yo *I*		**nosotros** *we (masculine)*	
tú *you (familiar)*		**nosotras** *we (feminine)*	
usted (Ud.) *you (formal)*		**ustedes (Uds.)** *you*	
él *he*		**ellos** *they (masculine)*	
ella *she*		**ellas** *they (feminine)*	

b. In Spanish, verbs change according to the subject pronoun or noun. Drop the ending **-ar** and add the appropriate ending for each subject.

yo	-o		yo	canto
tú	-as		tú	cantas
usted	-a		usted	canta
él ⎫ ella ⎭	-a		él ⎫ ella ⎭	canta
nosotros ⎫ nosotras ⎭	-amos		nosotros ⎫ nosotras ⎭	cantamos
ustedes	-an		ustedes	cantan
ellos ⎫ ellas ⎭	-an		ellos ⎫ ellas ⎭	cantan

We have just conjugated the verb **cantar** in the present tense.

Actividad

A

Identify each picture using the appropriate Spanish word.

1. _____ 2. _____ 3. _____

4. _____

5. _____

6. _____

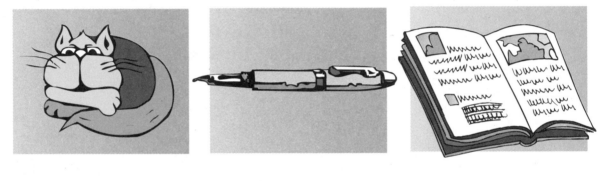

7. _____

8. _____

9. _____

10. _____

11. _____

12. _____

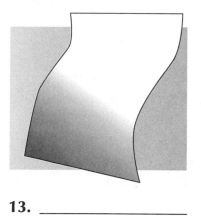

13. _____

14. _____

15. _____

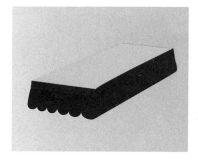

16. _____

17. _____

18. _____

Actividad

B

There are fifteen Spanish words hidden in this puzzle. See how quickly you can find them. Search from left to right, right to left, upwards, downwards, and diagonally.

```
M  A  B  U  E  L  O  S  O  E
A  M  A  B  F  L  O  R  D  T
D  I  S  C  O  Á  T  N  E  N
R  G  G  T  A  P  L  U  M  A
E  A  A  A  L  I  B  R  O  I
I  G  J  E  U  Z  V  X  R  D
L  I  P  S  M  E  S  A  R  U
H  A  M  N  N  U  L  Ñ  E  T
P  O  F  L  O  Q  R  I  P  S
M  E  R  B  L  O  H  N  T  E
```

Actividad

C

Find the hidden classroom objects. There are six classroom objects hidden in the picture. Circle them in the picture and list them below in Spanish.

1. _____   2. _____

3. _____   4. _____

5. _____   6. _____

Actividad

D

Here are ten pictures of people doing different activities. Describe each picture, using the correct form of one of the following verbs.

bailar	comprar	entrar	escuchar	mirar
cantar	contestar	escribir	hablar	trabajar

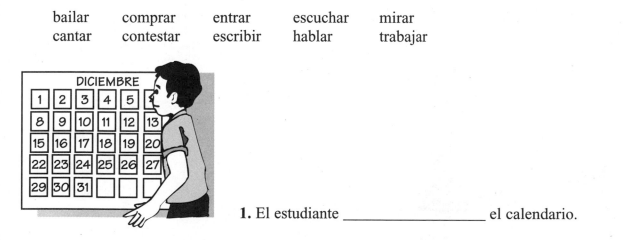

1. El estudiante _____ el calendario.

2. Nosotros _____.

3. Ellos _____ música.

4. Ellos _____ en la fiesta.

5. La mujer _____.

6. Los estudiantes _____.

7. El perro _____ en la casa.

8. Ellos _____ el auto.

9. Los hombres _____.

10. La muchacha _____ bien.

Actividad

E

Identify each picture with the appropriate Spanish word. Then read down the boxed column of letters to find the word that completes this sentence.

El español es _____.

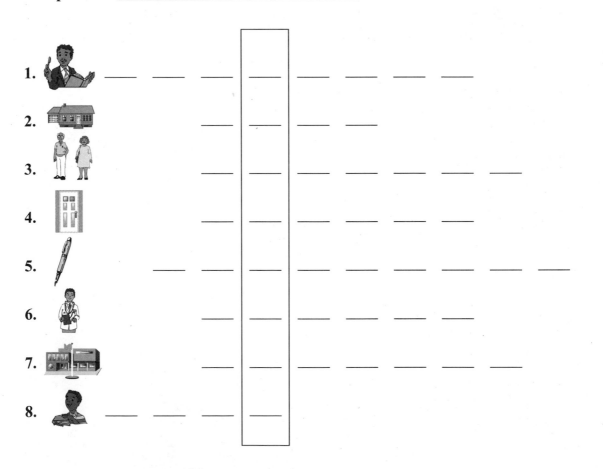

Actividad

F

Picture Story. Can you read this story? Much of it is in picture form. Whenever you come to a picture, read it as if it were a Spanish word.

Pepe es un ____ . Él estudia español en la ____ . La ____ de

Pepe se llama Isabel. El ____ se llama Jorge. La madre es ____ . Ella trabaja

en un ____ . El padre de Pepe es ____ . Él trabaja en una ____

moderna. Pepe va a la ____ de español con su ____ . En la

____ usa muchas cosas: un ____ , una ____ , un ____ y ____ .

En la ____ de Pepe hay dos animales. Sultán es un ____ y Patitas es

un ____ .

Actividad

G

Complete the sentences using the appropriate words from the list below.

clase	inteligente	papel
doctora	miran	pizarra
estudiantes	muy bien	pregunta

El profesor _____ cómo se dice el femenino de «doctor». Yo escribo la
                        1

palabra _____ en un _____ y voy a la _____.
                2   3   4

Mis amigos _____ la pizarra. Los _____ escuchan. El
                        5   6

profesor dice: _____, Antonio. Y dice a la _____: Antonio
                        7   8

es un muchacho muy _____.
                              9

Actividad

H

Let's Play Charades! One student volunteers to be the Master of Ceremonies. Another
one volunteers to go to the head of the class and mimics the action of one of the verbs
discussed in Lesson 5. The MC asks: **¿Qué hace...?** (What is . . . doing?). Whoever says
in Spanish what the volunteer is doing, goes to the head of the class next and mimics
another of those twelve actions. The MC asks again and students keep taking turns until
they are able to name and mimic one action.

   EXAMPLE: MC: ¿Qué hace María?
              Student: **María canta.**

SEGUNDA
Parte

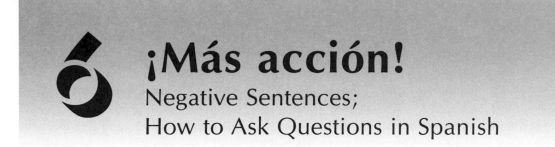

6 ¡Más acción!
Negative Sentences;
How to Ask Questions in Spanish

Look at the following sentences: can you figure out what's going on?

Max y Clara bailan.

Ricardo no baila.

Yo estudio la lección.

Yo no estudio la lección.

Ellos cantan.

Ellos no cantan.

Do you see what's happening here? If you want a sentence to be negative in Spanish, what word is placed directly in front of the verb? _____ If you wrote **no**, you are correct.

No matter what we say in English (*doesn't, don't, aren't, won't,* and the like), in Spanish the rule is always the same: To make a sentence negative, put the word **no** in front of the verb.

Here are some examples:

Ella *no* trabaja. $\begin{cases} \textit{She doesn't work.} \\ \textit{She isn't working.} \end{cases}$

Nosotros *no* entramos. $\begin{cases} \textit{We don't enter.} \\ \textit{We're not entering.} \end{cases}$

Usted *no* escucha. $\begin{cases} \textit{You don't listen.} \\ \textit{You're not listening.} \end{cases}$

Actividad

A _____

Carol is in a very argumentative mood. She contradicts everything people say. Express Carol's negative statements and write them on the space provided.

1. Yo hablo español en clase.   _____

2. Ustedes escuchan la radio.   _____

3. Tú contestas.   _____

4. Ellos caminan.   _____

5. María baila.   _____

6. Los estudiantes usan bolígrafos.   _____

7. Ella practica las palabras nuevas.   _____

8. La profesora mira la pizarra.   _____

9. El actor entra en el teatro.   _____

10. Los padres compran muchas cosas.   _____

2

¡**Magnífico!** Now you know how to make a Spanish sentence negative. But how would you ask a question in Spanish? It's just as simple. Look at the following:

Usted habla español.	*¿Habla usted español?*
Ella canta.	*¿Canta ella?*
Los estudiantes estudian.	*¿Estudian los estudiantes?*
Pedro trabaja en la casa.	*¿Trabaja Pedro en la casa?*

What did we do? We put the subject (**usted, ella, los estudiantes, Pedro**) after the verb when we ask a question. Observe that we do not use *do*, *does*, in Spanish questions. You have probably also noticed that, in addition to the regular question mark at the end, an upside-down question mark is placed at the beginning of a Spanish question. That's all there is to it.

Actividad

B
_____

Carol is in another one of her moods. Whenever someone says something, she doubts it and wants to make sure. Write Carol's questions.

1. Usted pregunta.   _____

2. Los muchachos contestan.   _____

3. El amigo entra.   _____

4. La madre canta. _____

5. Los hombres compran. _____

6. El hermano estudia. _____

7. Las hijas caminan. _____

8. El médico escucha. _____

9. La mujer trabaja. _____

10. Nosotras bailamos. _____

NOTE: If you want to ask a question in Spanish using the word _why_, look at the following:

¿Por qué canta Mariluz?	_Why is Mariluz singing?_
Ella canta porque está contenta.	_She sings because she is happy._

Did you notice that _why_ and _because_ are similar in Spanish? What is the difference? _Why_ is two words (**por qué,** with an accent mark) while _because_ (**porque**) is one word.

Actividad

Mr. O'Neil is making flashcards for his bilingual class. Place the letter of the English meaning with the matching Spanish card.

1. Usted no usa el lápiz. _____
a. They don't speak Spanish.
b. Is there a book in the class?

2. ¿Trabaja usted mucho? _____
c. You don't use the pencil.
d. Do you work hard (a lot)?

3. ¿Estudian ustedes? _____
e. The actor doesn't dance.
f. My teacher doesn't talk a lot.

4. Ella no contesta en la clase. _____
g. Are you studying?

5. ¿Es inteligente el doctor? _____
h. She doesn't answer in class.
i. Where are the girls?

6. ¿Hay un libro en la clase? _____
j. Is the doctor intelligent?

7. ¿Escuchas música? _____

8. ¿Dónde están las niñas? _____

9. El actor no baila. _____

10. ¿Canta él? _____

11. Ellos no hablan español. _____

12. Mi profesor no habla mucho. _____

k. Are you listening to music?
l. Does he sing?

Actividad

D

Work with a partner. Pick out the correct response to each question. Choose from the following suggestions.

EXAMPLE: ¿Por qué trabaja Ud.?
      Trabajo porque necesito dinero.

desea comprar un bolígrafo   está contento(a)
deseo aprender   no comprendo
deseo escuchar música

1. ¿Por qué canta la niña?

_____

2. ¿Por qué preguntas?

_____

3. ¿Por qué vas a la escuela?

_____

4. ¿Por qué tienes un radio?

_____

5. ¿Por qué entra Rafael en la tienda?

_____

Dígalo bien

■ The letters **b** and **v** are pronounced like *b* in *boat*.

*v*amos	*v*entana	*b*anco
auto*b*ús	*v*aso	nue*v*o
*b*onito	*b*ote	*b*usco
*b*lanco	*v*oy	*v*oto

*B*ueno, *V*icente. *V*amos a *b*uscar a *B*enito.
Las *b*ananas de *V*enezuela son *b*uenas y *b*aratas.

3

Here's a short story. Can you understand it?

Muchas personas, hombres y mujeres, usan el automóvil. ¿Por qué? Porque necesitan el automóvil para ir a trabajar. Muchos profesores y muchos estudiantes no usan el autobús para ir a la escuela. Usan el automóvil. Muchos doctores no van en autobús al hospital. Necesitan el automóvil. Y ¿qué necesita un automóvil? Necesita gasolina, mucha gasolina. También necesita un garaje.

usar *to use*
para ir a *to go to*
el autobús *bus*
a la *to the*
al *to the*
   necesitar *to need*
¿qué? *what?*
   gasolina *gas*
también *also*
el garaje *garage*

—¿Y tú, Horacio, ¿necesitas un auto nuevo?

nuevo *new*

— No, un auto usado está bien, un auto nuevo cuesta mucho dinero.

usado *used*
   cuesta *costs*
el dinero *money*

— Y tú, Héctor, ¿necesitas un auto nuevo?

— Sí, ¡claro!

¡claro! *of course*

— ¿Por qué?

— ¡Porque deseo impresionar a las muchachas!

Actividad

E

Answer the following questions in Spanish.

1. ¿Qué usan muchas personas?

_____

2. ¿Para qué usan el auto muchas personas?

_____

3. ¿Para qué necesitas tú un automóvil?

_____

4. ¿Qué necesita un automóvil?

_____

5. ¿Para qué necesita Héctor un auto?

_____

6. Y tú, ¿caminas a la escuela?

_____

Actividad

F

Say for what purpose you use the following.

EXAMPLE: Uso el libro para **estudiar**.

1. Uso la bicicleta para _____ al parque.

2. Uso el español para _____ en clase.

3. Uso mucho dinero para _____ un auto nuevo.

4. Usamos el autobús para _____ al cine.

5. Usamos la puerta para _____ .

6. Usamos la radio para _____ música.

NOTE: Perhaps you noticed that you say **al** (to the) when you go to a place that ends in -o or is considered masculine. And you use **a la** before a place that is considered feminine. Let's see if you understood this.

Actividad

G

Say where you are going.

EXAMPLES: **Voy a la escuela.**
Voy al hospital.

1. Voy _____ casa de Ana.

2. Voy _____ supermercado.

3. Voy _____ parque.

4. Voy _____ concierto.

5. Voy _____ garaje.

6. Voy _____ pizarra.

7. Voy _____ clase.

8. Voy _____ doctor.

Actividad

Ask your teacher if he or she does the activities illustrated in the pictures. Remember to use **usted** forms when speaking to your teacher.

1. _____

2. _____

3. _____

Actividad

Ask your friend if he or she does the activities illustrated in the pictures. Remember to use **tú** when speaking to your friend.

1. _____

2. _____

3. _____

4. _____

Actividad

J

You have been invited to a party, but you do not want to go. Using vocabulary in this lesson, write a brief note giving four reasons why you can't go to the party.

EXAMPLE: **No bailo con las muchachas (los muchachos).**

1. _____

2. _____

3. _____

4. _____

Actividad

K

Express the following phrases in Spanish.

1. a new car _____

2. a big park _____

3. a small garage _____

4. a used car _____

5. a good pen _____

6. a modern house _____

7. a famous actor _____

8. good things _____

9. a new book _____

Conversación

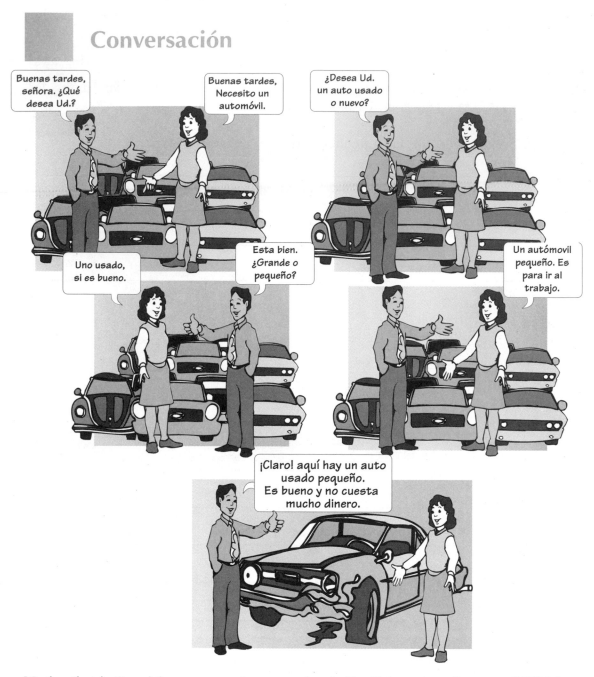

Notice that in Spanish you say **auto nuevo**, but in English you say "new car." Which word goes first in Spanish? _____ The thing or person described goes first. Let's see if you understand this.

Diálogo

Fill in what the second person in the dialogue would say. Choose from the following list:

Bueno...¡ Perfecto!
Un automóvil pequeño. Es para ir a trabajar.
Buenas tardes. Necesito un automóvil.
Usado, si es bueno.

Preguntas personales

Answer these personal questions in complete Spanish sentences.

1. ¿Bailas bien?

_____

2. ¿Cantas en clase?

_____

3. ¿Hablas español?

_____

4. ¿Escuchas música?

_____

Información personal

¡Felicitaciones! Congratulations! You have been picked the student most likely to succeed. Tell your friends what you do in your spare time to make you so successful. Start each sentence with **Yo...** or **Yo no...**

EXAMPLE: **Yo no miro mucha televisión.**

1. _____

2. _____

3. _____

4. _____

5. _____

Vamos a conversar

Your cousin Alejandro is asking you about a car you've seen and would like to get after graduation:

ALEJANDRO:	¿Qué tipo de automóvil deseas?
TÚ:	*(Tell him the kind of car you want.)*
ALEJANDRO:	¿Cuesta mucho dinero?
TÚ:	*(Tell him no, it's not a lot of money.)*
ALEJANDRO:	¿Es un auto nuevo?
TÚ:	*(Say it's a used car.)*
ALEJANDRO:	¿Para qué necesitas un auto?
TÚ:	*(Say to go to school.)*

Flying with the Gods —
Los Voladores de Papantla

Five men dressed in red velvet pants, embroidered sashes, and helmets decorated with multicolored feathers climb to a platform atop a swaying 100-foot pole. While four attach thick ropes to their ankles, the fifth man begins to play a flute and sound a small drum.

After a brief while, the four men release themselves from the platform into the air and begin a slow spiral around the pole, letting the ropes unwind from their bodies until they touch the ground. Each flyer has to make exactly thirteen revolutions around the pole before landing on his feet (four times thirteen is fifty-two, the number of years in the Aztec century).

This ceremony, known as **danza de los voladores**, is performed by Totonac Indians. It was originally a religious rite in honor of the rain god. Although the Spaniards abolished all forms of native worship, they allowed the flying dance to survive because they believed it was a daredevil sport rather than a sacred ceremony. It is still considered a daring act of bravery because of the danger. If a flyer falls too rapidly to the ground, he can be seriously injured or even killed.

The ceremony is held in front of an ancient pyramid at the town of Papantla, México.

Quick Quiz

1. The flyers of Papantla climb to the top of a _____ foot pole.

2. Four men attach ropes to their _____.

3. The flyers let themselves down, making exactly _____ revolutions around the pole.

4. The flying dance was originally a religious rite in honor of the _____.

5. Today the ceremony is considered an act of _____.

Let's Find Out More

1. How does this ceremony compare to "Bungee" jumping?

2. Which one would you prefer to practice?

3. Find out about other extraordinary ceremonies practiced in the Spanish-speaking world.

Vocabulario

WORDS TO KNOW

a *to* (motion)
al *to the* (m.)
a la *to the* (f.)
bueno(a) *good*
desear *to wish*
el dinero *money*
el garaje *garage*
la gasolina *gasoline*
ir (a) *to go (to)*
necesitar *to need*

nuevo(a) *new*
para *for, in order to*
pequeño(a) *small*
practicar *to practice*
¿qué? *what?*
si *if*
también *also*
uno(a) *one*
usado(a) *used*
usar *to use*

EXPRESSIONS

¡claro! *of course!*
¿para qué? *for what?*
para ir a *to go to*
buenas tardes *good afternoon*

uno nuevo *a new one*
cuesta mucho *it costs a lot*
Bueno..., *Well . . . ,*

7 Y el número es...

How to Count in Spanish:
(Numbers From 0 to 30)

Repeat the numbers aloud after your teacher.

0	cero	11	once	21	veintiuno
1	uno	12	doce	22	veintidós
2	dos	13	trece	23	veintitrés
3	tres	14	catorce	24	veinticuatro
4	cuatro	15	quince	25	veinticinco
5	cinco	16	dieciséis	26	veintiséis
6	seis	17	diecisiete	27	veintisiete
7	siete	18	dieciocho	28	veintiocho
8	ocho	19	diecinueve	29	veintinueve
9	nueve	20	veinte	30	treinta
10	diez				

Actividad

A

Write the Spanish word for the number of things you see.

1. _____

2. _____

3. _____

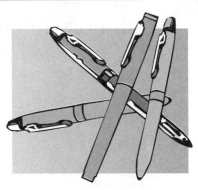

4. _____

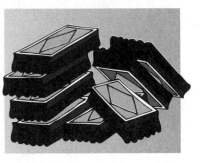

5. _____

6. _____

7. _____

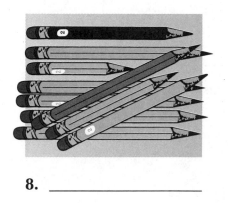

8. _____

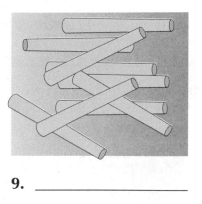

9. _____

Actividad

B

Match each Spanish number with its corresponding numeral. Write the numeral in the space provided.

1. cuatro _____ 5

2. dos _____ 20

3. trece _____ 9

4. veinte _____ 15

5. dieciocho _____ 4

6. quince _____ 2

7. cinco _____ 13

8. nueve _____ 18

Actividad

Find the hidden numbers and write them out in Spanish.

_____   _____

_____   _____

_____   _____

_____   _____

Dígalo bien

- In Spanish, the letter **c** is pronounced like *c* in *cake* when followed by **a**, **o**, or **u**.

*c*omprar	*c*omo	lo*c*o
*c*afé	pelí*c*ula	practi*c*ar
ban*c*o	¡*c*aramba!	*c*omer
Mar*c*os	fres*c*o	*c*asa

¿Cuándo compra Carmen la casa?
Carlos come coco en el comedor.

- When the letters **qu** are followed by **e** or **i**, they also sound like *c* in *cake*.

*qu*é	es*qu*iar	a*qu*el
ra*qu*eta	*qu*iero	*qu*eso
*qu*ién	*Qu*ito	blo*qu*e
pe*qu*eño	a*qu*í	par*qu*e

¿Quién quiere esquiar aquí en el parque?
Quiero aquella raqueta pequeña.

2

Here's a little poem about **diez gatitos** (ten little kittens). Try singing it to the tune of *Ten Little Indians*.

Uno, dos, tres gatitos,
cuatro, cinco, seis gatitos,
siete, ocho, nueve gatitos,
diez gatitos son.
10, 9, 8 gatitos,
7, 6, 5 gatitos,
4, 3, 2 gatitos,
un gatito es.

Actividad

You're announcing the results of a school race. Call off the numbers of the runners as they cross the finish line.

Actividad

Play the role of a telephone operator in Mexico. A classmate will ask you the number for one of the persons or places listed below. Say the number in Spanish.

> EXAMPLE: **el señor Montes: 4 25 6 8 1 13**
> **El número del señor Montes es cuatro veinticinco seis ocho uno trece.**

1. el señor López: 0 24 25 6 8 1
2. el doctor Ramos: 16 9 20 2 11
3. la señorita Fonseca: 21 14 13 27
4. el profesor: 30 15 28 04
5. la señora Soto: 23 10 0 9 24
6. la Farmacia Sonora: 17 16 7 4 18

7. el restaurante El Buen Sabor: 30 19 29 1 1
8. el Hotel Azteca: 5 6 3 22 25 3
9. el cine Acapulco: 28 4 5 0 6 8 0
10. la Línea Aérea Inca: 5 19 6 15 27 30

3 In this story, Luis and his sister Graciela make a small profit. Read on to find out how they do it. But first, learn your numbers, because there are lots of them in the story.

¡Somos ricos!

PERSONAJES:	Un niño que tiene siete años. Una niña que tiene seis años. Un vendedor de billetes de lotería. Un hombre
VENDEDOR:	¡El último billete! ¡El último billete!
NIÑO:	Deseamos comprar el billete. ¿Cuánto cuesta?
VENDEDOR:	Cuesta veinte centavos.
NIÑO:	Muy bien. Veinte centavos. Ocho, nueve, diez, once, doce, trece, catorce, quince, dieciséis, diecisiete. Tengo diecisiete centavos, señor. ¿Acepta usted diecisiete centavos?

tiene... años *is ... years old*
el vendedor *the seller*
 el billete *the ticket*
 la lotería *the lottery*
último *last*
¿cuánto cuesta? *How much does it cost?*
el centavo *cent, penny*
muy bien *very well*
(yo) tengo *I have*
aceptar *to accept*

VENDEDOR:	No, son veinte centavos.
NIÑA:	Yo tengo aquí tres centavos.
VENDEDOR:	Muy bien. Diecisiete y tres son veinte. Gracias, niños.
HOMBRE:	Yo deseo un billete también.
VENDEDOR:	Imposible: es el último billete.
HOMBRE:	Niños, ¿aceptan ustedes un dólar por el billete?
NIÑO:	¡Un dólar! ¡Somos ricos!

aquí *here*

muy bien *very well*

somos *we are*
ricos *rich*

Actividad

F

Complete these sentences, which are based on the story that you have just read.

1. El niño tiene _____ años.

2. La niña tiene _____ años.

3. Ellos desean comprar _____ .

4. El billete cuesta _____ centavos.

5. El niño tiene _____ centavos.

6. El hombre compra el billete por _____ dólar.

Actividad

G

Your teacher will read some numbers to you. Write the numbers you hear.

EXAMPLE: You hear **veinte** and you write: **20.**

1. _____   **2.** _____

3. _____   **4.** _____

5. _____   6. _____

7. _____   8. _____

9. _____   10. _____

Actividad

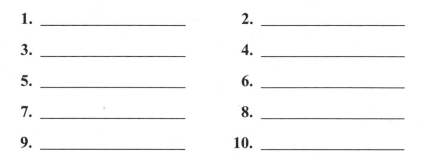

You will hear a number in English. Write the number in Spanish.

1. _____   2. _____

3. _____   4. _____

5. _____   6. _____

7. _____   8. _____

9. _____   10. _____

4 Now that you know the Spanish words for the numbers 0 to 30, let's try some arithmetic in Spanish. First you must learn the following expressions:

y *and* (+)   **dividido por** *divided by* (÷)
menos *minus, less* (−)   **es** *is, equals* (=)
por *times* (x)   **son** *are, equals* (=)

2 + 2 = 4	Dos y dos son cuatro.
5 − 4 = 1	Cinco menos cuatro es uno.
3 x 3 = 9	Tres por tres es nueve.
12 ÷ 2 = 6	Doce dividido por dos es seis.

Actividad

You're helping your little brother do his homework by reading the problems aloud. Help him write each problem in numerals.

1. Cinco y cinco son diez. _____

2. Veinte menos cinco es quince. _____

3. Nueve por dos es dieciocho. _____

4. Seis y tres son nueve. _____

5. Cuatro dividido por dos es dos. _____

6. Diecisiete menos dieciséis es uno. _____

7. Once por uno es once. _____

8. Veinte dividido por cinco es cuatro. _____

9. Dieciocho dividido por dos es nueve. _____

10. Dieciséis y tres son diecinueve. _____

Actividad

Your little brother also has to read some problems aloud. Help him say them in Spanish. Write the problems in Spanish, then read them aloud.

1. $2 + 3 = 5$ _____

2. $9 - 2 = 7$ _____

3. $4 \times 4 = 16$ _____

4. $8 \div 2 = 4$ _____

5. $22 + 3 = 25$ _____

6. $10 - 5 = 5$ _____

7. $24 + 5 = 29$ _____

8. $6 \div 3 = 2$ _____

9. $10 + 11 = 21$ _____

10. $18 - 7 = 11$ _____

Actividad

K

Circle the letter of the correct answer, and then read the entire problem aloud.

1. Cuatro menos dos es

    (a) 2   (b) 4   (c) 6   (d) 8

2. Ocho y tres son

    (a) 12   (b) 11   (c) 10   (d) 9

3. Seis dividido por tres es

    (a) 1   (b) 3   (c) 2   (d) 4

4. Cuatro y cuatro son

    (a) 8   (b) 20   (c) 0   (d) 16

5. Ocho y siete son

    (a) 15   (b) 1   (c) 16   (d) 3

6. Dos menos uno es

    (a) 3   (b) 1   (c) 2   (d) 4

7. Tres por tres es

(a) 6   (b) 8   (c) 9   (d) 2

8. Cuatro dividido por cuatro es

(a) 1   (b) 8   (c) 0   (d) 10

9. Tres y cuatro y cinco son

(a) 17   (b) 12   (c) 2   (d) 4

10. Veinte menos dieciocho es

(a) 10   (b) 9   (c) 2   (d) 8

Actividad

Add the columns in stages from top to bottom.

EXAMPLE:

Ocho y seis son catorce.
Catorce y dos son dieciséis.
Dieciséis y cuatro son veinte.

1. _____

_____

_____

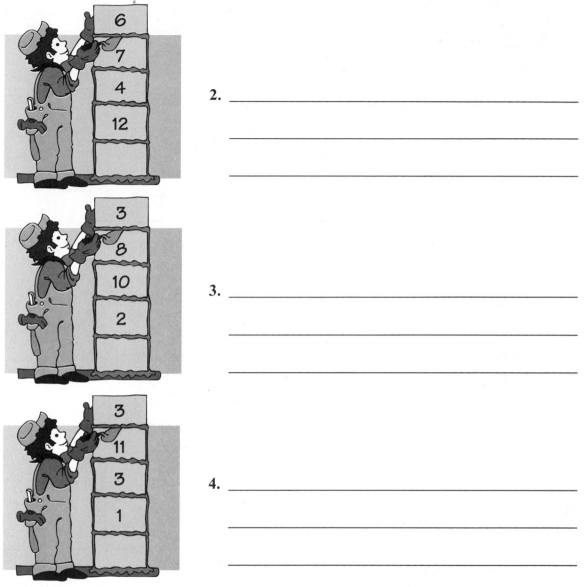

2. _____

_____

_____

3. _____

_____

_____

4. _____

_____

_____

Actividad

You have learned three forms of the verb **tener** (**tengo, tienes, tiene**) which is the verb used in Spanish to indicate age. Let's see if you have learned them.

1. El niño _____ seis años.

2. Tú _____ trece años.

3. Yo _____ doce años.

4. Ella _____ catorce años.

5. Pepe _____ quince años.

6. Tú no _____ once años.

Actividad

Work in pairs. Ask each other how many of the following objects you see in class. Give answers before asking the next question.

EXAMPLE: ¿Cuántas tizas hay?
Hay cuatro tizas.

1. ¿Cuántos cestos de papeles hay? **2.** ¿Cuántas ventanas hay?

3. ¿Cuántos estudiantes hay? **4.** ¿Cuántas puertas hay?

5. ¿Cuántos lápices hay? **6.** ¿Cuántos relojes hay?

7. ¿Cuántas sillas hay? **8.** ¿Cuántas pizarras hay?

9. ¿Cuántos cuadernos hay? **10.** ¿Cuántas niñas hay?

Conversación

¿Cuántos son siete y nueve?

Siete y nueve son quince.

¡claro que no! *of course not!, no way!*
¿qué tienes? *What's the matter with you?*
hoy *today*

generalmente *generally*
(tú) eres *you are*
el vendaje *bandage*
la mano *hand*

Diálogo

You're asking all the math questions now. Complete the dialogue, choosing from the following list of sentences.

¿Cuánto es veinte dividido por dos?　　　¿Cuántos son tres y cuatro?
¿Qué tienes hoy?　　　　　　　　　　　¿Cuánto es quince menos cinco?

Información personal

Your school club requires that every student fill out and ID card. Supply the requested information in Spanish, writing out all the numbers:

IDENTIFICACIÓN

1. Edad (age) _____ años

2. Número de hermanos: _____

3. Número de hermanas: _____

4. Número de personas en la familia: _____

5. Número de la casa: _____

6. Número de teléfono: _____

Vamos a conversar

You're at a refreshment stand in the park.

VENDEDOR: ¿Qué deseas?

TÚ: (Ask if he has ice cream.)

VENDEDOR: No hay de chocolate. Hay de vainilla.

TÚ: (Tell him you want vanilla ice cream.)

VENDEDOR: ¿Grande o pequeño?

TÚ: (Ask how much a small ice cream costs.)

VENDEDOR: El pequeño es treinta centavos.

TÚ: (Say here you have a dollar.)

LOS QUINCE: A SWEET FIFTEEN PARTY?

When a Spanish-American girl reaches fifteen years of age, it is a very special occasion. She is now a young lady and may begin to wear make-up, and perhaps to start dating. Traditionally, her proud parents hold an elaborate party and dance to present her into society.

La quinceañera (the young lady), dressed in a magnificent long gown, and accompanied by her parents, her date, and fourteen young couples (her court of honor) go to the ball where she changes to high-heel shoes to show she has become a woman. The climax of the event is **el baile de las quince parejas** (dance of the fifteen couples).

Los quince, as it is commonly called, sometimes involves hundreds of guests, takes a year of preparation, and costs thousands of dollars. In

Miami, there is even a *Miss Quinceañera Latina* pageant. A **quince** party can cost as much as $50,000! Many parents save for years for their daughter's coming out party. Although this celebration is common throughout Spanish America, no one really knows its exact origins. Some think the custom originated in Spain. One researcher claimed that **quinces** are an adaptation of an ancient ritual.

But one thing is certain, the birthday girl is surely made to feel like a "Princess for a Day."

 ## Quick Quiz

1. Generally, a young Hispanic lady may begin dating when she reaches the age of

   _____.

2. The name of the party is _____.

3. The name of the young lady is _____.

4. The climax of the festivities is _____.

5. The court of honor consists of _____.

6. Changing into high heel shoes signifies that the girl is now _____.

 ## Let's Find Out More

1. What are some similarities and differences between the **quince** and the "sweet sixteen"?
2. Go to the library and research if there are similar parties celebrated around the world.

Vocabulario

WORDS TO KNOW

aceptar *to accept*

el año *year*

aquí *here*

cl billete *ticket*

el centavo *cent, penny*

desear *to wish, to want*

el dólar *dollar*

el gatito, (la gatita) *kitten*

generalmente *generally*

el helado de chocolate *chocolate ice cream*

hoy *today*

la lotería *lottery*

menos *minus, less*

el número *number*

por *by; times (x)*

¿por qué? *why?*

porque *because*

rico(a) *rich*

el teléfono *telephone*

vainilla *vanilla*

el vendedor *seller*

NUMBERS

cero *zero*

uno *one*

dos *two*

tres *three*

cuatro *four*

cinco *five*

seis *six*

siete *seven*

ocho *eight*

nueve *nine*

diez *ten*

once *eleven*

doce *twelve*

trece *thirteen*

catorce *fourteen*

quince *fifteen*

dieciséis *sixteen*

diecisiete *seventeen*

dieciocho *eighteen*

diecinueve *nineteen*

veinte *twenty*

veintiuno *twenty-one*

veintidós *twenty-two*

veintitrés *twenty-three*

veinticuatro *twenty-four*

veinticinco *twenty-five*

veintiséis *twenty-six*

veintisiete *twenty-seven*

veintiocho *twenty-eight*

veintinueve *twenty-nine*

treinta *thirty*

EXPRESSIONS

¡claro que no! *of course not!, no way!*

¿cuánto cuesta? *how much does it cost?*

¿cuántos(as) hay? *how many are there?*

¿cuántos son... y... ? *how much is . . . and . . . ?*

eres *you are*

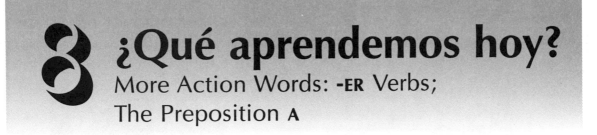

¿Qué aprendemos hoy?
More Action Words: -ER Verbs;
The Preposition A

The verbs that follow end in **-er**. Can you guess their meanings?

aprender

beber

comer

comprender

171

leer

responder

vender

ver

correr

saber*

* **saber** (to know) has an irregular form **sé** (I know). All other forms of the present are regular.

2

We just saw ten action words. Notice that these verbs don't end in **-ar** but in
_____. Do you recall how we made changes in **-ar** verbs by dropping **-ar**
and adding various endings? Well, we must do the same thing with **-er** verbs, but
the endings will be slightly different. Let's see what happens. A good example is
the verb **vender** (to sell). If you want to say *I sell*, remove the **-er** ending and add
the following:

yo	vend**o**	*I sell, I am selling*
tú	vend**es**	*you sell, you are selling* (familiar singular)
usted	vend**e**	*you sell, you are selling* (formal singular)
él ⎱ ella ⎰	vend**e**	*he sells, he is selling* / *she sells, she is selling*
nosotros ⎱ nosotras ⎰	vend**emos**	*we sell, we are selling*
ustedes	vend**en**	*you sell, you are selling* (plural)
ellos ⎱ ellas ⎰	vend**en**	*they sell, they are selling*

Actividad

A

Following the instructions given in point 2, write the forms for each subject in these **-er**
verbs. Note that **ver** retains letter **e** in the **yo** form: **Yo veo.**

	aprender	leer	ver
	(to learn)	(to read)	(to see)
1. yo	_____	_____	_____
2. tú	_____	_____	_____

3. Ud. _____ _____ _____

4. él _____ _____ _____

5. ella _____ _____ _____

6. nosotros _____ _____ _____

7. Uds. _____ _____ _____

8. ellos _____ _____ _____

9. ellas _____ _____ _____

3 Now let's compare an **-ar** verb with an **-er** verb. How are they similar and how are they different?

hablar _to speak_	**comprender** _to understand_
yo **habl***o*	yo **comprend***o*
tú **habl***as*	tú **comprend***es*
Ud. **habl***a*	Ud. **comprend***e*
él / ella **habl***a*	él / ella **comprend***e*
nosotros / nosotras **habl***amos*	nosotros / nosotras **comprend***emos*
Uds. **habl***an*	Uds. **comprend***en*
ellos / ellas **habl***an*	ellos / ellas **comprend***en*

Notice that **yo** has the same **-o** ending in both **-ar** and **-er** verbs: **yo hablo, yo comprendo.** In all other forms, however, the **-ar** verbs have endings that are **a**, or begin with **a**, while the **-er** verbs have endings that are **e** or begin with **e**.

Dígalo bien

■ In Spanish, the letter **c** is pronounced like *s* in *sent,* when followed by **e** or **i**.

*ci*ne	*ci*udad	na*ci*ón
aten*ci*ón	Bar*ce*lona	prin*ci*pal
*ci*nco	on*ce*	servi*ci*o
pre*ci*o	*ce*ro	*ce*rca

El *ci*ne está en el *ce*ntro de Bar*ce*lona.
Valen*ci*a está *ce*rca de la *ci*udad de Mur*ci*a.

■ The letter **z** is also pronounced like the *s* in *sent*:

lápi*z*	*z*apato	Ama*z*onas
pla*z*a	mo*z*o	pi*z*arra
die*z*	*Z*arago*z*a	Lá*z*aro
*z*ona	ta*z*a	ti*z*a

Esperanza Díaz lleva zapatos azules.
Mozo, quiero zumo de zanahoria en una taza.

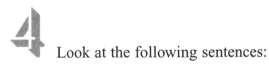

Look at the following sentences:

Ellos caminan *a* la tienda.	*They walk to the store.*
Ellos corren *a* la escuela.	*The run to the school.*

Note that in Spanish, the preposition **a** sometimes indicates motion to.

Corro *a* casa.   *I run home.*

If **a** comes directly before the article **el** (English *the*), the two words combine to form the word **al**.

Ellos van *al* cine.	*They go to the movies.*
Camino *al* teatro.	*I walk to the theater.*

Now look at these four sentences:

Yo veo la pizarra.	*I see the board.*
Yo veo la mesa.	*I see the table.*
Yo veo a la profesora.	*I see the teacher.*
Yo veo al profesor.	*I see the teacher.*

Which word in the above Spanish sentences IS NOT expressed in the English sentences? _____ If you said **a**, you are correct. The preposition **a** is placed after a verb and before the name of a person or pet. This use of **a** is called "personal a." What two Spanish words does **al** represent? _____ If you said **a el**, you are right.

Actividad

B
_____

Work with a partner. Ask each other where you are going. Use all of the following suggestions.

EXAMPLES: ¿Adónde vas?
               Voy a la escuela. ¿Y tú?
    OR:
               Voy al banco. ¿Y tú?

1. la fiesta   2. el doctor

3. el rodeo   4. el rancho

5. la pizarra   6. la clase

7. el tablón   8. el parque

9. la ventana   10. el teléfono

Actividad

Complete each sentence with **el, la, al,** or **a la** as needed.

1. Comprendemos _____ lección.

2. Comprendemos _____ presidente.

3. Yo no veo _____ muchacha.

4. Yo no veo _____ billete.

5. Los estudiantes escuchan _____ programa de radio.

6. Los estudiantes escuchan _____ señora Zamora.

7. María visita _____ abuela.

8. María visita _____ clase.

9. No comprendo _____ profesora.

10. No comprendo _____ pregunta.

5 Now let's read another fun story.

El gato habla también

Lupita, una muchacha que tiene once años, tiene un gato que se llama Patitas. Patitas es un gato bonito. Cuando Lupita va a la escuela, el gato no come. Cuando ella está en

se llama *called*
bonito *pretty*

casa, ella llama a Patitas, y él va a comer. Lupita siempre compra la comida para Patitas. Patitas es grande pero no come mucho. Come poco. Patitas es muy inteligente y aprende rápidamente. El gato está muy contento cuando ve a Lupita entrar en casa. Patitas desea correr al jardín. Cuando el gato dice «miau, miau» Lupita comprende y siempre responde:—¡Patitas, Patitas!—y va al jardín con el gato.

siempre *always*
la comida *the food*
pero *but*
poco *a little*
rápidamente *fast*
contento *happy*
al jardín *to the garden*

Actividad

D

Complete the sentences based on the story you have just read.

1. Lupita tiene _____ años.

2. Patitas es _____ de Lupita.

3. Patitas no necesita mucha _____ .

4. El gato está contento cuando _____ Lupita.

5. Cuando el gato dice «miau, miau» Lupita _____ .

Actividad

E

Say what the following people are doing by providing the correct forms of the verbs. Be sure to drop **-ar** or **-er** before adding the appropriate endings.

1. *(visitar)* Nosotros _____ a la profesora.

2. *(vender)* Pedro _____ billetes de lotería.

3. *(practicar)* Tú _____ la lección.

4. *(leer)* Usted _____ el periódico.

5. *(responder)*   Mi hermano _____ en español al profesor.

6. *(comprar)*   Ellos _____ muchos libros.

7. *(aprender)*   Ustedes _____ rápidamente.

8. *(trabajar)*   Mi padre _____ en una escuela moderna.

9. *(ver)*   Yo _____ a mi gato en el jardín.

10. *(correr)*   Ella _____ al parque con su perro.

Actividad

F

Now, read each sentence in **Actividad E** and have a classmate say it in the negative.

1. _____

2. _____

3. _____

4. _____

5. _____

6. _____

7. _____

8. _____

9. _____

10. _____

Actividad

G

Repeat each sentence in **Actividad F** and have a classmate change it into a question.

1. _____

2. _____

3. _____

4. _____

5. _____

6. _____

7. _____

8. _____

9. _____

10. _____

Actividad

H

What is everyone doing? Match the following sentences with the pictures they describe.

Nosotras leemos un libro.

La gata come.

El muchacho vende periódicos.

Yo respondo en la clase.

El hombre bebe café.

Los estudiantes aprenden mucho.

El muchacho no comprende.

Mi amigo tiene un perro.

Vemos al gatito.

Ellos corren al cine.

1. _____

2. _____

3. _____

4. _____

5. _____

6. _____

7. _____

8. _____

9. _____

10. _____

Actividad

You want to EMPHASIZE or make clear who is doing the action. Fill in the blanks with the correct subject pronoun.

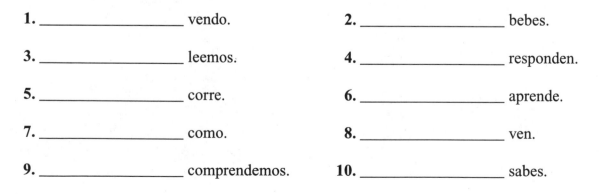

1. _____ vendo.

2. _____ bebes.

3. _____ leemos.

4. _____ responden.

5. _____ corre.

6. _____ aprende.

7. _____ como.

8. _____ ven.

9. _____ comprendemos.

10. _____ sabes.

Conversación

yo prefiero *I prefer*
todos *all* (plural)
hasta luego *so long*

Diálogo

Complete the dialogue by using expressions chosen from the following list:

¡Oh, sí! Él comprende mucho.   ¿Come mucho Rambolito?
Hasta luego, Roberto.   Voy al parque con mi gato Chiquito.

Información personal

Your school counselor wants to find out a few things about you. Finish each sentence in a way that tells us something about you.

EXAMPLE: **Leo el periódico.**

1. Aprendo _____.

2. Como _____.

3. Corro _____.

4. Leo _____.

5. Trabajo _____.

6. Escucho _____.

Vamos a conversar

You and a neighbor (**una vecina**) are talking about your cat.

VECINA: Es un gato bonito. ¿Cómo se llama?

TÚ: *(Tell her its name.)*

VECINA: No es muy grande.

TÚ: *(Say it's a kitten.)*

VECINA: ¿Come mucho?

TÚ: *(Disagree. Tell her it does not eat much.)*

VECINA: Los gatos son estúpidos. ¿Verdad?

TÚ: *(Disagree. Tell her they are very intelligent and learn fast.)*

¡Fiesta!

Having a party? Then, you'll need a long stick or bat. In many Spanish-speaking countries, no party—especially a birthday party—is complete without a **piñata**.

Piñatas are clay pots or wire-mesh frames covered with brightly colored crepe paper. They come in all shapes and sizes: a striped donkey, a woolly sheep, or even an intergalactic ship. Piñatas are filled with candies, nuts, fruits, and sometimes coins or little toys.

The piñata is hung from tree limb or—if indoors—from a rafter in the house. Then it is raised and lowered by a rope. The children take turns swinging at the piñata with a long stick to break it open. To make it more

challenging, they are blindfolded. When someone breaks it, the candy and other goodies shower to the ground and a wild scramble ensues to gather as much loot as possible. While one child tries to break the piñata, the others sing:

Dale, dale, dale,	*Hit it, hit it, hit it,*
no pierdas el tino.	*don't loose your aim.*
Porque si lo pierdes,	*Because if you do,*
pierdes el camino.	*you'll lose your way.*

Another popular jingle is:

Yo no quiero oro,	*I don't want gold,*
ni quiero plata.	*I don't want silver.*
Yo lo que quiero es	*What I want*
romper la piñata.	*is to break the piñata.*

Quick Quiz

1. La piñata is a _____ covered with brightly colored paper.

2. Piñatas are filled with _____ .

3. The piñata is _____ and _____ by a rope.

4. The children are _____ so that they won't see.

5. A long stick is used to _____ the piñata.

Let's Find Out More

1. Construct a piñata of papier maché or cardboard and cover it with crepe paper of different colors.

2. Find out which are some of the games played at birthday parties in the United States?

Vocabulario

WORDS TO KNOW

admirar *to admire*

aprender *to learn*

beber *to drink*

bonito *pretty*

comer *to eat*

la comida *meal*

comprender *to understand*

contento *happy*

correr *to run*

el jardín *garden*

leer *to read*

pero *but*

rápidamente *rapidly*

responder *to answer*

siempre *always*

todos *all*

vender *to sell*

ver *to see*

EXPRESSIONS

hasta luego *so long*

prefiero *I prefer*

tiene *she, he has*

¿Cómo es?

How to Describe Things in Spanish

The words that follow are all adjectives. They describe the people, animals, and objects in the pictures. Can you guess their meanings?

grande

pequeño

bonito

feo

inteligente

estúpido

rico

pobre

viejo

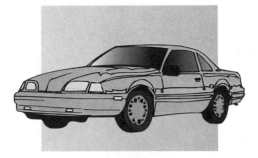

nuevo

alto

bajo

difícil

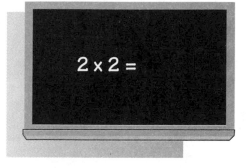

fácil

moreno*

rubio

* Footnote: **Moreno** means either dark-skinned or dark-haired, though sometimes it means both. Also, **alto** and **bajo** are used to describe people's height.

Actividad

A

Kathy is learning Spanish. She wants to learn to describe things and has made a list of common adjectives. Help her by providing an appropriate subject for each adjective.

EXAMPLE: **Un auto americano.**

1. americano(a)

2. colombiano(a)

3. delicioso(a)

4. diferente

5. elegante

6. especial

7. estúpido(a)

8. excelente

9. famoso(a)

10. horrible

Dígalo bien

- In Spanish, the letter **j** is pronounced like *h* in *home*.

jardín	ba*j*o	gara*j*e
*j*oven	venda*j*e	traba*j*o
*j*ulio	hi*j*o	*J*osé
*j*unio	vie*j*o	mu*j*er

El hi*j*o de *J*osé traba*j*a en San *J*uan.
Una mu*j*er muy vie*j*a está en el *j*ardín.

- The letter **g,** in the combinations **ge** and **gi,** has the same sound as **j**.

inteli*g*ente	Ar*g*entina	Jor*g*e
*g*eneralmente	pá*g*ina	ori*g*inal
*g*eneroso	*G*erardo	*g*itano

***G*erardo es *g*eneralmente *g*eneroso.**
El *g*eneral es ar*g*entino.

2

Now see if you can understand this story:

Mi amigo Jorge

Jorge es un muchacho cubano. Es guapo, alto y moreno. Es también inteligente. Sus amigos dicen que es bueno y generoso con todos. Le gusta la música moderna, y baila muy bien. Es un muchacho perfecto (¡en su opinión!).

muchacho *boy*

amigos *friends*

dicen *say*

bueno *good*

le gusta... *(he/she) likes...*

Actividad

B

Make a list of all the adjectives used to describe Jorge.

1. _____

2. _____

3. _____

4. _____

5. _____

6. _____

7. _____

8. _____

Actividad

C

Read each of the following untrue statements to a classmate, who will then change all the words in boldface to make the statements true.

1. Jorge es un muchacho **colombiano**. _____

2. Jorge es **bajo** y **rubio**. _____

3. Jorge es **estúpido**. _____

4. Jorge es un muchacho **feo**. _____

Here is another story. See how much you can understand.

Mi amiga Alicia

Alicia es una muchacha cubana. Es guapa, alta y morena. Es también inteligente. Sus amigas dicen que ella es interesante y que también es muy generosa con todos. Le gustan los deportes. Su deporte favorito es el tenis. Es una muchacha perfecta (¡en su opinión!).

el deporte *the sport*
su *his, her*

Actividad

D

Make a list of all the adjectives used to described Alicia.

1. _____   2. _____

3. _____   4. _____

5. _____   6. _____

7. _____   8. _____

Actividad

E

Read each of the following untrue statements to a classmate, who will then change all the words in boldface to make the sentences true.

1. Alicia es una muchacha **colombiana**. _____

2. Alicia es **baja** y **rubia**. _____

3. Alicia es **estúpida**. _____

4. Alicia es una muchacha **fea**. _____

3

Have you been observant? Look at the adjectives that describe Jorge. Compare them with the adjectives that describe Alicia. Read the adjectives aloud from left to right after your teacher.

JORGE	**ALICIA**
cuban*o*	**cuban***a*
alt*o*	**alt***a*
moren*o*	**moren***a*
generos*o*	**generos***a*
perfect*o*	**perfect***a*

Notice that Spanish adjectives agree in gender with the person or thing it describes.

Which letter do the MASCULINE forms of the adjective end in? _____

Which letter do the FEMININE forms of the adjective end in? _____

That's right. Adjectives that end in **-o** describe MASCULINE nouns and those ending in **-a** describe FEMININE nouns.

Actividad

F
_____

Your little sister is describing some people. Complete her sentences with the correct form of the adjective.

1. Eugenia es _____ (*rubio, rubia*).

2. Carmen es _____ (*rico, rica*).

3. El abuelo es _____ (*viejo, vieja*).

4. La señora es _____ (*famoso, famosa*).

5. La doctora es _____ (*flaco, flaca*).

6. Geraldo es _____ (*moreno, morena*).

Actividad

G
_____

Roberto is describing some things. Complete his sentences by choosing the adjective that best describes the subject.

1. El tren es _____ (*rápido, rápida*).

2. La fruta es _____ (*delicioso, deliciosa*).

3. Leemos un libro _____ (*romántico, romántica*).

4. La escuela es _____ (*moderno, moderna*).

5. El automóvil es _____ (*nuevo, nueva*).

6. La música es _____ (*magnífico, magnífica*).

7. El café es _____ (*colombiano, colombiana*).

Have you noticed that in Spanish adjectives are usually placed AFTER the noun?

      el tren *rápido*   *the fast train*
      la fruta *deliciosa*   *the delicious fruit*

Remember this as we learn more adjectives.

Actividad

Complete the sentences by choosing the appropriate Spanish forms of the adjectives.

1. (*Mexican*) La profesora _____ trabaja mucho.

2. (*pretty*) La muchacha _____ baila.

3. (*good*) Yo uso una pluma _____.

4. (*dark*) La madre es _____.

5. (*ugly*) El sombrero es _____.

6. (*fast*) Usted usa un automóvil _____.

7. (*old*) ¿Usas una bicicleta _____?

8. (*little*) Mi gato es muy _____.

9. (*perfect*) La profesora busca un libro _____.

10. (*romantic*) Ellas escuchan música _____.

4 Now look at these adjectives that could be used to describe either Jorge or Alicia.

JORGE

inteligente
interesante
joven
pobre
popular

ALICIA

inteligente
interesante
joven
pobre
popular

What do you notice about the adjectives in both columns? _____

That's right, they do not end in **-o** or **-a**. Remember the folowing rule:

When an adjective ends in **-e** (or any letter other than **-o** and **-a**) the masculine and the feminine forms are the same.

un libro *fácil*   **una lección** *fácil.*

There is one major exception: most adjectives of nationality, whatever their masculine form, have feminine forms ending in **-a**.

el muchacho *español*   **la muchacha** *española*

> **el médico** *francés*   **la bicicleta** *francesa*
> **el actor** *inglés*   **la actriz** *inglesa*

Notice that adjectives of nationality in Spanish DO NOT begin with capital letters.

Actividad

Read the first part of the sentence to a classmate, who will then complete the second part with the correct form of the adjective. Try doing this activity as quickly as possible.

1. Pablo es popular; Kim es _____ también.

2. La bicicleta es grande; el auto es _____ también.

3. El libro es fácil; la lección es _____ también.

4. El actor es francés; la actriz es _____ también.

5. El insecto es tropical; la fruta es _____ también.

There is still more to learn about adjectives. Can you finish describing the people in the second column?

rico	**inteligente**	**ricos**	_____
perfecto	**alto**	**perfectos**	_____
moreno	**cubano**	**morenos**	_____
elegante		**elegantes**	_____

Look at the left column. How many persons are we describing? _____
Now look at the right column. Which letter did we have to add to the adjective to show that we are describing more than one? We added the letter _____.

Can you finish another set of descriptions?

americana **perfecta**
alta **morena**
inteligente **elegante**
rica

americanas _____
altas
inteligentes _____
ricas _____

Look at the left column. What is the gender of the noun we are describing? _____
How many people are we describing in the left column? _____ How many female persons are we describing? _____ Now look at the adjectives in the right column. How many female persons are we describing? _____ Which letter did we have to add to the adjective to show that we are describing more than one? We added the letter _____.

Remember this rule:

> Adjectives in Spanish agree in GENDER and NUMBER with the person or thing they describe.

Now complete the right column for these adjectives:

joven	**jóvenes**
popular	**populares**
difícil	_____
fácil	_____
original	_____

Which letters did we have to add to the adjectives in the left to show that we are describing more than one? We added the letters _____.

Here is the complete rule:

> To form the plural, adjectives ending in a vowel add **-s**; adjectives ending in a consonant add **-es**.

Actividad

Mr. Estévez is testing his class in Spanish grammar. The students must complete the sentences with the correct forms of the adjective.

1. Las puertas son _____ (_grande, grandes_).

2. Mi hermana María es _____ (_bonito, bonitos, bonita, bonitas_).

3. Los hombres son _____ (_rico, rica, ricos, ricas_).

4. Las matemáticas no son _____ (_difícil, difíciles_).

5. Hay trenes _____ (_rápido, rápidos, rápida, rápidas_).

6. El gato es un animal _____ (_pequeño, pequeña, pequeños, pequeñas_).

7. El señor Gil es un profesor _____ (_inteligente, inteligentes_).

8. Tengo dos relojes _____ (*italiano, italiana, italianos, italianas*).

9. Escribo con lápices _____ (*perfecto, perfecta, perfectos, perfectas*).

10. Leo los periódicos _____ (*importante, importantes*).

Actividad

K

You're describing various pictures in your book. Match the expressions with the correct pictures.

el hombre viejo　　　　　las actividades fáciles
el libro importante　　　el animal grande
las mesas pequeñas　　　el hombre pobre
los estudiantes contentos　el auto nuevo
los gatos gordos　　　　los perros flacos

1. _____　　**2.** _____

3. _____　　**4.** _____

5. _____

6. _____

7. _____

8. _____

9. _____

10. _____

Actividad

Your new Chilean pen pal has asked you to describe some people and objects. Complete your descriptions with the correct Spanish form of the adjectives in parentheses.

1. (modern) La casa es _____.

2. (elegant) Las mujeres son _____.

3. (difficult) Tú contestas las preguntas _____.

4. (fast) Los autos son _____.

5. (old) Comemos en un restaurante _____.

6. (important) El español es _____.

7. (small) Marina y Luz son niñas _____.

8. (famous) La doctora es _____.

9. (poor) El señor Rodríguez es _____.

10. (pretty) Las flores son muy _____.

Comunicación

Your two best friends, boy and girl, want to join the school club of which you are a member. Write a note to the president of the club describing them.

Él es _____   Ella es _____

_____   _____

_____   _____

_____   _____

_____   _____

Conversación

así, así *so so*
¡madre mía! *my goodness!*

Diálogo

Fill in the correct responses in the dialog. Choose from the following list.

Buenos días, señor Martínez.   ¡Madre mía!
¿Cómo está usted?   ¿Qué guapo es su hijo!
Así, así.   es perfecto, ¿verdad?

Información personal

Your prospective summer employer has asked you to briefly describe yourself. Using some of the adjectives you have learned, write five sentences about yourself. Start each sentence with **Yo soy** (I am).

1. _____ .

2. _____ .

3. _____ .

4. _____ .

5. _____ .

Vamos a conversar

Your friend Marcos is asking you about a new girl in class.

MARCOS: ¿Cómo se llama la estudiante nueva en tu clase?

TÚ: (*Tell him her name.*)

MARCOS: ¿Cómo es?

TÚ: (*Say that she's short, blond and very elegant.*)

MARCOS: ¿Qué deportes y qué música prefiere?

TÚ: (*Say that she prefers tennis and popular music.*)

MARCOS: ¿Es francesa?

TÚ: (*Say no. Say that she's Italian.*)

Escríbalo

Describe a male character and a female character in a popular movie or TV sitcom. Write five sentences for each.

_____

_____

_____

_____

_____

_____

_____

CANDY SKULLS?

November 2 is a very special day in Latin America: **el Día de los Muertos**, (The Day of the Dead.) It's a time when relatives and loved ones who have passed on are remembered. In many countries, such as Mexico, this day is celebrated in a very interesting way. Families visit the cemetery bringing food and flowers to the graves of their loved ones. Fruit and cakes are placed on the graves to nourish the spirits in case they get hungry.

This is an old Mexican tradition. Before the arrival of Columbus, the Aztecs held a festival for their god of death. Today, this holiday is a happy one, not a day of mourning. The day is spent having a family picnic. Sometimes families remember their ancestors with candles and flowers and keep watch all night. Children show the way to the cemetery by sprinkling flower petals along the route.

Sugar candies are decorated with pink and blue icing and shaped like skulls, bones, skeletons, and coffins. Sometimes children and grown-ups are given funny bread skeletons that bear their names.

Rather than being a sad occasion, **el Día de los Muertos** is a happy one. It both celebrates life and pays respect to departed ancestors and loved ones.

Quick Quiz

1. Families visit the cemeteries with flowers and _____.

2. This tradition goes as far as the Aztecs, who held a festival for their _____.

3. The icing on sugar candies is _____ and _____.

4. Breads are sometimes decorated with funny _____.

Let's Find Out More

1. Research in the library and write a comparison between **el Día de los Muertos** and *All Saints' Day.*
2. Research the different meanings that skulls, bones, and skeletons have in the United States.

Vocabulario

WORDS TO KNOW

la actriz *actress*
alto *tall*
bajo *short*
colombiano *Colombian*
cubano *Cuban*
el deporte *sport*
difícil *difficult*

estúpido *stupid*
fácil *easy*
feo *ugly*
flaco *skinny*
francés *French*
gordo *fat*

italiano *Italian*
joven *young*
naturalmente *naturally*
nuevo *new*
su *his, her*
viejo *old*

EXPRESSIONS

¡madre mía! *my goodness!*
le gusta *(he/she) likes* . . .
así así *so so*

Repaso II
(Lecciones 6–9)

LECCIÓN 6

a. To make a sentence negative in Spanish, put **no** directly before the verb.

> **Enrique *no* habla inglés.**   *Enrique doesn't speak English.*
> **Nosotros *no* comprendemos.**   *We don't understand.*

b. To ask a question, put the the verb first, followed by the subject. An inverted question mark is placed at the beginning of a question.

> **¿*Ven ellos* la pizarra?**   *Do they see the blackboard?*
> **¿*Va María* al cine hoy?**   *Is María going to the movies today?*

LECCIÓN 7

0 cero	11 once	21 veintiuno
1 uno	12 doce	22 veintidós
2 dos	13 trece	23 veintitrés
3 tres	14 catorce	24 veinticuatro
4 cuatro	15 quince	25 veinticinco
5 cinco	16 dieciséis	26 veintiséis
6 seis	17 diecisiete	27 veintisiete
7 siete	18 dieciocho	28 veintiocho
8 ocho	19 diecinueve	29 veintinueve
9 nueve	20 veinte	30 treinta
10 diez		

+ **y**   - **menos**   x **por**   ÷ **dividido**   = **es, son**

LECCIÓN 8

a. To conjugate an **-er** verb, drop the **-er** ending and add the corresponding ones for the different subjects. Let's take **comprender** (to understand). Just drop the **-er** ending and add the following.

yo	-o	yo	comprend*o*
tú	-es	tú	comprend*es*
usted	-e	usted	comprend*e*
él ⎱ ella ⎰	-e	él ⎱ ella ⎰	comprend*e*
nosotros ⎱ nosotras ⎰	-emos	nosotros ⎱ nosotras ⎰	comprend*emos*
ustedes	-en	ustedes	comprend*en*
ellos ⎱ ellas ⎰	-en	ellos ⎱ ellas ⎰	comprend*en*

b. The preposition **a** is placed after a verb if the action is directed to a person or a pet. This **a** is called "personal **a**":

> **Yo veo *a* mi amiga.**

But:

> **Yo veo la escuela.**

The combination **a** + **el** forms the contraction **al**.

> **Escuchamos *al* profesor.**

c. Verbs of motion also require the preposition **a**. (When followed by the definite article **el**, they form one word: **al**.)

> **Camino *a la* escuela.**
> **Vamos *al* cine.**

LECCIÓN 9

a. Adjectives agree in GENDER and NUMBER with the nouns they describe. Masculine, feminine, and plural nouns will be described by masculine, feminine, and plural adjectives, respectively.

la escuela moderna	**las escuelas modernas**
el libro americano	**los libros americanos**

b. Adjectives that do not end in **-o** have the same form in the masculine and feminine, except for adjectives of nationality, which have feminine forms in **-a**.

el niño inteligente	**la niña inteligente**

But:

el actor *español*	**la actriz *española***

c. Adjective ending in a consonant, add **-es** in the plural.

el baile popular	**los bailes populares**
la pregunta difícil	**las preguntas difíciles**

d. Spanish adjectives usually follow the noun.

el libro *interesante*	*the interesting book*
la doctora *mexicana*	*the Mexican doctor*

Actividad

A

Here are nine pictures of people doing different things. Complete the description below each picture by using the correct form of one of the following verbs.

aprender	comprender	responder
beber	correr	vender
comer	leer	ver

1. Yo _____ agua.

2. Carmen _____ un sandwich.

3. Ellas _____ un periódico.

4. El niño no _____ .

5. Los niños _____ en el parque.

6. Ricardo _____ matemáticas.

7. El hombre _____ un sombrero.

8. La señorita no _____ al burro.

9. La muchacha _____ bien.

Actividad

Hidden in the puzzle below are: 9 adjectives, 4 verbs, 3 nouns, and 2 numbers.

See how many you can find and circle the hidden words, then write them in the spaces below. The words in the puzzle may be read from left to right, right to left, upwards, downwards, or diagonally.

```
A  M  U  N  D  O  D  R  O  G
M  M  O  D  E  R  N  O  B  E
O  D  E  Q  D  R  I  C  O  V
L  E  E  R  V  E  R  C  N  E
F  N  R  E  I  H  A  D  I  I
Á  Í  B  M  F  C  M  O  T  N
C  D  O  O  L  P  A  S  O  T
I  R  P  C  O  S  C  N  S  E
L  A  R  E  R  R  O  C  O  X
F  J  R  U  B  I  O  F  E  O
```

ADJECTIVES   VERBS

_____   _____   _____

_____   _____   _____

_____   _____   _____

_____   _____   _____

_____

NOUNS   NUMBERS

_____   _____

_____   _____

_____

Actividad

Crucigrama.

HORIZONTALES		VERTICALES	
1. American	9. ugly	1. to learn	6. young
4. nine	10. two	2. number	8. to eat
5. rich	12. seven	3. to read	11. six
7. to listen	13. romantic		

Actividad

D

Are you a good detective? Match the names and their descriptions with their corresponding pictures.

Jacinta: doce años, bonita, rubia, baja, tímida
Federico: veinte años, moreno, alto, inteligente
Elena: diecinueve años, morena, alta, rica, elegante
Máximo: quince años, rubio, bajo, popular.

1. _____

_____

_____

2. _____

_____

_____

3. _____

_____

_____

4. _____

_____

_____

Actividad

E

Answer each question correctly.

1. ¿Cuántos hay?

_____

2. ¿Cuánto cuesta?

_____

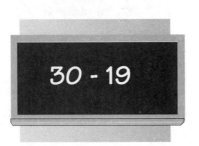

3. ¿Cuánto es?

_____

4. ¿Cuántos años tiene?

_____

5. ¿Cuántos tienes?

_____

6. ¿Cuántos hay?

_____

7. ¿Cuánto es?

8. El número es…

_____

_____

9. Los números son…

_____

Actividad

All of the following people are saying some numbers. What are they?

¿Cuánto es? … centavos.

1. _____

Mi número de teléfono es…

2. _____

3 x 5 es…

3. _____

Dos, por favor. … dólares.

4. _____

El número es…

5. _____

El primero es el número…

6. _____

Los números son…

7. _____

Los números son…

8. _____

Actividad

Would you like to know your future? Follow these simple rules to see what the cards have in store for you. Choose a number between two and seven. Starting in the upper left corner and moving from left to right, write down all the letters that appear under the Spanish number at which you stopped.

tres F	cuatro U	dos T	siete M	cinco C	seis V	siete U	seis I
cuatro N	seis D	dos R	dos A	seis A	tres O	cuatro A	tres R
dos B	siete C	tres T	dos A	siete H	tres U	cuatro U	siete O
cuatro T	siete S	cinco A	cuatro O	siete A	dos J	cinco S	seis C
cuatro M	tres N	cinco A	dos O	seis O	cinco B	tres A	cuatro O
dos F	tres G	seis N	tres R	cuatro D	siete M	seis T	cuatro E
siete I	dos A	cuatro R	dos C	siete G	seis E	cuatro N	tres A
cuatro O	cinco O	siete O	cinco N	tres N	seis N	tres D	dos I
cinco I	seis T	siete S	tres E	seis A	cinco T	dos L	cinco A

Actividad

Select the correct adjective form.

1. Ellos no tienen un centavo. Son muy *(pobre, pobres)*.
2. Los helados son *(delicioso, deliciosa, deliciosos, deliciosas)*.
3. Los muchachos necesitan un automóvil *(nuevo, nueva, nuevos, nuevas)*.
4. Tengo sólo los dos *(último, última, últimos, últimas)* billetes.
5. Aquí hay muchas flores *(bonito, bonita, bonitos, bonitas)*.
6. Una pregunta es difícil, pero las otras son *(fácil, fáciles)*.

Actividad

Complete each sentence with the appropriate definite article. If necessary, use **a**, **al**, or **a la**.

1. Veo _____ profesora.
2. Admiramos _____ actor.
3. Ella vende _____ bicicleta.
4. No comprendo _____ vendedor.
5. ¿Escuchas _____ teléfono?
6. Respondo _____ doctor que como bien.
7. Miro _____ profesor cuando habla.
8. Practico _____ deportes.

Actividad

Work with a partner. Take turns asking each other where you are going. Choose from the following places.

EXAMPLE: ¿Adónde vas?

Voy al cine. ¿Y tú?

1. la clase de música
2. el fútbol
3. el jardín
4. la escuela
5. el hospital
6. la casa de la abuela
7. el parque

Actividad

K

Can you read this story? Much of it is in picture form. Whenever you come to a picture, read it as if it were a Spanish word.

Emiliano es un [image] joven. Él es [image] pero es muy popular. Lorenzo,

el amigo de Emiliano, es muy [image] y tiene un [image] nuevo. Emiliano

va a [image] en [image]. Lorenzo es muy generoso. Los [image] van

con Lorenzo porque no desean [image] a la escuela. Emiliano no tiene

[image] para [image] un automóvil. Él compra un [image] de lotería.

¡Buena suerte!

TERCERA
Parte

10 ¿Qué eres tú?
Professions and Trades;
The Verb **SER**

Here are several people in action. Can you tell what their jobs are?

el cantante   la cantante

el doctor   la doctora
el médico   la médica

el dentista   la dentista

el abogado   la abogada

229

el secretario   la secretaria

el enfermero   la enfermera

el policía   la policía

el cartero   la cartera

el vendedor   la vendedora

el mecánico   la mecánica

Actividad

A

Your school is publishing a career catalog. Match the occupations with the correct pictures. Choose from this list.

una abogada   un enfermero   un policía
un cartero   una mecánica   un secretario
un dentista   una pianista   una vendedora
una doctora

1. _____

2. _____

3. _____

4. _____

5. _____

6. _____

7. _____

8. _____

Actividad

B

The following pictures are being added to the catalog. Identify each occupation.

1. _____

2. _____

3. _____

4. _____

5. _____

6. _____

7. _____

8. _____

Dígalo bien

When the Spanish letter **g** is followed by **a**, **o**, or **u**, it is pronounced like *g* in *go*.

*ga*solina	la*go*	*ga*to
*gu*sto	di*ga*	ami*go*
re*gu*lar	ten*go*	*go*rdo

El *ga*to es *go*rdo.
Ten*go* la *ga*solina en el *ga*raje.

2

One of the most important verbs in the Spanish language is the verb **ser** (to be). It is irregular because it doesn't follow the rules for **-er** verbs that we learned in Lesson 7. Here are the forms of **ser**. MEMORIZE them.

yo	soy	*I am*	nosotros nosotras } somos		*we are*
tú	eres	*you are* (familiar)			
Ud.	es	*you are* (formal)	Uds.	son	*you are* (plural)
él ella } es		*he is* *she is*	ellos ellas } son		*they are*

Ser is used to indicate nationalities, professions, and individual characteristics.

Elena es dominicana. *Elena is Dominican.*
Alberto es mecánico. *Alberto is a mechanic.*
Los autos son modernos. *The cars are modern.*

Actividad

Choose five people you know and write their professions. Write complete sentences. Remember that it is not necessary to use **un** or **una**.

EXAMPLE: **Mi hermano es abogado.**

1. _____

2. _____

3. _____

4. _____

5. _____

Actividad

D

The students in your Spanish class are describing or asking about different people. Complete each sentence with the correct form of the verb **ser**.

1. Manuel _____ mexicano.

2. ¿ _____ tú española?

3. Ella _____ secretaria.

4. ¿ _____ Ud. abogado?

5. María _____ dentista.

6. Mis padres _____ jóvenes.

7. Ellos _____ vendedores.

8. ¿ _____ Uds. los hermanos de José?

9. Nosotros _____ importantes.

10. Yo _____ estudiante.

Actividad

E

For each of the completed sentences above, make a question to a classmate, who will answer in the negative.

> EXAMPLE: ¿Es Manuel mexicano?
> **No, Manuel no es mexicano.**

1. _____

   _____

2. _____

   _____

3. _____

_____

4. _____

_____

5. _____

_____

6. _____

_____

7. _____

_____

8. _____

_____

9. _____

_____

10. _____

_____

Actividad

Here are some sentences in which a form of **ser** is used. Can you match these sentences with the pictures they describe? Write the descriptions in the blanks.

Luis es guapo.
Yo soy inteligente.
Ella es rica.
Nosotras somos bonitas.

Tú eres rubio.
Ellas son inglesas.
Ellos no son altos.
Ud. es importante.

1. _____

2. _____

3. _____

4. _____

5. _____

6. _____

7. _____

8. _____

3

Here's a short story about a new girl in school, and Mr. Fernández, the teacher of the class.

Necesito un amigo*

EL SEÑOR FERNÁNDEZ:	Buenos días, ¿cómo te llamas?
ANTONIA:	Me llamo Antonia Campos.
EL SEÑOR FERNÁNDEZ:	Antonia, ¿hablas inglés?
ANTONIA:	No mucho... Hablamos español en casa. Soy de Venezuela.
EL SEÑOR FERNÁNDEZ:	Ah, venezolana. ¿Tus padres están aquí?
ANTONIA:	Sí, señor. Mi padre es mecánico. Mi madre trabaja también. Es enfermera en un hospital.
EL SEÑOR FERNÁNDEZ:	¡Estupendo! ¡Fantástico! Estoy muy contento.
ANTONIA:	¿Contento? ¿Por qué? No comprendo.
EL SEÑOR FERNÁNDEZ:	Siempre tengo problemas con mi auto. Necesito un buen mecánico. Y voy todos los años al hospital para mi examen físico. Ahora tengo una amiga allí.
ANTONIA:	¿Habla Ud. en serio?
LOS OTROS ESTUDIANTES:	¡Ja, ja! Otra broma del señor Fernández. Es muy cómico.

en casa *at home*

venezolana *Venezuelan*

muy contento *very happy*

todos los años *every year*

allí *there*

en serio *seriously*

otra *another*

broma *joke*

cómico *funny*

* Footnote: The verbs **necesitar** and **tener**, when used in a general sense, do not require the personal **a**: **Necesito un amigo** but **Necesito a mi amigo**.

Actividad

G

These statements are based on the preceding story. Read a statement to a classmate, who will say **Sí** if it is true, or **No** if it is false. If the statement is false, your partner will correct the information in boldface.

1. Antonia Campos es **la profesora** de la clase. _____

2. El señor Fernández habla **español**. _____

3. **Antonia Campos** no habla inglés. _____

4. El padre de Antonia trabaja **en un hospital**. _____

5. Antonia es **dominicana**. _____

6. La madre de Antonia **no trabaja**. _____

7. Antonia habla **inglés** en casa. _____

8. El profesor **no habla** en serio. _____

Actividad

H

Work with a partner. Take turns at asking and answering the following questions.

1. ¿Es francesa Antonia?

_____

2. ¿Es enfermero el padre de Antonia?

_____

3. ¿Dónde trabaja la madre de Antonia?

_____

4. ¿Tiene Antonia problemas con su auto?

_____

5. ¿Es el señor Fernández serio o cómico?

_____

Conversación

nunca *never*   **enfermo(a)** *sick*
ser *to be*   **¿quién?** *who?*

Diálogo

Choose the best answers to the questions from the following list.

Yo soy un estudiante pobre.
Es un actor famoso. Tiene mucho dinero

Es mi hermana.
No, es policía.

Información personal

Using some of the adjectives in the list below, say something about these people.

famoso (a)	cómico (a)
inteligente	bajo (a)
pobre	rubio (a)
moreno (a)	rico (a)
alto (a)	

1. Mi actor favorito es _____.

2. Mi médico es _____.

3. Mi dentista es _____.

4. Mi profesor(a) es _____.

5. Mi cantante favorito(a) es _____.

6. La secretaria de la escuela es _____.

Vamos a conversar

You have just transferred to a school in Mexico. Mr. Ramos, the counselor, is going to ask you some personal questions.

EL SEÑOR RAMOS:	¿Cómo te llamas?
TÚ:	*(Tell him your name.)*
EL SEÑOR RAMOS:	¿Hablas inglés?
TÚ:	*(Say that you speak English, but at home you speak Spanish.)*
EL SEÑOR RAMOS:	¿Dónde trabaja tu papá?
TÚ:	*(Tell him your father works in a hospital.)*
EL SEÑOR RAMOS:	¿Trabaja tu mamá también?
TÚ:	*(Say your mother works at home.)*

Escríbalo

The school guidance department wants to find out about the students' career plans. Write a short statement (4 sentences) about what you like to be. You could begin your sentences with **Deseo ser...** (I wish to be…) or **Deseo estudiar...** (I wish to study…) and continue with your preferences (**Prefiero...**). You may use a negative statement like **No deseo trabajar con computadoras**.

_____

_____

_____

_____

LOS CLAVADISTAS—DEATH-DEFYING DIVERS

The most famous nightime attraction of Acapulco, Mexico, is the diving of daring cliff-divers at **La Quebrada**—the Gorge. From a tiny torchlit ledge in the craggy rock wall, a young man plunges 136 feet (equal to a fifteen-story building) into a narrow cove bordered by treacherous rocks. It all happens in an instant and the success of the spectacular dive depends on skill and split-second timing. To make sure there is enough water below, the diver must enter the water at the precise moment that the tide swirls in, filling the shallow inlet. The surf immediately recedes, leaving the water level dangerously low. One false start or slip of the foot and the diver will be smashed on the rocks below.

After a dive, the diver climbs up the rocks, dripping and smiling, to gather the donations and applause of the crowd.

There are four of these heart-stopping dives every evening of the year. The **clavadistas** certainly have an unusual profession.

Quick Quiz

1. The cliff-divers at **La Quebrada** are called _____ .

2. The jump equals falling from _____ stories.

3. The depth of the water changes with the _____ .

4. The success of a dive depends on split-second _____ .

5. When the surf recedes, the _____ is dangerously low.

Let's Find Out More

1. Go to the library or visit a travel agency and find more information about Acapulco. Write a short composition.

2. Find out about other famous Mexican vacation spots. Write down their location, major attractions, and other interesting facts.

Vocabulario

WORDS TO KNOW

la abogada _lawyer_ (f.)

el abogado _lawyer_ (m.)

allí _over there_

broma _joke_

el (la) cantante _singer_

la cartera _letter carrier_ (f.)

el cartero _letter carrier_ (m.)

cómico(a) _funny_

el (la) dentista _dentist_

la enfermera _nurse_ (f.)

el enfermero _nurse_ (m.)

la mecánica _mechanic_ (f.)

el mecánico _mechanic_ (m.)

la médica _physician_ (f.)

el médico *physician* (m.)

nunca *never*

el (la) policía *police officer*

¿quién? *who*

la secretaria *secretary* (f.)

el secretario *secretary* (m.)

venezolano(a) *Venezuelan*

EXPRESSIONS

en serio *seriously*

estar enfermo(a) *to be sick*

¡estupendo!, ¡fantástico! *great*

todos los años *every year*

Más actividades
-IR Verbs

The following words are also verbs. Can you guess their meanings by looking at the pictures?

abrir

cubrir

dividir

escribir

sufrir

recibir

salir   **descubrir**

Do you recall the changes you did with **-ar** and **-er** verbs? You dropped **-ar** and **-er** and added the corresponding endings. You must do the same with **-ir** verbs. Here's an example with the verb **vivir** (to live).

yo	viv*o*	*I live, I am living*
tú	viv*es*	*you live, you are living*
Ud.	viv*e*	*you live, you are living*
él ⎱ ella ⎰	viv*e*	*he lives, he is living* *she lives, she is living*
nosotros ⎱ nosotras ⎰	viv*imos*	*we live, we are living*
Uds.	viv*en*	*you live, you are living*
ellos ⎱ ellas ⎰	viv*en*	*they live, they are living*

If you compare the **-er** and **-ir** verbs, what do you notice? The endings for **-ir** verbs are almost the same as those for **-er** verbs! The only exception is the ending for **nosotros**. The **-er** ending for **nosotros** is **-emos**, but the **-ir** ending for **nosotros** is **-imos**. That makes things simple. Let's take another verb. Can you add the proper endings?

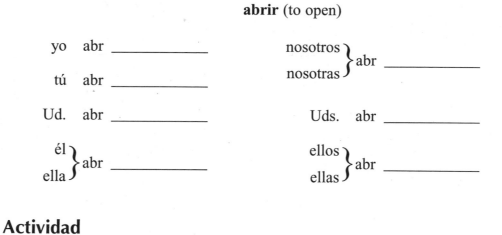

abrir (to open)

yo   abr _____

tú   abr _____

Ud.   abr _____

él }
ella } abr _____

nosotros }
nosotras } abr _____

Uds.   abr _____

ellos }
ellas } abr _____

Actividad

A

Let's practice with other **-ir** verbs. Give the forms for each subject.

	descubrir	**dividir**	**recibir**
yo	_____	_____	_____
tú	_____	_____	_____
Ud.	_____	_____	_____
él	_____	_____	_____
ella	_____	_____	_____
nosotros	_____	_____	_____
Uds.	_____	_____	_____
ellos	_____	_____	_____
ellas	_____	_____	_____

Actividad

B

Ms. Ramírez is testing her students' comprehension. She wants them to match the sentences with the pictures they describe.

Él abre la ventana.　　　　　Ella escribe en el cuaderno.
Tú vives con tu familia.　　　Yo recibo una bicicleta.
Ellos descubren los chocolates.　Ud. cubre la mesa.

1. _____

2. _____

3. _____

4. _____

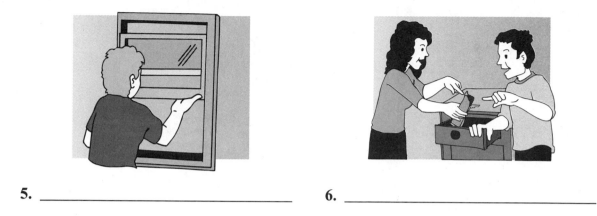

5. _____   6. _____

Actividad

The students of the bilingual class are preparing flash cards. Match the Spanish cards with the English meanings and write the matching letter in the space provided.

1. yo abro _____

2. ellos reciben _____

3. Uds. viven _____

4. tú escribes _____

5. nosotros escribimos _____

6. él vive _____

7. ellos deciden _____

8. ellos viven _____

9. ella recibe _____

10. él divide _____

11. Ud. cubre _____

12. tú vives _____

13. nosotros dividimos _____

14. yo escribo _____

15. ellos abren _____

a. I write
b. you live *(plural)*
c. they open
d. she receives
e. we divide
f. you cover *(formal)*
g. you write *(informal)*
h. you live *(singular)*
i. they receive
j. I open
k. we write
l. he lives
m. he divides
n. they live
o. they decide

2 Here's one important **-ir** verb: **salir** (to leave, to go out, to come out). It has an irregular **yo** form, **salgo** and it is followed by **de** if you mention the place you're "going out of".

Yo *salgo.*	*I'm going out.*
Yo *salgo de...*	*I'm leaving the . . .*

Actividad

D

Everybody's leaving! Complete the sentences with the correct forms of **salir**. Add **de** if necessary.

1. Ellos _____ mañana para Madrid.

2. Yo _____ la clase.

3. Ella _____ con su perro.

4. ¿Cuándo _____ tú _____ la casa?

5. ¿ _____ ustedes ahora?

6. ¿ _____ nosotros hoy también?

7. Ud. no _____ la casa.

Another important **-ir** verb is **decir** (to say). Like **salir**, the verb **decir** has a different form for **yo**. We say **yo digo** (I say, I am saying). The rest is almost regular. Note, however, that, except for **nosotros**, we have to change the first vowel of the verb from **e** to **i**.

yo	**d***i***go**	*I say, I am saying*
tú	**d***i***ces**	*you say, you are saying*
usted	**d***i***ce**	*you say, you are saying*

| él | } | | *he says, he is saying* |
| ella | } | **dice** | *they say, they are saying* |

| nosotros | } | | |
| nosotras | } | **decimos** | *we say, we are saying* |

| ustedes | **dicen** | *you say, you are saying* |

| ellos | } | | |
| ellas | } | **dicen** | *they say, they are saying* |

Actividad

E

Now, you complete the sentences with the correct form of **decir**.

1. El profesor _____ «¡repitan!»

2. Tú _____ buenas tardes

3. Nosotros _____ hasta mañana.

4. ¿Qué _____ tú?

5. ¿Qué _____ los estudiantes?

3

Now we are ready to compare all three groups of verbs: **-ar**, **-er**, and **-ir**.

	comprar	vender	decidir
yo	**compro**	**vendo**	**decido**
tú	**compras**	**vendes**	**decides**

Ud.	compr*a*	vend*e*	decid*e*
él ella	compr*a*	vend*e*	decid*e*
nosotros nosotras	compramos	vendemos	decidimos
Uds.	compran	venden	deciden
ellos ellas	compran	venden	deciden

Actividad

Three actions are described below each picture. Underline the one that correctly describes the picture.

1. **a.** yo escribo
    b. yo entro
    c. yo pregunto

2. **a.** él abre
    b. él baila
    c. él vende

3. **a.** nosotros recibimos
   b. nosotros cantamos
   c. nosotros respondemos

4. **a.** ellos compran
   b. ellos corren
   c. ellos usan

5. **a.** él sale
   b. él divide
   c. él canta

6. **a.** Ud. come
   b. Ud. bebe
   c. Ud. estudia

7. **a.** Rosita escucha
   b. Rosita abre
   c. Rosita divide

8. **a.** María y Raúl deciden
   b. María y Raúl viven
   c. María y Raúl entran

9. **a.** yo visito
   b. yo camino
   c. yo trabajo

10. **a.** Francisca lee
    b. Francisca escribe
    c. Francisca mira

Actividad

This test will show you if you really know your action words. Complete each sentence with the correct form of the verb.

1. (*salir*) Yo _____ del automóvil.

2. (*decidir*) Uds. _____ si vamos.

3. (*leer*) Nosotros _____ el periódico.

4. (*visitar*) Yo _____ a mi amigo.

5. (*responder*) Ella _____ en la clase.

6. (*recibir*) Ellos _____ mucho dinero.

7. (*beber*) Tú _____ una soda.

8. (*abrir*) Marisol _____ la puerta.

9. (*vivir*) María y yo _____ en Chicago.

10. (*desear*) Yo _____ correr en el parque.

Actividad

Now, here's another challenge. Read the completed statements above to a classmate who will change the subject pronoun of each sentence. You complete the sentence with the appropriate verb form for the subject your classmate gave you. Take turns.

> EXAMPLE: Yo salgo del automóvil.
> **Nosotros salimos del automóvil.**

Actividad

Some verbs have minor irregularities in the **yo** form. See if you have learned them.

1. *(ver)* Yo no _____ mi libro aquí.

2. *(salir)* Yo _____ de la casa con mi perro.

3. *(tener)* Yo _____ muchas amigas.

4. *(saber)* Yo no _____ bailar.

5. *(ser)* Yo _____ vendedor de autos.

6. *(ir)* Yo _____ a México todos los años.

Dígalo bien

■ When it appears at the beginning or in the middle of a word, the letter **y** is pronounced like the *y* in *yarn* or the *j* in *jet*.

ya	**playa**	**mayo**
yo	**coyote**	**Maya**
ayer	*Yucatán*	**vaya**

Yolanda y *yo* llegamos ayer.
En mayo vaya a una playa en *Yucatán*.

4 Here's a story with lots of **-ar**, **-er**, and **-ir** verbs.

El misterio de la casa abandonada

Dos policías hablan.

—Mira, la casa número 13 de la Calle Sonora está abandonada. Nadie vive allí. Pero muchas personas dicen que salen unos ruidos misteriosos de la casa. Vamos a ir allá para ver si descubrimos la razón.

El policía Ordóñez va a la casa. Está desierta. Entra por la puerta y mira por todas partes. Escucha un momento. Silencio. De repente, hay un ruido en el otro cuarto de la casa y él pregunta:

—¿Quién está ahí?

Nadie responde. Ordóñez saca la pistola y abre la puerta. ¿Qué ve el policía? Ve una gata con cinco gatitos. Ahora comprende todo. No hay más misterio.

la calle *street*
nadie *nobody*
ruido *noise*
allá *there*
razón *reason*
desierta *deserted*
por todas partes *everywhere*
de repente *suddenly*
el cuarto *room*
ahí *there*
sacar *to take out*

Actividad

Complete the following sentences according to the story above.

1. El policía Ordóñez va _____.

2. La casa está en el número 13 de la Calle _____.

3. El policía escucha un _____.

4. El policía desea _____ la razón de los ruidos.

5. Ordóñez _____ por la puerta y _____ por todas partes.

6. El policía _____ la pistola.

7. Cuando abre la puerta ve _____.

8. Ahora él _____ todo.

Actividad

K _____

When you use **nosotros(as)**, you have to choose among all three endings (**-amos, -emos, -imos**). Let's see if you have learned this. Complete all sentences with the **nosotros** form.

1. (*comer*) _____ frutas.

2. (*hablar*) _____ español.

3. *(vivir)* _____ en un hotel.

4. *(ver)* _____ la película.

5. *(comprender)* _____ el misterio.

6. *(escribir)* _____ en el papel.

7. *(leer)* _____ el periódico.

8. *(aprender)* _____ las expresiones.

9. *(salir)* _____ a todas partes.

Actividad

Here's a story with missing words. Read the pictures as words. Fill in the blanks with verbs that complete the sentences logically. Have fun!

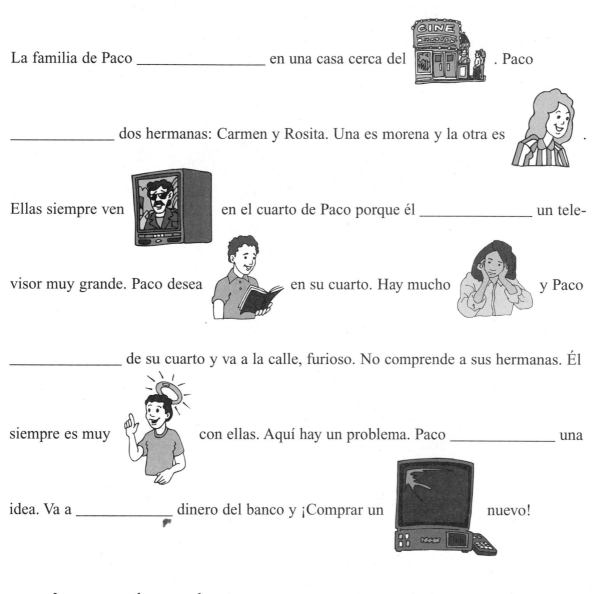

La familia de Paco _____ en una casa cerca del [CINE] . Paco

_____ dos hermanas: Carmen y Rosita. Una es morena y la otra es _____ .

Ellas siempre ven [televisor] en el cuarto de Paco porque él _____ un tele-

visor muy grande. Paco desea [leer] en su cuarto. Hay mucho [ruido] y Paco

_____ de su cuarto y va a la calle, furioso. No comprende a sus hermanas. Él

siempre es muy [idea] con ellas. Aquí hay un problema. Paco _____ una

idea. Va a _____ dinero del banco y ¡Comprar un [televisor] nuevo!

cerca de... *near the . . . , close to . . .*
televisor *TV set*

Conversación

sufrir *to suffer*

¿Por qué? *Why?*

porque *because*

el trabajo *work*

Hago la tarea *I do my homework*

¿Qué haces? *What are you doing?*

¿No sabes nada… ? *Don't you know anything . . . ?*

Diálogo

Fill in the words that are missing from the dialog. Choose from the following list.

Tengo mucho trabajo.
Comprendo mucho.
¡Claro! Pero somos ocho personas.

Sufro mucho.
Tengo mucho dinero.
Escribo una historia de mi familia.

Información personal

Describe yourself and your family by filling in the blanks.

1. Me llamo _____ .

2. Soy _____ .

3. Vivo _____ .

4. Yo _____ un auto.

5. Somos _____ hermanos (hermanas) en mi familia.

6. Se llaman _____ .

7. Mi padre es _____ .

8. Mi padre trabaja _____ días por semana.

9. Mi mamá trabaja en _____ .

10. Mis abuelos viven en _____ .

Vamos a conversar

You're answering some questions posed by the police.

LA POLICÍA: ¿Dónde vive Ud.?

TÚ: (*Tell her on what street you live.*)

LA POLICÍA: ¿Cuál es el número de su casa?

TÚ: (*Tell her your house number.*)

LA POLICÍA: ¿Pasa Ud. por aquí generalmente?

TÚ: (*Say that you pass by every day.*)

LA POLICÍA: ¿Quién vive en esta casa?

TÚ: (*Say that you don't know and that they say nobody lives in the house.*)

PUERTO RICO IN NEW YORK

Isn't Puerto Rico an island in the Caribbean? Of course. It's a beautiful, tropical island, one hundred miles long and thirty-five miles wide (the fourth largest island in the Caribbean), about one thousand miles southwest of Florida, with a population of over three and a half million people. Puerto Rico is a commonwealth of the United States, and Puerto Ricans are U.S. citizens, though Spanish is still the main language spoken.

It is said that there really are "two Puerto Ricos." In addition to the people living on the island, there are over two and a half million Puerto Ricans (about two out-of-every-five Puerto Ricans, or forty percent of the total population of this small island) residing on the United States mainland. About half of them live in New York City, which boasts a Puerto Rican population second only in size to that of San Juan, Puerto Rico's capital and largest city.

Puerto Ricans in New York City amount to more than ten percent of the city's population. New York is truly a bilingual city, with the use of Spanish on most public notices and signs; advertisements in Spanish on billboards, in subway cars, and on buses; Spanish-speaking radio stations, Spanish-language TV channels, and more than a dozen Spanish-language newspapers, including the most popular — El Diario/La Prensa, staffed mainly by Puerto Ricans.

The main Puerto Rican community is a district called Spanish Harlem or **El barrio** (The Neighborhood). Some consider themselves **neoyorquinos**; others **hispanos** or **boricuas** (from **Borinquen**, the old Indian name of the island).

Walk along East 116th Street, El Barrio's main street and in **La Marqueta** (the market), and you will see many **bodegas** (grocery stores), **cafés** and restaurants, giving the area a distinct Puerto Rican flavor.

These establishments have introduced many Americans of diverse ethnic groups to Puerto Rican food. Some typical Puerto Rican delicacies are: **arroz con gandules** (yellow rice with pork and pigeon peas), **mofongo** (mashed fried green plantains), **píononos** (fried ripe plantains with ground meat) and a variety of pastries and desserts such as **brazos gitanos** (jelly rolls), and **flan de coco** (coconut custard).

Do you want to experience Puerto Rican culture? Do you want to taste the flavor of Caribbean food? Then, by all means, pay a visit to **El Barrio** in "**Nueva York**."

Quick Quiz

1. Puerto Rico is an island in the _____ Sea.

2. It is about _____ miles from Florida.

3. There are about _____ people living on the island and _____ living on the United States mainland.

4. **Arroz con gandules** consists of _____.

5. In Spanish, New York is _____ and New Yorker is _____.

Let's Find Out More

1. Go to a travel agent and get materials on Puerto Rico. Why is the island such a magnet for tourists? What are its attractions?

2. Obtain a copy of a newspaper written in Spanish. See if you can read some of it.

3. See if your supermarket has a section for Caribbean food and report your findings to the class.

4. Send a postcard to the Goya Company. Ask for a recipe book of typical Puerto Rican dishes and share it with your classmates.

Vocabulario

WORDS TO KNOW

abrir *to open*

ahí *there*

la calle *street*

con *with*

el cuarto *room*

cubrir *to cover*

decidir *to decide*

descubrir *to discover*

dividir *to divide*

escribir *to write*

nada *nothing*

nadie *nobody*

la razón *reason*

recibir *to receive*

el ruido *noise*

saber *to know*

sacar *to take out*

salir *to leave*

sufrir *to suffer*   **el trabajo** *work* (noun)
la tarea *homework*   **vivir** *to live*
el televisor *TV set*

EXPRESSIONS

de repente *all of a sudden*
hago *I do, I am doing*
¿no sabes nada? *don't you know anything?*
por todas partes *everywhere*
¿qué haces? *what are you doing?*
¿quién está ahí? *who is there?*

12 ¿Dónde está usted?
The Verb ESTAR;
Expressions with ESTAR

We have already learned one verb that means *to be*: **ser**. And you have used expressions with **estar**, such as **¿Dónde estás?** and **¿Cómo estás?** Let's learn more about **estar** (to be).

Yo *estoy* aquí.

Él *está* allí.

Él *está* en el parque.

Ella *está* en la cafetería.

Él *está* enfermo.

Ella *está* bien.

269

Ud. *está* triste.

Uds. *están* cansados.

Nosotros *estamos* contentos.

Ellos *están* sentados.

El agua *está* caliente.

El agua *está* fría.

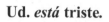

Let's look at the forms of **estar**. You can see that **estar**, like **ser**, is somewhat irregular.

yo	estoy	*I am*
tú	estás	*you are* (familiar)
Ud.	está	*you're* (formal)

| él ⎫ está | *he is* |
| ella ⎭ | *she is* |

| nosotros ⎫ estamos | *we are* |
| nosotras ⎭ | |

| Uds.   están | *you are* (plural) |

| ellos ⎫ están | *they are* |
| ellas ⎭ | |

Now the question is: When do you use **ser** and when do you use **estar**? For example, if you want to say *I am*, do you say **yo soy** or **yo estoy**? If you want to say *she is*, do you say **ella es** or **ella está**?

You can't just use whichever verb you feel like using. There are rules. The following examples show three special uses of the verb **estar**.

¿Cómo *está* Ud.?	*How are you?*
Yo *estoy* bien, gracias.	*I'm well, thank you.*
No *estoy* bien; *estoy* enfermo.	*I'm not well; I'm sick.*

Can you figure out why one uses forms of estar in the three sentences above? The reason is that they ask or talk about someone's HEALTH.

¿Dónde *está* la casa?	*Where is the house?*
Madrid *está* en España.	*Madrid is in Spain.*
Juan *está* en el parque.	*Juan is in the park.*

In the above sentences, we are telling the LOCATION of someone or something.

María *está* contenta.	*María is happy.*
***Estamos* cansados.**	*We are tired.*
La sopa *está* fría.	*The soup is cold.*

Note that the CONDITION of the persons or things in the above sentences can quickly change.

María *está* **contenta.** (That's how she feels right now.)
Estamos **cansados.** (With a little rest, that will change.)
La sopa *está* **fría.** (It was hot and got cold.)

Therefore, the CONDITION of these persons or things is not permanent but temporary.

Here, then, are the simple rules. There are three situations in which we use a form of **estar**.

a. HEALTH. If we ask about or talk about someone's health.

Yo *estoy* **bien.** *I'm well.*
Juan *está* **enfermo.** *Juan is sick.*

b. LOCATION. If we ask about or talk about where something or someone is.

Los estudiantes están en la clase. *The students are in the classroom.*

c. TEMPORARY CONDITION. If the adjective describes a temporary condition that can change back and forth.

El café *está* **caliente/frío.** *The coffee is hot/cold.*
María *está* **triste/contenta.** *María is sad/happy.*
La puerta *está* **abierta/cerrada.** *The door is open/closed.*
Luis *está* **sentado.** *Luis is seated (sitting).*

Now you know the three situations in which you use **estar**. In all other situations, use the verb **ser**.

NOTE: Sometimes it is not so easy to decide whether a condition is "temporary" or "permanent." Temporary conditions vary often. In Spanish, some conditions are usually regarded as permanent characteristics. Adjectives like **rico**, **pobre**, **gordo**, **flaco**, **joven**, and **viejo** are usually considered permanent characteristics. Therefore, people say in Spanish:

Yo *soy* **rico.** La abuela es vieja.
Mi amigo *es* **pobre.** Los muchachos son gordos.

However, **estar loco** (to be crazy) can be considered permanent!

Actividad

A

Complete the sentences with the correct forms of **estar**, then explain why you use **estar** instead of **ser**.

1. Ellos _____ en Madrid.

2. Carolina _____ enferma.

3. Nosotros _____ contentos ahora.

4. ¿Cómo _____ Ud.?

5. ¿Cómo _____ Uds.?

6. ¿Dónde _____ mi padre?

7. Las sodas _____ frías.

8. Los muchachos _____ sentados en la silla.

9. ¡Cuánto trabajo! Yo _____ cansado.

10. Mi hermano no _____ bien hoy.

Let's review the two verbs meaning to be. Repeat the forms aloud after your teacher.

SER			ESTAR	
yo	**soy**	*I am*	**yo**	**estoy**
tú	**eres**	*you are*	**tú**	**estás**
Ud.	**es**	*you are*	**Uds.**	**están**
él } **ella** }	**es**	*he is* *she is*	**él** } **ella** }	**estás**
nosotros } **nosotras** }	**somos**	*we are*	**nosotros** } **nosotras** }	**estamos**

Uds.	son	*you are*	Uds.	están
ellos ellas } son		*they are*	ellos ellas } están	

Actividad

Match the sentences with the correct pictures:

Mi abuelo es mecánico.
El agua está caliente.
Ellas son abogadas.

¿Es mexicana la muchacha?
El médico está en el hospital.
Las ventanas están cerradas.

1. _____

2. _____

3. _____

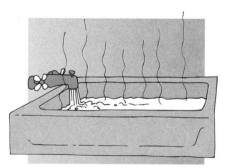

4. _____

5. _____   6. _____

Actividad

C _____

Work with a partner. Your are supervising things at a party. Ask your partner in Spanish for a report on how things are going.

1. Is the soup hot?
2. Are the sodas cold?
3. Is the music good?
4. Are the windows open?
5. Are the girls sitting?
6. Are all happy?

3 Now read this story about poor Rosita, who seems very sick. But, is she really?

¡Pobre niña!

¡Pobre Rosita! Ella no está bien. Está en casa todo el día porque está enferma. No desea leer. No desea mirar la televisión. La madre de Rosita está triste también cuando ella ve a la muchacha enferma.

todo el día *all day*

MADRE: ¡Mi pobre hija! ¿Sufres mucho?

       sufrir *suffer*

ROSITA: Sí, sufro mucho, mamá. Ay, ay, ay, ¡qué dolor!

       el dolor *the pain*

MADRE: Necesitas un médico. ¿Dónde está el doctor Curante?

Entra el doctor Curante. Es joven y guapo. Él sabe mucho sobre medicina. También comprende a las muchachas.

EL DOCTOR CURANTE: ¿Dónde está la niña enferma? ¡Ajá! Aquí está. ¿Cómo estás, Rosita? ¿Por qué estás triste? Mañana es día de fiesta. No hay clases.

       el día de fiesta *holiday*

ROSITA: ¿No hay clases? ¿Es día de fiesta? ¡Ay, gracias! ¿Sabe usted? Estoy bien ahora.

Actividad

D

Complete each sentence with the correct word, using the story you have just read.

1. Rosita no _____ bien hoy.

2. Está en _____ porque está _____.

3. Rosita _____ mucho.

4. La muchacha necesita un _____.

5. ¿Dónde _____ el doctor?

6. El doctor Curante _____ joven.

7. ¿Cómo _____, Rosita? ¿Por qué _____ triste?

8. Mañana _____ día de fiesta.

9. No _____ clases.

10. Ahora Rosita _____ contenta.

Actividad

E

Using the story, make up a false sentence and tell it to a classmate, who will have to correct it. Take turns.

    EXAMPLE: Rosita está en el cine.
              No, Rosita está en casa.

Actividad

F

Invent three sentences on your own, each with a different use of estar.

1. health   _____

2. location   _____

3. condition   _____

Actividad

G

Invent three sentences on your own, each with a different use of ser.

1. nationality _____

2. profession _____

3. individual characteristics _____

Actividad

H

Your little sister has to do her Spanish homework. Help her choose between forms of **estar** and **ser**. Underline the correct form.

1. Ricardo (*es, está*) contento hoy.

2. Yo (*soy, estoy*) cantante.

3. Ella (*es, está*) secretaria.

4. ¿Quién (*es, está*) Ud.?

5. ¿Dónde (*son, están*) mis padres?

6. Uds. (*son, estan*) inteligentes.

7. El abuelo (*es, está*) inteligente.

8. Nosotros (*somos, estamos*) bien, gracias.

9. Mi profesor (*es, está*) en la clase.

10. Las casas (*son, están*) grandes.

Conversación

Lo siento *I'm sorry.*
¿Qué pasa? *What's happening, What's wrong?*
el resfriado *the cold*

Diálogo

Complete the dialog with expressions chosen from the following list:

adiós	enferma	muchas gracias
a la escuela	estás	mucho dinero
caliente	eres	pasa
comer	estudiar	un resfriado

¿Cómo _____, niña?

No muy bien. Estoy _____.

¿Qué _____?

No deseo _____.

Tienes _____.
Estás _____.

Necesito _____ para un examen mañana.

Preguntas personales

Can you give honest, complete answers to these questions? Try your best.

1. ¿Cuándo estás contento(a) ?

_____

2. ¿Dónde está tu escuela? (¿en qué calle?)

_____

3. ¿Cuántos programas de televisión ves? ¿Cuáles son?

_____

4. ¿Eres serio(a) o cómico(a)?

_____

Información personal

The computer pen-pal service is assembling a personality profile for every student. You are asked to answer the following questions truthfully.

	Sí	No
1. ¿Eres estudioso (estudiosa)?		
2. ¿Estás contento (contenta) en la escuela?		
3. ¿Eres alto (alta)?		
4. ¿Estás enfermo (enferma) el día de examen?		
5. ¿Eres una persona responsable?		
6. ¿Te gusta la música popular?		
7. ¿Eres rubio (rubia)?		
8. ¿Estás cansado (cansada) todo el día?		
9. ¿Eres un(a) joven popular?		
10. ¿Estás bien hoy?		

After you check the boxes, describe yourself using at least five complete Spanish sentences.

_____

_____

_____

_____

_____

Vamos a conversar

You're not feeling well today. The doctor is visiting you at home.

DOCTORA: Hola, ¿cómo estás?

TÚ: *(Tell her you're sick.)*

DOCTORA: Pobre muchacho! ¿Comes bien?

TÚ: *(Say you don't want to eat.)*

DOCTORA: Tienes dolor?

TÚ: *(Tell her yes, you're suffering a lot)*

DOCTORA: No es muy serio. Sólo necesitas unas medicinas.

TÚ: *(Tell her O.K. and thank her.)*

Escríbalo

You have been sent to the nurse's office by your teacher because don't look well. Tell her in three or four sentences how badly you feel today.

_____

_____

_____

_____

LITTLE HAVANA

Wouldn't it be great to be able to go on a visit to an exotic place where you could practice your Spanish by speaking with the native people, going to their festivals, and trying out delicious foods in Spanish-speaking restaurants? And, all this without the hassle of getting a tourist permit or passport or even leaving the United States.

Well, why not go to Little Havana? Where is Little Havana? It's right in the center of the city of Miami, not far from Miami Beach. Since 1959, hundreds of thousands of Cubans have left Cuba to settle in the United States—the majority of them in Miami. Today there are about three quarters of a million Cuban-Americans in Miami—about half the total population of the city. With the additional immigration of tens of thousands of Central and South Americans, Miami has taken on a distinct Latin flavor. Nearly all stores display signs both in Spanish and English. (Even the most typical of American foods—hot dogs—are advertised as **perros calientes**).

There are Spanish newspapers, magazines, and radio and television programs. Miami's largest event is the **Carnaval de Miami**, a week-long Cuban celebration with parades, concerts, fireworks, and entertainment rivaling the Mardi Gras of New Orleans. More than one million people fill the heart of the Cuban district every March to enjoy the non-stop festivities.

Walking along **Calle Ocho**, the main street and soul of Little Havana, gives you the feeling of being in Cuba. Enterprising Cubans have revitalized the economy of the state. Business is bustling everywhere. You can buy products unavailable in many other cities of the United States: tropical fruits and vegetables, **guayaberas** (Cuban shirts), tiny cups of Cuban expresso coffee, **guarapo** (sugar cane juice), and ice-cold **batidos** (tropical fruit shakes).

Feeling hungry? Let's drop in on a Cuban restaurant. The food here is delicious and reasonably priced. Cuban food is flavorful but not at all spicy (**picante**).

"Waiter, bring us an order of **ropa vieja** (shredded beef cooked with tomatoes and peppers—literally : "old clothes"), **moros y cristianos** (black beans cooked with rice—literally Moors and Christians), and **plátanos fritos** (fried plantains). For dessert we'll have **cascos de guayaba con queso** (guava shells in syrup with farmer's cheese) and to drink, a **batido de mango** (a mango milkshake)."

Quick Quiz

1. Little Havana is located in the city of _____.

2. The majority of the Spanish-speaking people there came from _____.

3. The main street of Little Havana is called _____.

4. **Ropa vieja,** which means "old clothes" is really shredded _____.

5. Black beans cooked with rice are called _____.

Let's Find Out More

1. Obtain a Spanish or Spanish-American cookbook from the library and compare Cuban food to American, Mexican, and Spanish foods.

2. Make up a menu featuring typical Cuban foods (rice and beans, fried plantains and so on).

3. Visit a Spanish or Latin American restaurant. Sample the various foods.

4. Have each student prepare a Cuban or other Latin American dish. Have a Latin food festival.

5. Look at a map and locate the island of Cuba.

6. Find out more about Cuban history. Write a short essay on the topic.

Vocabulario

WORDS TO KNOW

abierto(a) *open*
el agua (f.) *water*
caliente *hot*
cansado(a) *tired*
cerrado(a) *closed*
el cumpleaños *birthday*

el dolor *pain*
frío(a) *cold*
el resfriado *cold* (sickness)
sentado(a) *seated, sitting*
triste *sad*

EXPRESSIONS

día de fiesta *holiday*
¿qué pasa? *what's happening?, what's wrong?*
todo el día *all day*
todos los días *every day*
no es nada *it's nothing*

lo siento *I'm sorry*
por favor *please*

Do you want to learn how to tell time in Spanish? Look at the illustrations and figure out what the sentences mean.

¿Qué hora es?

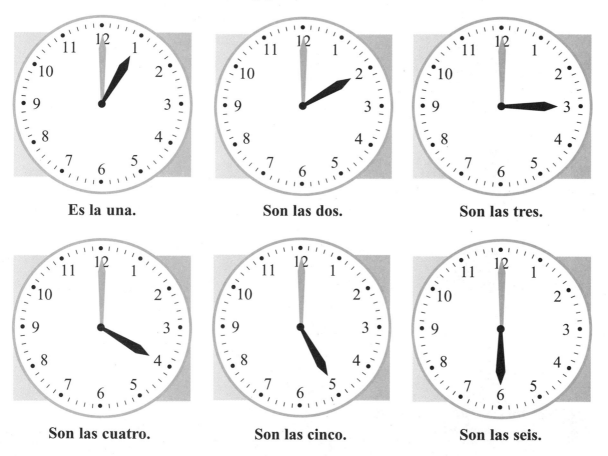

Es la una.	**Son las dos.**	**Son las tres.**
Son las cuatro.	**Son las cinco.**	**Son las seis.**

Now see if you can do the rest.

Note these other expressions for 12:00 o'clock:

Es mediodía. *It's 12:00 noon.*   **Es medianoche.** *It's 12:00 midnight.*

How do you say "What time is it?" in Spanish? _____ What Spanish word means "it's" when saying "it's one o'clock"? _____ What Spanish word means "it's" when saying any other hour? _____ How do you say "It's noon"? _____ How do you say "It's midnight"?

_____

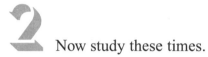
Now study these times.

Es la una y cinco.

Son las dos y cinco.

Son las tres y cinco.

Son las cuatro y cinco.

Continue writing these times.

Any problems so far? Let's see if you can express the following times.

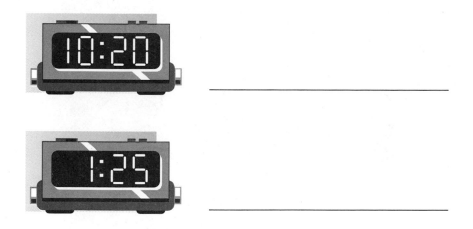

_____

_____

How do you express time AFTER the hour? _____ That's right. To express time AFTER the hour, we use the Spanish word **y** (and) plus the number of minutes.

What time is it now? Write each answer in full.

_____

_____

_____

Now study these times.

Es la una menos cinco.

Son las dos menos cinco.

Son las tres menos cinco.

Son las cuatro menos cinco.

Can you write what time it is?

_____

_____

_____

How would you say the following times?

_____

_____

How do you express time BEFORE the hour? _____
That's right. To express time BEFORE the next hour, we use the Spanish word **menos** and subtract the number of minutes from the next hour.

How would you express?

_____

_____

4 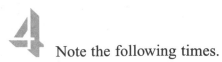 Note the following times.

Es la una y cuarto.

Es la una menos cuarto.

Son las dos y cuarto.

Son las dos menos cuarto.

Son las tres y cuarto.

Son las tres menos cuarto.

Son las cuatro y cuarto.

Son las cuatro menos cuarto.

How would you express the following times?

_____

_____

_____

_____

What's the Spanish word for "a quarter"? _____

How do you say "a quarter after"? _____

How do you say "a quarter before"? _____

The words "quarter" and "four" in Spanish are similar. What is the difference?

_____

Now study these times.

Es la una y media.

Son las dos y media.

Son las tres y media.

Son las cuatro y media.

How would you say?

_____

_____

_____

_____

What is the special word for "half past"? _____

How do you express "half past" the hour? _____

Actividad

A_____

Write out these times in numbers.

EXAMPLE: Es la una. **1:00**

1. Son las dos menos cuarto. _____

2. Son las siete y media. _____

3. Son las once y diez. _____

4. Son las doce y cuarto. _____

5. Es la una y cuarto. _____

6. Son las nueve y veinte. _____

7. Son las tres menos diez. _____

8. Son las cinco menos veinticinco. _____

9. Son las diez y trece. _____

10. Son las cuatro menos veintinueve. _____

Actividad

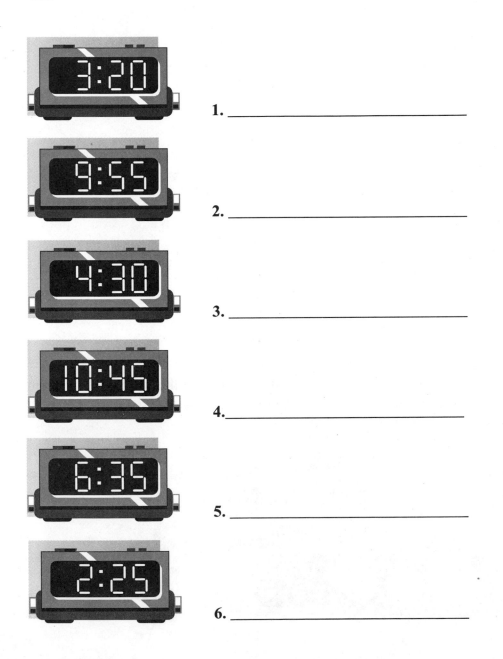

Going in circles, take turns at asking **¿Qué hora es, por favor?** or **¿Qué hora tienes?**
Answer the following cues given. Make sure answers begin with the Spanish equivalent of
"It's."

1. _____

2. _____

3. _____

4. _____

5. _____

6. _____

7. _____

8. _____

9. _____

10. _____

Actividad

Crazy clock shop. Agustín is really confused. All of the clocks in this shop have different times, except two of them showing the same correct time. Can you tell which is the correct time? And can you tell what time does each clock show?

1. _____

2. _____

3. _____

4. _____

5. _____

6. _____

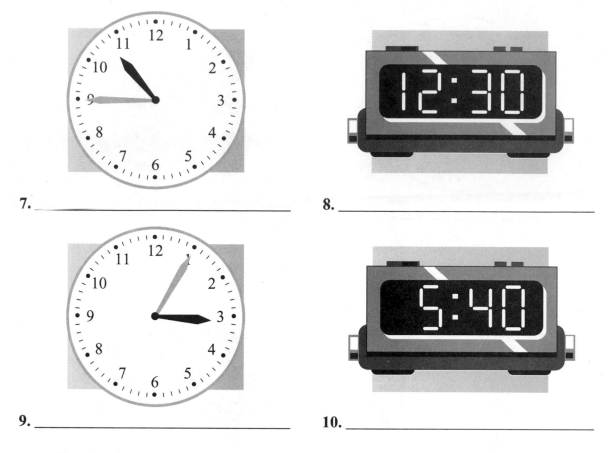

7. _____ 8. _____

9. _____ 10. _____

Actividad

Here are some broken clocks. Each one has the minute hand missing. In your notebook, draw each clock with its minute hand in place.

1. Son las dos menos cinco.

2. Son las tres y diez.

3. Son las cuatro y veinticinco.

6. Es la una menos diez.

4. Son las nueve y cinco.

7. Son las cinco menos veinticinco.

5. Son las once y cuarto.

8. Son las seis menos veinte.

9. Son las doce menos diez.

10. Es mediodía.

5 Now that you know how to answer when someone asks **¿Qué hora es?**, let's learn how to reply if someone asks, for example:

    ¿A qué hora es la clase?   *At what time is the class?*

Here's one possible answer:

    La clase es *a las dos*.   *The class is at two.*

If you want to express "at + time," which Spanish word must you use before the time? _____

If you want to be specific about the time of day, here is what you must do.

    La clase de español es a las ocho *de la mañana*.   *The Spanish class is at 8 A.M.*
    Yo practico la lección a la una *de la tarde*.   *I practice the lesson at 1 P.M.*
    Son las nueve *de la noche*.   *It's 9 P.M.*

How do you express "in the morning" or "A.M." in Spanish? _____

How do you express "in the afternoon" or "P.M."? _____

How do you express "in the evening" or "P.M."? _____

Actividad

Write out in Spanish.

1. 6:35 P.M. _____

2. 2:15 A.M. _____

3. 3:45 P.M. _____

4. 7:55 A.M. _____

5. 10:25 P.M. _____

6. 5:10 P.M. _____

Actividad

Here are people doing different activities during the day. Write the most likely answer to the question **¿Qué hora es?**

a. Es la una y media de la mañana.

b. Son las siete de la mañana.

c. Son las tres de la tarde.

1. _____

a. Son las nueve y media de la noche.

b. Son las cuatro de la tarde.

c. Son las siete y media de la mañana.

2. _____

a. Son las ocho y diez de la mañana.

b. Son las once de la noche.

c. Es la una y cuarto de la tarde.

3. _____

a. Son las siete menos veinte de la noche.

b. Son las dos de la mañana.

c. Es mediodía.

4. _____

a. Son las tres de la tarde.

b. Son las once y media de la noche.

c. Son las dos menos veinte de la mañana.

5. _____

a. Son las ocho de la mañana.

b. Son las cuatro y media de la mañana.

c. Son las nueve de la noche.

6. _____

a. Son las dos y media de la tarde.

b. Son las cuatro y cinco de la mañana.

c. Son las siete y cuarto de la noche.

7. _____

a. Son las tres de la mañana.

b. Son las diez menos diez de la noche.

c. Es la una de la tarde.

8. _____

a. Son las cuatro menos diez de la tarde.

b. Son las siete y cuarto de la noche.

c. Son las once de la noche.

9. _____

a. Es medianoche.

b. Son las diez y cinco de la mañana.

c. Son las cinco y media de la tarde.

10. _____

6

Read this conversation and act it out in groups of three students, as if it were a mini-play.

FRANCISCO:	Pepe, ¿Qué hora es?
PEPE:	Son las nueve y cuarto.
FRANCISCO:	¡Ay caramba! Hay un examen en la clase de matemáticas hoy a las nueve y media. Vamos Rosita. ¡Es tarde!
ROSITA:	No hay problema.
FRANCISCO:	¿No hay problema? El profesor López va a estar furioso.
ROSITA:	Creo que no.
FRANCISCO:	¿Por qué no?
ROSITA:	¿No sabes? El señor López está ausente hoy.
FRANCISCO:	¡Ay, qué suerte!

¡caramba! *goodness, gosh*

Es tarde. *It's late.*

Creo que no. *I don't think so.*

¡Qué suerte! *What luck!*

Actividad

G

Answer the following questions in Spanish.

1. ¿Con quién habla Francisco?

_____

2. ¿Qué hora es en el reloj de Pepe?

_____

3. ¿Qué dice Rosita?

_____

4. ¿En qué clase tiene un examen Francisco?

_____

5. ¿Por qué no hay examen hoy?

_____

Actividad

Some words in Spanish, just like some words in English, are used in more than one way. How many of the following can you figure out? Choose from:

mañana   tarde   noche

1. Son las seis de la _____.

2. Buenas _____, muchachos. ¿Cómo están ustedes?

3. Así, así. Hay un examen difícil _____.

4. ¿A qué hora? A las nueve de la _____.

5. Bueno, vamos a estudiar toda la _____.

6. Y ahora vamos a casa. Es _____. Son las siete de la _____.

7. Buenas _____. Hasta _____.

 ## Información personal

Complete the sentences with an appropriate time.

1. Yo voy a la escuela a _____.

2. Entro a la clase de español a _____.

3. Hago (*I do*) mis tareas (*homework*) a _____.

4. Veo televisión a _____.

5. Como a _____.

Actividad

Work with a partner. Take turns asking and answering questions about your daily schedule of activities.

EXAMPLE: ¿A qué hora vas al parque?
Yo voy al parque a las seis.

Conversación

la película *film, movie*
Voy a ver *I'm going to see*

Diálogo

Fill in the words that are missing from the dialog. Choose from the following list.

¿por qué?	hora	película	ver
las cuatro y cuarto	televisión	programa	sorpresa
Cuál	Cómo	¡Caramba!	también

¿Qué _____ es?

Son _____.
¿Por qué?

Hay un _____ importante
en la _____ a la seis.

¿_____ programa?

Es una _____
cómica.

¿_____
se llama la película?

«El hijo de Drácula»

Yo deseo _____
la película _____.

Vamos a conversar

You rush into your Spanish class (Late Again!). Your teacher wants to know why this happens so often.

PROFESOR:	¿Sabes qué hora es?
TÚ:	(*Say it's 9:30.*)
PROFESOR:	¿Y sabes a qué hora es la clase?
TÚ:	(*Tell him the class is at 9:00.*)
PROFESOR:	Mañana hay un examen. ¿A qué hora vas estar aquí?
TÚ:	(*Tell him you're going to be in class at 9:00.*)
PROFESOR:	Muy bien. A las nueve, ¿verdad?
TÚ:	(*Say yes, that you're going to buy a new watch.*)

Escríbalo

Your coach wants to get in touch with you sometime during the day. Write a short note (5 sentences) telling what you are doing at various times during the day.

_____

_____

_____

_____

_____

WHAT TIME IS IT, ANYWAY?

What would you think if you opened a Spanish television guide and saw that the soccer game (**partido de fútbol**) starts at 19.30? What about being at the train station and seeing that your train departs at 22.10?

Most Spanish-speaking countries use a 24-hour system (known in the U.S. as military time) for official time. It is used for schedules for planes, trains, radio and television programs, sports, and entertainment events.

At first look, it might seem confusing, but using the 24-hour system, there is no need to specify **de la mañana** or **de la tarde** (A.M. or P.M.). All you have to do is subtract 12 from the numbers between 13 and 24 and you obtain the conventional time. If the official time is less than 12, it means A.M.; if it is more, it means P.M. For instance, 08.00 means 8:00 A.M., 13.30 means 1:30 in the afternoon, and 23.00 means 11 o'clock in the evening.

To understand this a little better, here is an illustration of what you may see in an airport of a Spanish-speaking country:

LLEGADAS/ARRIVALS		SALIDAS/DEPARTURES	
Nueva York	17.30	París	17.50
San Juan	18.00	Buenos Aires	18.15
Bogotá	18.25	San Francisco	19.30
Lima	21.30	Montevideo	20.15

But don't let this fool you. The 24-hour system is only used in official contexts, never in casual conversation. If you are trying to get together with your Spanish-speaking friends, don't tell them that you will meet them at 16.30. You just say *a* **las cuatro y media**, and by context, they will know you mean 4:30 P.M.

Quick Quiz

1. Most Spanish-speaking countries use the _____ system to tell the official time.

2. This system makes it unnecessary to use _____ or _____.

3. In casual conversation, 4:30 P.M. in Spanish is _____.

4. The plane from New York arrives at _____ in conventional time.

5. The plane to Montevideo departs at _____ in conventional time.

Let's Find Out More

1. Find out in what other countries and organizations is the 24-hour system used to tell the time.

2. What other differences are there in mesurements, other than time, between the United States and Spanish-speaking countries? Compare weight, temperature, etc.

Vocabulario

WORDS TO KNOW

ausente *absent*
la medianoche *midnight*
un programa *program*
la película *film, movie*
el mediodía *noon*

EXPRESSIONS

a las (dos) *at (two) o'clock*
¡caramba! *gosh!, my goodness!*
creo que no *I don't think (so)*
de la mañana *A.M.*
de la noche *P.M.*
de la tarde *P.M.*
es la una *it's one o'clock*

no hay problema *no problem*
por favor *please*
¿por qué no? *why not?*
¿qué hora es? *what time is it?*
¡qué suerte! *what luck!*
son las dos *it's two o'clock*

Repaso III
(Lecciones 10–13)

LECCIÓN 10

The verb **ser** is an irregular verb that means *to be*. Remember all of its forms.

yo	soy	nosotros ⎫ somos
tú	eres	nosotras ⎭
Ud.	es	Uds.	son
él ⎫ es	ellos ⎫ son
ella ⎭	ellas ⎭

LECCIÓN 11

a. To conjugate an **-ir** verb, drop the **-ir** ending and add the appropriate endings for each pronoun. Let's take the verb **vivir** (to live).

yo	-o	yo	viv*o*
tú	-es	tú	viv*es*
Ud.	-e	Ud.	viv*e*
él ⎫ -e	él ⎫ viv*e*
ella ⎭	ella ⎭
nosotros ⎫ -imos	nosotros ⎫ viv*imos*
nosotras ⎭	nosotras ⎭
Uds.	-en	Uds.	viv*en*
ellos ⎫ -en	ellos ⎫ viv*en*
ellas ⎭	ellas ⎭

318

b. The verb **salir** (to leave, to go out) has an irregular **yo** form (**salgo**) and is followed by **de** before the name of a place.

    Yo *salgo de* **la escuela a las dos.**

Do you remember other similar irregular forms? Yes, you are right:

    tengo (I have) and **hago** (I do, make).

LECCIÓN 12

a. There is another Spanish verb meaning *to be*: the irregular verb **estar**. Remember all its forms.

yo	estoy	nosotros } nosotras }	estamos
tú	estás		
Ud.	está	Uds.	están
él } ella }	está	ellos } ellas }	están

b. Ser is used when expressing individual characteristics, professions and nationalities.

La muchacha *es* **inteligente.**	*The girl is intelligent.*
La señora *es* **enfermera.**	*The woman is a nurse.*
El médico *es* **mexicano.**	*The doctor is Mexican.*

Estar is used when talking about health, when referring to location, and when describing a temporary condition.

La niña *está* **bien.**	*The girl is fine.*
¿Dónde *está* **Roberto?**	*Where is Roberto?*
Estamos **muy contentos.**	*We are very happy.*

LECCIÓN 13

a. Time is expressed as follows:

¿Qué hora es?	What time is it?
Es la una.	It's one o'clock.

Son las dos.	*It's two o'clock.*
Son las dos y diez.	*It's 2:10.*
Son las dos y cuarto.	*It's 2:15.*
Son las dos y media.	*It's 2:30.*
Son las tres menos veinte.	*It's 2:40.*
Es mediodía.	*It's 12 noon.*
Es medianoche.	*It's 12 midnight.*
Son las seis de la mañana.	*It's 6 A.M.*
Son las cuatro de la tarde.	*It's 4 P.M.*
Son las ocho de la noche.	*It's 8 P.M.*

b. To express *at + time*, use **a**.

¿*A* qué hora miras tú televisión?	*At what time do you watch TV?*
***A* las ocho de la noche.**	*At eight P.M.*

Actividad

A

Two letters are missing from each profession. Which are they?

1. mé __ __ co

2. a __ o __ ada

3. de __ __ ista

4. me __ áni __ o

5. polí __ í __

6. sec __ __ taria

7. c __ __ tante

8. car __ e __ o

Actividad

B

Here are some pictures of people doing things. Describe each picture using the correct form of one of the following verbs.

abrir	descubrir	recibir
cubrir	dividir	salir
decidir	escribir	vivir

1. Los alumnos _____ a
las tres.

2. Él _____ la pluma.

3. La profesora _____
la ventana.

4. Nosotros _____ la
computadora.

5. Tú _____ en tu auto.

6. Ud. _____ a una
amiga.

7. Las niñas _____
frutas.

8. Ella _____ la bicicleta
nueva.

Actividad

Work with a partner, and alternate roles. Just say no, following the example.

> EXAMPLE: ¿Haces una lista? (tarea)
> **No, hago la tarea.**

1. ¿Tienes mucho dinero? (*trabajo*)
3. ¿Eres cantante? (*abogado -a*)
5. ¿Sales de casa a las nueve? (*ocho*)
7. ¿Tienes frío? (*calor*)
9. ¿Eres profesor -a? (*alumno -a*)

2. ¿Estás triste? (*contento*)
4. ¿Eres, estúpido? (*inteligente*)
6. ¿Estás enfermo? (*muy bien*)
8. ¿Vas a la escuela? (*parque*)

Actividad

Carlos could not leave the house today, so he wrote his girlfriend a message in Spanish on the window of his room. He had to write it in reverse form, so that his girlfriend could read it from the street. Can you read the message? (Hint: A mirror might help.)

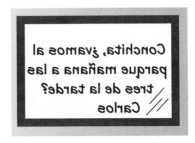

Conchita, ¿vamos al
parque mañana a las
tres de la tarde?
Carlos

Actividad

Complete the crosswrod puzzle with the Spanish equivalent for the clues given.

Crucigrama

HORIZONTALES		VERTICALES	
5. to write	**12.** to cover	**1.** we open	**6.** to know
7. they do	**13.** you leave	**2.** you are (**tú**)	**10.** you take out (**Uds.**)
8. to go	**15.** I do	**3.** she goes	**11.** I know
9. you know (**tú**)	**16.** he lives	**4.** to discover	**14.** to see
11. I am			

Actividad

F

Write something related to the pictures using forms of **estar** or **ser**.

EXAMPLES:

Él *es* médico.

Ellas *están* contentas.

1. _____

2. _____

3. _____

4. _____

5. _____

6. _____

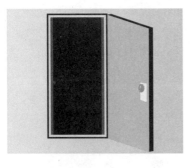

7. _____

8. _____

9._____

10. _____

Actividad

G

Describe some popular personality you like (or dislike). Include the following details.

Use **ser** and **estar**.

EXAMPLE: Julio Iglesias.
Es español.
Está en España.

1. nationality
2. profession
3. a personal characteristic

4. where person is or lives
5. state of health
6. attitude or emotional condition

Actividad

H

Can you understand this story? Whenever you come to a picture, read it as if it were a Spanish word.

Mi familia

Mi hermano pequeño tiene 10 años. Es [image] y [image]. Él está en [image]

ahora. Somos muy diferentes. Yo soy [image] y [image]. Yo estoy en la [image]

ahora y [image] una composición en la [image] de español. Yo deseo

ser [image] o [image]. Mi hermano desea ser [image]. Él tiene muchos [image]

pequeños. Bueno, voy a [image]. Es tarde y la [image] está [image].

Mi mamá está [image] si yo voy tarde a [image] y mi [image] está furioso. Termino aquí y

[image] a casa.

CUARTA
Parte

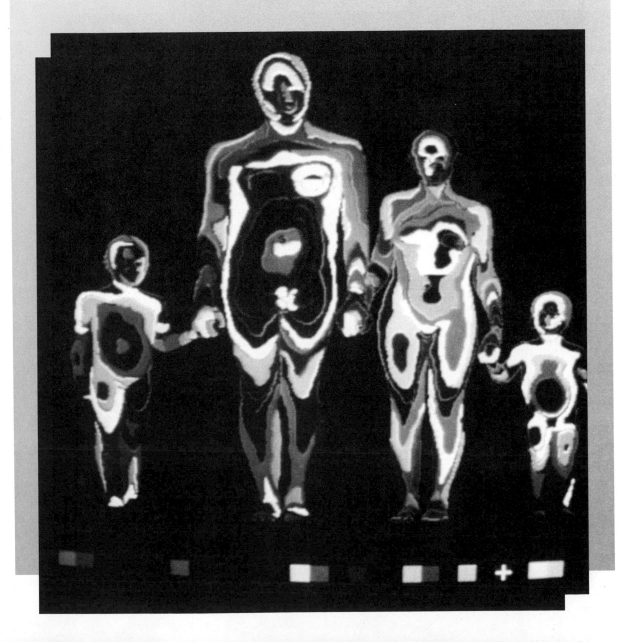

14 El cuerpo
Parts of the Body;
The Verb **TENER**;
Expressions With **TENER**

Let's learn the parts of the body in Spanish. Look at the pictures and the Spanish words and try to figure out their meanings.

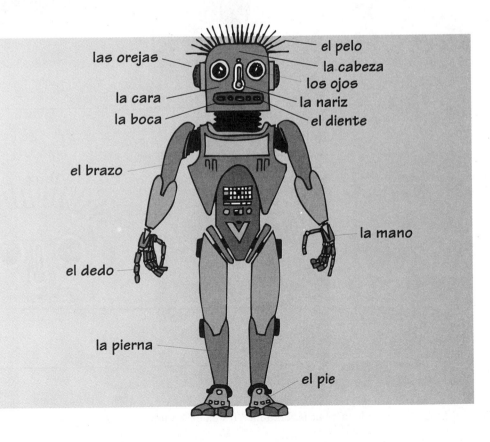

las orejas
el pelo
la cabeza
los ojos
la cara
la nariz
la boca
el diente
el brazo
la mano
el dedo
la pierna
el pie

Actividad

A

This robot may look different, but the parts of his body are the same as yours and mine. Study them and match the Spanish words with the correct pictures.

la boca	el dedo	la oreja
el brazo	la mano*	el pelo
la cabeza	la nariz	el pie
la cara	los ojos	la pierna

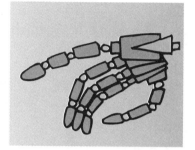 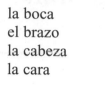 

1. _____ 2. _____ 3. _____

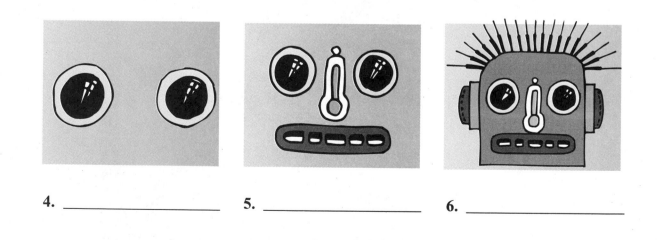

4. _____ 5. _____ 6. _____

*Did you notice that **mano** ends in **o** but is feminine? It's an exception to the general rule.

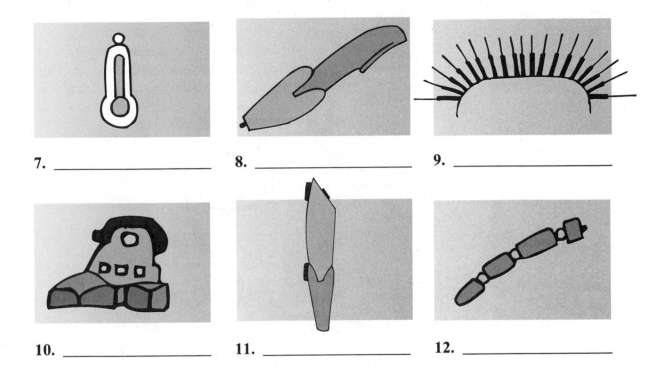

7. _____ 8. _____ 9. _____

10. _____ 11. _____ 12. _____

Actividad

B

Every part of the body has a function. Using the verbs on the right column, match the part of the body with the action it can perform.

EXAMPLE: **Los ojos son para ver.**

1. Los ojos son _____.

2. Las piernas son _____.

3. Las manos son _____.

4. La boca es _____.

5. Los pies son _____.

6. Las orejas son _____.

7. Los dedos son _____.

hablar
escribir
escuchar
trabajar
ver
correr
caminar

2 Now that you are an expert on the body, you are ready to read the amazing story of Dr. Gustavo Guacamole, his assistant Rosalinda, and their wonderful creation. This story contains all the forms of the irregular Spanish verb **tener** (to have). See if you can find them all.

Robotón el Magnífico

CUÁNDO:	El futuro
DÓNDE:	Un laboratorio en una ciudad misteriosa. Los habitantes de la ciudad no están contentos. Todos están muy tristes porque tienen un dictador brutal y cruel: Héctor el Horrible.
QUIÉN:	El doctor Gustavo Guacamole, un científico famoso y brillante, y Rosalinda, su asistente.

la ciudad *city*
los habitantes *inhabitants*

su asistente *his assistant*

EL DOCTOR:	Nuestros soldados son viejos y gordos. Sólo desean comer y vivir bien. No desean combatir a nuestro horrible dictador. Todos los habitantes tienen miedo.	**soldados** *soldiers* **sólo** *only* **tienen miedo** *are afraid*
ROSALINDA:	Tengo una idea. Vamos a construir un hombre mecánico, un robot superior, que va a destruir al dictador.	**vamos a** *we are going to*
EL DOCTOR:	¿Tenemos las partes necesarias?	
ROSALINDA:	Sí, es fácil, pero no tenemos mucho tiempo. Vamos al laboratorio. (Más tarde en el laboratorio.) Ahora vamos a hacer una criatura nueva. ¡Mira! Tenemos la cabeza: la cara, los dientes, los ojos y las orejas.	**el tiempo** *time* **más tarde** *later*
EL DOCTOR:	Y ahora el cuerpo, las manos, los dedos, las piernas y los pies.	**el cuerpo** *body*
ROSALINDA:	Necesitamos un cerebro.	
EL DOCTOR:	Tengo una mini-computadora.	**el cerebro** *brain*
ROSALINDA:	¡Ah, perfecto! Ahora tenemos a Robotón- el superhombre metálico.	
EL DOCTOR:	Robotón, tiene que combatir al dictador.	
ROBOTÓN:	¿Combatir yo? No, señor. Yo sólo voy a bailar, y a cantar, y a correr y...	**combatir** *to fight*

Actividad

Ask a classmate to read each statement and say if it is true or false. If it is false, your classmate must change the words in boldface to make the statement true.

1. Es un laboratorio en **la ciudad de Madrid**.

_____

2. Todos los habitantes están **contentos**.

_____

3. **El doctor** no desea combatir al dictador.

_____

4. **El doctor** tiene una idea.

_____

5. Rosalinda hace un **hombre mecánico**.

_____

6. Rosalinda dice que Robotón va a destruir **al dictador**.

_____

7. Robotón desea **bailar**.

_____

Actividad

D
_____

Fill in the names of the labeled parts of the body.

Actividad

Look at each picture and write the Spanish word for the part of the body it associates with.

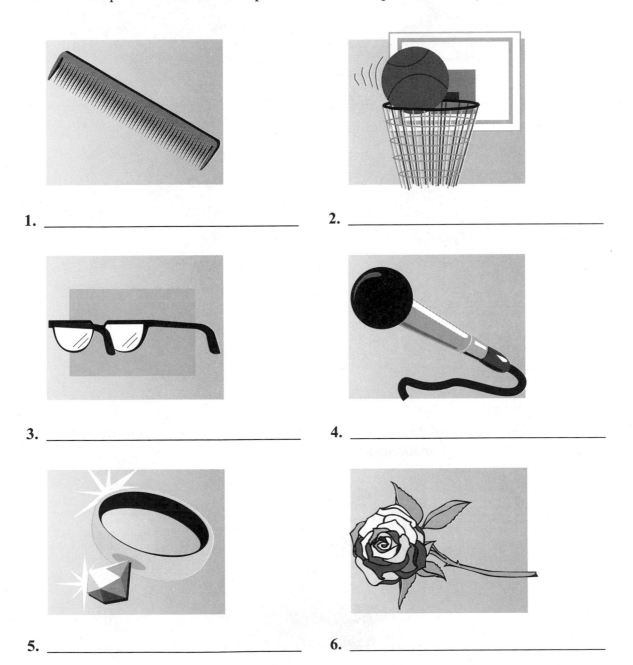

1. _____

2. _____

3. _____

4. _____

5. _____

6. _____

7. _____

8. _____

9. _____

10. _____

Actividad

F

You are playing a game of "Simon says" with your friends. Which of your friends are out of the game? Put a check mark next to each incorrect response.

EXAMPLE:

Simón dice:— el pelo.

Simón dice:— la nariz. ✔

Simón dice:—la pierna.

Simón dice:—los ojos.

Simón dice:—la boca.

Simón dice:—la cabeza.

Simón dice:—el brazo.

Simón dice:—las orejas.

Actividad

Now let's have some more fun! You and your classmates take turns in playing "Simón dice."

3 Did you find the forms of the irregular verb **tener** in the story about Robotón el Magnífico? Here are the forms of **tener**. MEMORIZE them:

yo	**tengo**	*I have*
tú	**tienes**	*you have*
Ud.	**tiene**	*you have*
él } **ella** }	**tiene**	*he has* *she has*
nosotros } **nosotras** }	**tenemos**	*we have*
Uds.	**tienen**	*you have*
ellos } **ellas** }	**tienen**	*they have*

Actividad

H

Mr. Soto's students have been asked to describe themselves and each other. Complete each statement by filling in a subject pronoun or name of a person.

1. _____ tiene los ojos negros.

2. _____ tienen el pelo rubio.

3. _____ tengo la cara bonita.

4. _____ tiene la nariz grande.

5. _____ tienes la boca pequeña.

6. _____ tenemos los pies enormes.

7. _____ tienes los brazos flacos.

8. _____ tiene los dientes blancos.

Actividad

Here are some sentences in which a form of **tener** is used. Can you match these sentences with the pictures they describe?

El robot tiene dos cabezas.
Tengo las orejas pequeñas.
Ellos tienen el pelo rubio.
Yo tengo las piernas flacas.
Ud. tiene las manos delicadas.

Él tiene el pelo negro.
Ellas tienen la cara bonita.
Tú tienes la boca perfecta.
Él tiene la nariz fea.
Ud. tiene los pies grandes.

1. _____

2. _____

3. _____

4. _____

5. _____

6. _____

7. _____

8. _____

9. _____

10. _____

Actividad

J

Complete the following descriptions with the correct forms of the verb **tener**.

1. Ellas _____ el pelo negro.

2. María _____ los ojos grandes.

3. Ud. _____ las manos pequeñas.

4. Yo _____ el pelo rubio.

5. Nosotros _____ los dedos rápidos.

6. Tú _____ las orejas bonitas.

7. Uds. _____ los ojos bonitos.

8. Pedro _____ los pies cansados.

Actividad

K

Read this riddle and see if you can find the answer.

No soy mexicano. No soy cubano. Soy de los Estados Unidos, pero estoy en todas partes. Soy muy popular. Estoy en la televisión todos los días. Soy cómico y mi cuerpo es negro. Mis orejas son grandes y mis pies también. Todos saben mi nombre. Mi amiga se llama Minnie. Y yo me llamo Miguelito. ¿Quién soy yo?

Actividad

Read each description and see which animal it refers to. Choose from the following.

el burro	el elefante	el león	el perro
el camello	el gato	el mono	el tigre

1. Es muy cómico. _____

2. Tiene su casa en el jardín. _____

3. Tiene mucho pelo en la cabeza. _____

4. Vive en el desierto. _____

5. Tiene orejas grandes. _____

6. Es pequeño. _____

7. Tiene el cuerpo grande y gordo. _____

8. Vive en Asia. _____

4 More about **tener**. There are some very common Spanish expressions that use the verb **tener**. The equivalent expressions in English use the verb *to be*.

tengo miedo	*I am frightened, scared* (literally, *I have fear*)
tienes calor	*you are warm* (literally, *you have warmth*)
tiene frío	*he (she) is cold*
tiene hambre	*he (she) is hungry*
tienes sed	*you are thirsty*
tienen sueño	*they are sleepy*
tenemos razón	*we are right*
no tienen razón	*they are wrong*
tengo dos años	*I am two years old*

Note that these expressions with **tener** are generally used when the subject is a living creature. When the subject is not a living creature, use the verb **estar.**

El café *está* caliente.	*The coffee is warm.*
Las sodas *están* frías.	*The sodas are cold.*

Actividad

M

Find out your classmates' age.

EXAMPLE: ¿Cuántos años tienes?
Tengo catorce años. ¿Y tú?

Actividad

N

The following human-interest pictures are being prepared for a Spanish help book. It's your job to label them:

Tienes doce años.	Tienen calor.
Tengo hambre.	Tiene frío.
Tenemos sed.	El niño tiene sueño.

1. _____   2. _____

3. _____

4. _____

5. _____

6. _____

Actividad

Circle the sentence that is equivalent to the English expression.

1. I am very thirsty.

a. Tengo mucha hambre.
b. Tengo mucha sed.
c. Tengo razón.
d. Estoy muy cansado(a).

2. He is wrong.

    a. No tiene miedo.   b. No tiene razón.
    c. Tiene sueño.   d. Tiene razón.

3. Is she fourteen years old?

    a. ¿Tienes cuarenta años?   b ¿Tiene ella cuatro años?
    c. ¿Tiene ella catorce años?   d. ¿No tiene catorce años?

4. They are hungry.
    a. Tienen hambre.   b. Están enfermos.
    c. Tienen calor.   d. Tienen sueño.

Actividad

Match each English sentence with its equivalent in Spanish. Write the correct letter in the space provided.

1. You're thirsty. _____   **a.** Tiene hambre.
    b. Ud. tiene sed.
2. We're hot. _____   **c.** Tienes frío.
    d. Tenemos calor.
3. I'm sleepy. _____   **e.** Tienen trece años.
    f. Tengo sueño.
4. They're thirteen years old. _____   **g.** Tienen razón.
    h. No tiene razón.
5. He's wrong. _____   **i.** ¿Cuántos años tienes?
    j. ¿Tienen Uds. hambre?
6. How old are you? _____

7. He's hungry. _____

8. You're cold. _____

9. She's wrong. _____

10. They're right. _____

Actividad

You ask your friends, "**¿Vamos al cine?**" and this is what they answered. Take turns reading your friends' answers with a classmate.

The next day you asked some of your classmates in the Spanish class. They all said yes! Could both you and your classmate find several different ways of saying yes to the question?

1. _____ 2. _____

3. _____ 4. _____

5. _____ 6. _____

Diálogo

Identify yourself with the person in each picture as you answer the question **¿Qué te pasa?**

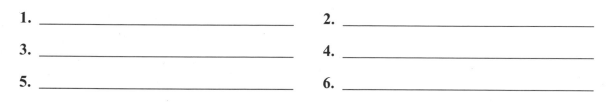

1. _____ 2. _____

3. _____ 4. _____

5. _____

Preguntas personales

1. ¿Cuántos años tienes?

_____

2. ¿Tienes hambre?

_____

3. ¿Tienes siempre razón?

_____

4. ¿A qué hora tienes sueño?

_____

Información personal

Draw your own robot creation and label the parts of the robot's body. Then write three sentences describing the robot.

1. _____

2. _____

3. _____

BODY LANGUAGE

Visiting a Spanish-speaking country? If you anticipate having some problems with the language, and you are thinking of using gestures to communicate, be careful, because you could run into trouble.

For example, someone draws a semicircle with his or her hand, separating and closing up their fingers: you should know that they are refering to something that was stolen. You go to a hotel and ask an employee for a room. The employee answers by turning a hand palm-up opening and closing the tips of the fingers repeatedly: that means that the place is crowded. Also, your friend puts his or her thumb against the lips: your friend is asking you to get something to drink.

But gestures are not the only difference you will notice regarding body language. There are also differences in the way friends and relatives greet each other. People of Spanish heritage are usually very affectionate and warm with family and friends, or when meeting new people. They readily express their feelings and have more physical contact than Americans. Kissing each other on the cheeks when meeting and again when parting is common practice among female friends and friends of the opposite sex. Shaking hands (**darse la mano**) is almost required, and it is usually accompanied with a tap on the back (**una palmada**) or a hug (**un abrazo**).

In most Spanish-American countries, people greet their friends with one kiss. However, in some countries, like Spain, two kisses, one on each cheek, are customary.

Remember: **hablar con las manos** (talking with your hands) is OK, but keep in mind that there is no such a thing as an international code for gestures or body language.

Quick Quiz

1. The sign for stealing in the Spanish-speaking world is _____.

2. Touching the tip of your fingers against each other means _____.

3. People of Spanish heritage are very _____ with friends and relatives.

4. **Darse la mano** means _____, and it is usually accompanied by **una**

_____.

5. Gestures and body language are _____ among cultures.

Let's Find Out More

1. Make a list of common gestures among Americans. Find out if they have the same meaning in the Spanish-speaking world. Compare the two.

2. Find out about ways to greet people in different cultures. Discuss them in class.

Vocabulario

WORDS TO KNOW

la boca *mouth*	**el cuerpo** *body*	**los ojos** *eyes*
el brazo *arm*	**el dedo** *finger*	**la oreja** *(outer) ear*
la cabeza *head*	**el diente** *tooth*	**el pelo** *hair*
la cara *face*	**el futuro** *future*	**el pie** *foot*
la ciudad *city*	**la mano** *hand*	**la pierna** *leg*
la computadora *computer*	**la nariz** *nose*	**el tiempo** *time, weather*
	negro *black, dark*	

EXPRESSIONS

tengo calor *I am warm, hot*

tengo doce años *I am twelve years old*

tengo frío *I am cold*

tengo hambre *I am hungry*

tengo miedo *I am afraid*

tengo razón *I am right*

tengo sed *I am thirsty*

tengo sueño *I am sleepy*

vamos a... *we are going to . . . , let's . . .*

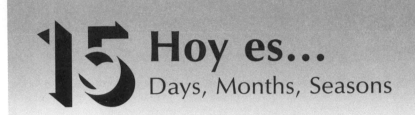

Hoy es...
Days, Months, Seasons

Let's learn the days of the week in Spanish. You will notice that they are not written with capital letters. Note also that in Spanish-speaking countries Monday (not Sunday) is the first day of the week.

			JUNIO			
lunes	martes	miércoles	jueves	viernes	sábado	domingo
1	2	3	4	5	6	7
8	9	10	11	12	13	14
15	16	17	18	19	20	21
22	23	24	25	26	27	28
29	30					

un día

sábado	domingo
6	7

un fin de semana

lunes	martes	miércoles	jueves	viernes	sábado	domingo
1	2	3	4	5	6	7

una semana

In Spanish, the days of the week are considered masculine.

Un poema

**Lunes, martes, miércoles, tres;
jueves, viernes, sábado, seis.
Y el domingo siete es.**

Actividad

Can you recognize the names of the days of the week? Fill in the blanks with the appropriate letters.

1. __ o __ in __o   **2.** m __ __ __ __ s   **3.** __ i __ r __ e __

4. j __ __ v __ __   **5.** m __ __ r __ __ l __ __   **6.** __ u __ e __

7. __ á __ a __ o

Actividad

B

Jorge is a very smart little boy. Whenever someone tells him what day it is, he wants to show off that he knows which days go before and after. Can you figure out what days he would say?

1. _____ martes _____

2. _____ jueves _____

3. _____ sábado _____

4. _____ lunes _____

Actividad

C

Now, you try this with your classmates. Tell a day of the week to a student next to you, who will then repeat the name of the day and add the name of the day that follows.

2 All the kids at school are discussing their favorite days of the week.

¿Qué día de la semana es tu día favorito? ¿Por qué?

PÍA: El viernes veo una película con mis amigas.

CARLOS: El sábado practico tenis con mi amigo.

JOSÉ: El domingo veo el fútbol en la televisión.

VICTORIA: El lunes, el martes, el miércoles, el jueves y el viernes. Prefiero los días de clase.

GUADALUPE: El miércoles tengo una clase especial después de la escuela. Trabajo con las computadoras.

después de *after*

ANDRÉS: Prefiero el fin de semana porque no voy a la escuela. Estoy cansado de estudiar.

Actividad

D

Do you remember each person's favorite day(s)? Match the person on the left with their favorite day or days on the right. Write the matching letter in the space provided.

1. Andrés   _____

2. José   _____

3. Victoria   _____

4. Carlos   _____

5. Pía   _____

6. Guadalupe   _____

a. el sábado
b. el viernes
c. el miércoles
d. el sábado y el domingo
e. el domingo
f. el lunes, el martes, el miércoles, el jueves, el viernes

Actividad

E

Write in Spanish why each person prefers a particular day of the week.

1. Carlos _____

2. Victoria _____

3. Guadalupe _____

4. Pía _____

5. Andrés _____

6. José _____

Actividad

F

Look at the calendar and identify the days of the week in the questions.

EXAMPLE: **¿Qué día es el seis?**
Es domingo.

ENERO

lunes	martes	miércoles	jueves	viernes	sábado	domingo
	1	2	3	4	5	6
7	8	9	10	11	12	13
14	15	16	17	18	19	20
21	22	23	24	25	26	27
28	29	30	31			

1. ¿Qué día es el veintitrés? _____

2. ¿Qué día es el siete? _____

3. ¿Qué día es el trece? _____

4. ¿Qué día es el treinta y uno? _____

5. ¿Qué día es el ocho? _____

6. ¿Qué día es el doce? _____

7. ¿Qué día es el nueve? _____

8. ¿Qué día es el dieciocho? _____

Actividad

a. Work with a partner. Ask each other what your favorite day is and why.

¿Cuál es tu día de la semana favorito? _____

¿Por qué? _____

b. Find out about your classmate's schedule. Take turns asking and answering questions.
¿Qué días tienes clases de matemáticas? ¿de inglés? ¿de computadoras?

_____

3

Let's learn the months of the year in Spanish. Look at the pictures and try to figure out what the words mean.

enero

febrero

marzo

abril

mayo

junio

julio

agosto

septiembre

octubre

noviembre

diciembre

Actividad

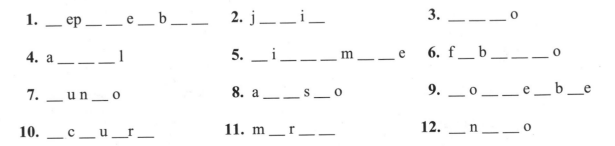

If you have learned the names of the months of the year, you will recognize them though some letters are missing. Write the missing letters.

1. __ ep __ __ e __ b __ __

2. j __ __ i __

3. __ __ __ o

4. a __ __ __ __ l

5. __ i __ __ __ m __ __ e

6. f __ b __ __ __ __ o

7. __ u n __ o

8. a __ __ s __ o

9. __ o __ __ e __ b __ e

10. __ c __ u __ r __

11. m __ r __ __ __

12. __ n __ __ o

Actividad

Identify which month is being described.

1. Llueve mucho. _____

2. Es el mes del Día de Acción de Gracias. _____

3. Es el último mes del año. _____

4. Hace mucho calor. _____

5. Es el mes número uno del año. _____

6. Es el mes de los matrimonios. _____

7. Es el mes de las flores. _____

8. Hace mucho frío. _____

9. Terminan las vacaciones. _____

a. enero
b. agosto
c. noviembre
d. febrero
e. mayo
f. septiembre
g. diciembre
h. abril
i. junio

4 Let's learn the four seasons in Spanish. Look at the pictures and figure out what the words mean.

la primavera

el verano

el otoño

el invierno

Actividad

Look at each picture and identify in Spanish the season it represents.

1. _____

2. _____

3. _____

4. _____

Actividad

K

Let's see if you have learned the seasons.

1. El año termina en _____.

2. En octubre estamos en _____.

3. Mayo es un mes lindo de _____.

4. En las vacaciones estamos en _____.

5. Después del verano es _____.

6. En _____ hace mucho frío.

7. Después de la primavera es _____.

5

Here's a group of students talking about their favorite months of the year. See how much you can understand.

¿Qué estación prefieres tú? ¿Cuál es tu mes favorito? ¿Por qué?

FELIPE:	El verano, porque en julio y agosto estoy de vacaciones.
LIDIA:	El invierno, porque la Navidad es en diciembre.
PEPE:	Yo prefiero el otoño, porque en octubre hay fútbol.
RODRIGO:	La primavera. En abril corro en el parque.
GABRIELA:	El invierno. Prefiero febrero porque hace frío.
MÓNICA:	El otoño. En septiembre me gusta ir a la escuela.
MARÍA:	La primavera. En mayo hay muchas flores bonitas.

la Navidad *Christmas*

Actividad

Answer according to the story above.

1. ¿Quién prefiere el invierno porque hace frío?

_____

2. ¿Cuándo hay flores bonitas?

_____

3. ¿En qué mes hay fútbol?

_____

4. ¿Quién prefiere el otoño?

_____

5. ¿Cuál es la estación favorita de María?

_____

Actividad

M

Identify each person's preference in the story and write in Spanish why they prefer a particular month.

1. (María) _____

2. (Lidia) _____

3. (Felipe) _____

4. (Pepe) _____

5. (Mónica) _____

6. (Gabriela) _____

7. (Rodrigo) _____

Actividad

N

Find out what your classmates prefer. Work in pairs.

1. ¿Cuál es tu estación favorita? _____

2. ¿Por qué? _____

3. ¿Cuál es tu mes favorito? _____

4. ¿Por qué? _____

Actividad

Name the season for each month.

1. abril _____

2. junio _____

3. diciembre _____

4. octubre _____

5. mayo _____

6. agosto _____

7. septiembre _____

8. febrero _____

9. marzo _____

10. julio _____

11. noviembre _____

12. enero _____

6 Now let's see how the date is expressed in Spanish.

¿Qué día es hoy? (What is today's date?)

ABRIL						
L	M	M	J	V	S	D
1	②	3	4	5	6	7
8	9	10	11	12	13	14
15	16	17	18	19	20	21
22	23	24	25	26	27	28
29	30	31				

JULIO						
L	M	M	J	V	S	D
1	2	3	4	5	6	7
8	9	10	⑪	12	13	14
15	16	17	18	19	20	21
22	23	24	25	26	27	28
29	30	31				

Es el dos de abril. **Es el once de julio.**

Es el veintiuno de septiembre.

Es el treinta de diciembre.

To express the date in Spanish, use: Hoy **es el** + (date) + **de** + (month).

To express the date in Spanish for the first day of the month, use: **Hoy es** + **el** + **primero** + **de** + (month).

If you want to include the day of the week: **Es lunes**, **tres de mayo**, or **Hoy es lunes, tres de mayo**.

Hoy es el primero de enero.

Actividad

You're setting up a calendar of events for the Spanish club. Write the following dates in Spanish.

1. June 4 _____

2. January 11 _____

3. May 15 _____

4. December 21 _____

5. September 27 _____

6. April 30 _____

7. Tuesday, February 14 _____

8. Thursday, August 7 _____

9. Sunday, March 31 _____

10. Monday, November 1 _____

11. Wednesday, July 16 _____

12. Saturday, October 13 _____

Actividad

Answer by giving the dates in Spanish for these important events.

1. ¿Cuándo es el Día de la Independencia? _____

2. ¿Cuándo es el Día de las Madres? _____

3. ¿Qué día es Navidad? _____

4. ¿Cuál es tu día favorito? _____

5. ¿Qué día es hoy? _____

Conversación

Diálogo

Play the role of the second person in the dialogue. Write an original response to each dialogue line following the directions given.

¿Cuál es tu mes favorito?

_____
(Tell which one.)

¿Por qué te gusta ese mes?

_____
(Tell why.)

Yo prefiero el mes de agosto. Es el mes de mi cumpleaños.

_____
(Ask how the other person celebrates his or her birthday.)

Tengo una fiesta con mis amigos y mi familia.

_____
(Give your reaction.)

Información personal

1. ¿Qué día es hoy?

_____

2. ¿Cuándo es tu cumpleaños?

_____

3. ¿En qué mes tienes vacaciones?

_____

4. ¿En qué estación hace frío en tu ciudad?

_____

5. ¿En qué estación tienes calor?

_____

Plan de la semana

List the things you plan to do for the week so that you won't forget.

EXAMPLE: sábado   **No voy a la escuela.**
           (fecha) **15 de mayo**   **Visitamos a los abuelos.**

lunes	
(fecha) _____	_____
	_____

martes

(fecha) _____ | _____
_____

miércoles

(fecha) _____ | _____
_____

jueves

(fecha) _____ | _____
_____

viernes

(fecha) _____ | _____
_____

sábado

(fecha) _____ | _____
_____

domingo

(fecha) _____ | _____
_____

Vamos a conversar

Work with a partner to do this dialogue.

TÚ:	¿Cuándo es tu cumpleaños?
OTRO ESTUDIANTE::	*(Say that it's on Thursday and add the date.)*
TÚ:	¡Feliz cumpleaños!
OTRO ESTUDIANTE::	*(Say many thanks.)*
TÚ:	¿Y qué día es la fiesta?
OTRO ESTUDIANTE::	*(Say it's tomorrow, and add the date.)*
TÚ:	¿A qué hora?
OTRO ESTUDIANTE::	*(Say it's at 4.)*

¿Sabías que...?

WHEN IS YOUR NAME DAY?— EL DÍA DE TU SANTO

A common practice among Spanish-speaking people is to name their children after a saint who is celebrated on the day they are born. In the Spanish **almanaque** (calendar), there are complete lists of all the saints that are celebrated each day.

It is customary for people to then celebrate the day of the saint after whom they are named (**el Día del Santo**). It's also called Name Day.

For example, if a girl is born on July 16, the parents would usually give their daughter the name of Carmen. All girls with the name Carmen would celebrate their Name Day on July 16. So their birthday and their name day would be on the same day.

375

Many parents, however, prefer to give their children a name different from the saint celebrated on the day they are born. For example, if a boy is born on September 2 and his parents name him Juan, the child can then celebrate the two days: his birthday on September 2 and his saint's day on June 24. And how would we sing happy birthday to Juan? In many Spanish-speaking lands, they sing "Happy Birthday" in Spanish. Here's how it goes. (Sing it to the tune of "Happy Birthday to You.")

> **Cumpleaños feliz**
> **te deseamos a ti.**
> **Que tengas, Juanito,**
> **cumpleaños feliz.**

Quick Quiz

1. Spanish-speaking people usually give their children names of _____.

2. Besides birthdays, people usually celebrate el **Día del** _____.

3. Parents would probably name their daughter _____ if she were born on July 16.

4. A saint's day is also called _____ day.

5. Some people celebrate their _____ and their name day on different days.

Let's Find Out More

1. Make a list of three or four important saints' days in the calendar.

2. Find out what are the most common Spanish names (male and female) that are also names of saints?

3. Are there equivalents as common in the United States?

Vocabulario

WORDS TO KNOW

abril *April*
agosto *August*
después de *after*
diciembre *December*
el domingo *Sunday*
enero *January*
la estación *season*
febrero *February*
el invierno *winter*
el jueves *Thursday*
julio *July*
junio *June*

el lunes *Monday*
el martes *Tuesday*
marzo *March*
mayo *May*
el mes *month*
el miércoles
  Wednesday
la Navidad
  Christmas
noviembre
  November
octubre *October*

el otoño *autumn*
la primavera *spring*
el primero *the first*
el sábado *Saturday*
la semana *week*
septiembre
  September
el verano *summer*
el viernes *Friday*

EXPRESSIONS

¿Cuál? *Which (one)?*
¡Feliz cumpleaños! *Happy Birthday!*

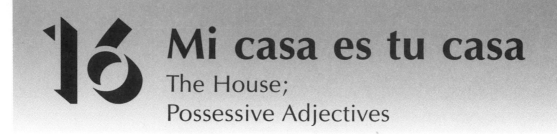

Mi casa es tu casa

The House;
Possessive Adjectives

Look at the pictures and try to guess the meanings of the words.

la casa

el patio

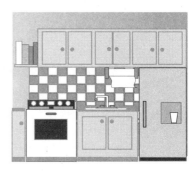

la cocina

el comedor

el cuarto de baño

la sala

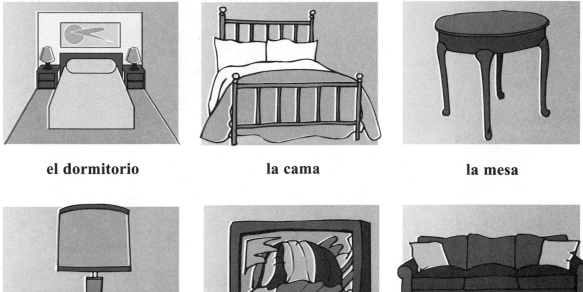

| **el dormitorio** | **la cama** | **la mesa** |

la lámpara   **el televisor**   **el sofá***

Actividad

A

You are making a picture album of your house. Label the pictures and remember to add the correct articles (**el** or **la**).

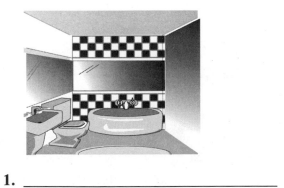

1. _____   2. _____

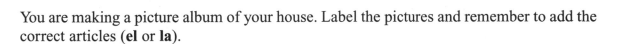

*The noun **sofá** ends in **á**, but takes the article **el** because it's a masculine noun.

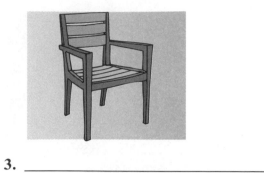

3. _____

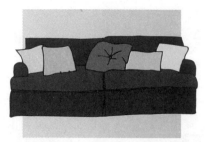

4. _____

5. _____

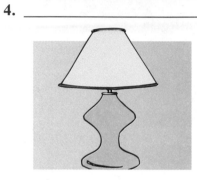

6. _____

7. _____

8. _____

9. _____

10. _____

Actividad

B

You've just moved into a big new house. The movers are asking you where to put some of your things. Tell them.

EXAMPLE: 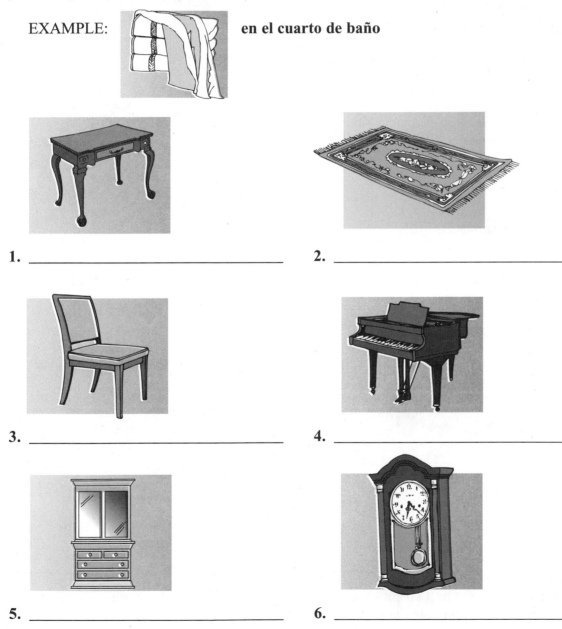 **en el cuarto de baño**

1. _____

2. _____

3. _____

4. _____

5. _____

6. _____

7. _____

8. _____

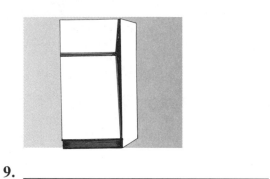

9. _____

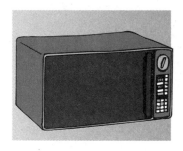

10. _____

11. _____

12. _____

Actividad

The movers came. The two following pictures show what was there and what they left behind. See if you can name what the movers took.

_____   _____

_____   _____

_____   _____

_____   _____

_____   _____

Actividad

D

Interview a classmate and let a classmate interview you. Here are some suggestions.

¿Dónde vives?   ¿Hay un reloj en tu casa? ¿Dónde está?
¿Vives en un apartamento?   ¿Dónde estudias?
¿Tienes un patio o jardín?   ¿Dónde ves televisión?
¿Tienes ventanas?

2

You already know that possession or belonging is indicated with the words **de**, **del**, and **de la**.

la hermana *de* **Cecilia**   **la ventana** *de la* **cocina**
el libro *de* **Pepe**   **la puerta** *del* **apartamento**

Actividad

F

How would you express these in Spanish?

1. the kitchen clock
2. the dining room lamp
3. Roberto's family
4. Anita's dog
5. Pepe's dad
6. Rosa's radio
7. grandma's garden

 Now let's learn how to say that something belongs to someone. You will learn possessive adjectives. Pay special attention to each group of sentences.

Es *mi* libro.   **Son *mis* libros.**
Es *mi* amiga.   **Son *mis* amigas.**

Look at the nouns in the left column. Underline them. Are these nouns singular or plural?

_____ What does **mi** mean? _____ Here's the rule:

> There are two words in Spanish for my: **mi** and **mis**. **Mi** is used when the noun it refers to is singular; **mis** is used when the noun is plural.

Actividad

F

All of these belong to you. Complete the phrases with **mi** or **mis**.

1. _____ hermanos

2. _____ casa

3. _____ silla

4. _____ amigas

5. _____ libros   **6.** _____ papeles

7. _____ dinero   **8.** _____ televisor

9. _____ películas   **10.** _____ dormitorio

Actividad

G
_____

Here are some of your relatives. Express your relationship.

1. La madre de mi padre es _____.

2. La hija de mi madre es _____.

3. La madre de mi madre es _____.

4. Los hijos de mis padres son _____.

5. Los padres de mi padre son _____.

Let's see other possessive adjectives.

¿Necesitas *tu* **libro?**   ¿Necesitas *tus* **libros?**
¿Dónde está *tu* **pluma?**   ¿Dónde están *tus* **plumas?**

What do **tu** and **tus** mean? _____

When do you use **tu**? _____

When do you use **tus**? _____

When you use **tu** or **tus**, are you being familiar or formal? _____

What distinguishes **tu** (your) from **tú** (you)? Yes, you guessed right. It's the accent mark that distinguishes one from the other.

Actividad

H

All of these refer to your best friend. Complete with **tu** or **tus**.

1. _____ escuela

2. _____ clases

3. _____ padres

4. _____ lámpara

5. _____ teléfono

6. _____ flores

7. _____ abuelos

8. _____ número

9. _____ bicicleta

10. _____ amigos

Now look at the next group of possessive adjectives.

Él tiene *su* perro.

Ella tiene *su* perro.

Nurse asks: **¿Dónde está *su* perro?**

Él corre con *sus* perros.

Ellos tienen *su* perro.

When do you use **su**? _____

When would you use **sus**? _____

Note that **su** and **sus** have four possible meanings in English:

su libro {
your book (formal)
his book
her book
their book
}

sus libros {
your books (formal)
his books
her books
their books
}

Actividad

Fill in with **su** or **sus**, as needed.

1. _____ trabajo

2. _____ abogado

3. _____ papeles

4. _____ comida

5. _____ pelo

6. _____ dormitorios

7. _____ piernas

8. _____ lámpara

9. _____ apartamento

10. _____ sillas

Actividad

Express in Spanish.

1. his brother _____.

2. her brother _____.

3. his father _____.

4. your sons (*Ud.*)_____.

5. your flowers (*tú*) _____.

6. her secretary _____.

7. their cars _____.

8. your doctor (*Ud.*) _____.

9. his lamps _____.

10. her grandfather _____.

Let's learn more about possessive adjectives.

Es *nuestro* gato.

Son *nuestros* gatos.

Es *nuestra* abuela.

Son *nuestras* abuelas.

Which subject pronoun do **nuestro**, **nuestros**, **nuestra**, and **nuestras** bring to mind?

_____

What do **nuestro**, **nuestros**, **nuestra**, **nuestras** mean? _____

When do you use:

nuestro? _____

nuestros? _____

nuestra? _____

nuestras? _____

Actividad

K

_____

All of these belong to us. Fill in the correct possessive adjective, **nuestro**, **nuestros**, **nuestra**, **nuestras**.

1. _____ patio

2. _____ trabajo

3. _____ familia

4. _____ ojos

5. _____ frutas   6. _____ manos

7. _____ cama   8. _____ comedor

9. _____ sofás   10. _____ secretarias

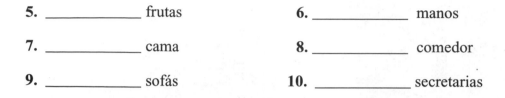

Let's summarize the possessive adjectives that we've learned.

mi, mis	*my*
tu, tus	*your* (familiar)
nuestro, nuestra, nuestros, nuestras	our
su, sus	*your* (formal) *his, her* *your* (plural) *their*

Actividad

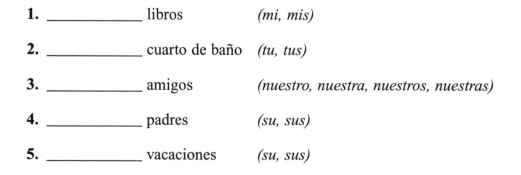

Choose the appropriate possessive adjective.

1. _____ libros   *(mi, mis)*

2. _____ cuarto de baño   *(tu, tus)*

3. _____ amigos   *(nuestro, nuestra, nuestros, nuestras)*

4. _____ padres   *(su, sus)*

5. _____ vacaciones   *(su, sus)*

6. _____ lección   *(mi, mis)*

7. _____ boca   *(su, sus)*

8. _____ bicicleta   *(su, sus)*

9. _____ dinero   *(nuestro, nuestra, nuestros, nuestras)*

10. _____ flores   *(tu, tus)*

Actividad

M

Your cousin is writing a short story in which he uses many possessive adjectives. How would he say the following?

1. your *(familiar)* newspaper   _____

2. our city   _____

3. my car   _____

4. my money   _____

5. your *(familiar)* hands   _____

6. our living room   _____

7. their newspapers   _____

8. her girlfriends   _____

9. your *(formal)* physician   _____

10. our bodies   _____

Actividad

N

Ask a classmate about various personal items. You may use your imagination or select from the list of suggestions.

bicicleta	cuadernos	libros de inglés
billetes	dinero	película
bolígrafos	helado	perro
comida		

EXAMPLE: ¿Dónde está nuestro auto?
Está en el garaje.

5

Now it's time to read another fun story. Let's see how much you can understand.

Laura and Luis look like any young married couple shopping to furnish their apartment.

Laura y Luis

VENDEDOR:	Buenos días. ¿Qué desean?
LAURA:	Un sofá, no muy grande.
LUIS:	Es para un apartamento pequeño.
VENDEDOR:	Muy bien. Aquí tienen una buena selección de sofás.
LUIS:	Me gusta el sofá azul.
LAURA:	Sí, es muy bonito. ¿Cuánto cuesta?
VENDEDOR:	El sofá es más barato si compran también una silla. Por el mismo precio tienen los dos y dos lámparas.

me gusta *I like*
azul *blue*

barato *cheap*
el mismo precio *the same price*

LUIS:	Perfecto. También queremos ver las camas y una mesa para la cocina.
VENDEDOR:	No hay problema, señores. ¿Para cuándo van a necesitar todo?
LAURA:	Tenemos tiempo. En dos o tres años.
VENDEDOR:	¿Dos o tres años? ¡No comprendo!
LUIS:	Bueno, primero la graduación... el trabajo... y después, la boda.
LAURA:	Sí. Ahora sólo queremos saber los precios.
VENDEDOR:	¡Madre mía!

primero *first*
después *afterwards*
la boda *wedding*
queremos *we want*

Actividad

Complete the sentences based on the story that you just read.

1. Laura y Luis desean ver _____.

2. El apartamento es _____.

3. Luis prefiere el sofá _____.

4. También desean ver _____.

5. Y necesitan una mesa para _____.

6. Van a necesitar el sofá en _____ años.

7. Después de la graduación, Luis necesita _____.

8. El vendedor no _____.

Conversación

sobre *on*

Diálogo

Using the picture cues, complete the dialog with the correct Spanish words.

Información personal

This is going to be your first apartment. Fill it with furniture and label the objects in Spanish.

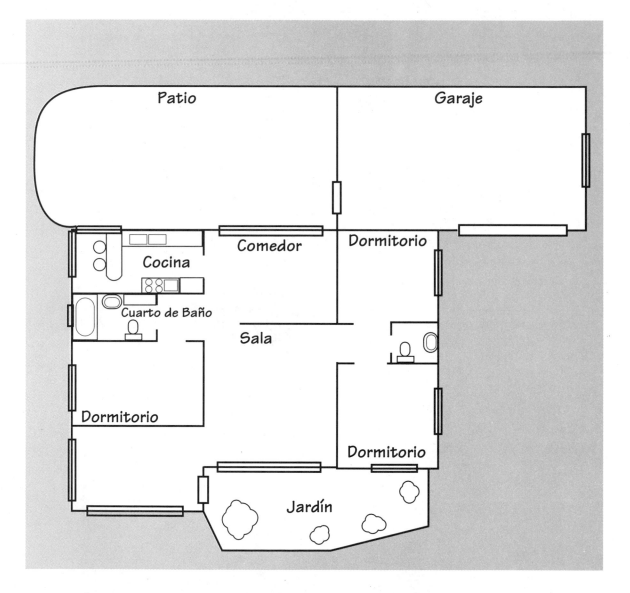

Describe your house and the furniture in each room in at least five sentences.

_____

_____

_____

_____

_____

_____

Vamos a conversar

You are discussing with your parents about how you are going to fix up your room.

TUS PADRES:	¿Qué necesitas para tu cuarto?
TÚ:	*(Tell them the room isn't big. You don't need much.)*
TUS PADRES:	¿Entonces, qué necesitas?
TÚ:	*(A couch, a chair and a desk.)*
TUS PADRES:	¿Eso es todo?
TÚ:	*(Say that you also need a lamp.)*
TUS PADRES:	No hay problema. ¿Cuándo quieres ir a la tienda?
TÚ:	*(Say tomorrow.)*

THE CITY OF THE ANGELS

It sounds like this place might be found somewhere in Heaven. Actually, if you know its name in Spanish, you will easily recognize it as the city of Los Angeles.

One hundred twenty miles north of the Mexican border, Los Angeles is, of course, in California, a part of the great Southwest of the United States. (The people living in Los Angeles called themselves *Angelenos*.)

The city itself has a total area of more than 460 square miles sprawling in all directions, making it the largest city in area in the United States and one of the largest urban areas in the entire world.

In 1781, a Spanish missionary, Father Junípero Serra, and the Spanish governor of the Mexican province of Alta California, Don Felipe de Neve, founded a town called **El Pueblo de Nuestra Señora**, **Reina de los Angeles, de Porciuncula** (The Town of Our Lady, Queen of the Angels, of Porciuncula). The first part of the name was dropped when Los Angeles became a Mexican city after gaining independence from Spain. And after the Mexican-American War, the United States took over the northern part

of what had been Mexico. Thousands of Spaniards and Mexican citizens suddenly became Americans living in the southwestern United States. (It is said that most Mexican Americans did not come to the United States; the United States came to them.)

Los Angeles now has the largest Mexican population of any city except for Mexico City. About forty percent of its population (almost three million people) is of Hispanic origin, primarily Mexican.

Originally, forty-four settlers lived around a plaza or town square by the Porciuncula River. The old plaza is now a park. One section of the city has been closed to traffic and is preserved as a replica of the Mexican street of a century ago. This street, the city's oldest, founded in 1781, is Olvera Street. It has been restored as a typical old Mexican marketplace. Shops and booths line along both sides of the street. Shoppers leisurely browse in the colorful stalls filled with ponchos, sarapes, sombreros, and other Mexican goods while munching on tortilla chips or a taco.

Today, Los Angeles, usually referred to as L.A., is home to the glitz and excitement of Hollywood and the film industry. It offers myriad attractions such as Disneyland, Six Flags, Knotts Berry Farm, and Universal Studios. Wealthy shoppers delight in Beverly Hills' swanky Rodeo Drive, and sports fans enjoy major league baseball, basketball, football, and hockey. But a casual stroll along Olvera Street through **La Ciudad de los Ángeles** transports one to a more peaceful time—time when this land was part of Mexico. For many it symbolizes the historic and enduring presence of Mexican and Hispanic cultures.

Quick Quiz

1. Los Angeles was founded in _____.

2. In English, Los Angeles means_____.

3. The United States took over northern Mexico after the _____ war.

399

4. The American city with the largest Mexican population is _____.

5. The oldest street in Los Angeles is_____.

Let's Find Out More

1. Write a short composition about Junípero Serra. Mention who he was and what he accomplished.

2. Read about "El Camino Real". Draw a map illustrating the "Camino Real."

3. What is the Mission of San Juan de Capistrano famous for?

4. Study the Mexican-American War. What were some of its results? How do they affect us today?

Vocabulario

WORDS TO KNOW

azul *blue*
el apartamento
  apartment
barato *cheap*
la cama *bed*
la cocina *kitchen*
el comedor *dining*
  room
el cuarto de baño
  bathroom

después *afterwards*
el dormitorio
  bedroom
finalmente *finally*
la lámpara *lamp*
nuestro(a)
nuestros(as) *our*
el patio *patio,*
  courtyard
el precio *price*

primero *first*
la sala *living room*
sobre *on, on top of*
el sofá couch
su(s) *your* (formal),
  his, her, their
la tienda *store*

EXPRESSIONS

me gusta *I like*
el mismo precio *the same price*

17 Más números
Numbers from 31 to 100

You are now ready to count to 100. (You may want to review first the numbers 1 to 30 in Lesson 7.)

31	treinta y uno	40	cuarenta
32	treinta y dos	50	cincuenta
33	treinta y tres	60	sesenta
34	treinta y cuatro	70	setenta
35	treinta y cinco	80	ochenta
36	treinta y seis	90	noventa
37	treinta y siete	100	cien
38	treinta y ocho		
39	treinta y nueve		

As you may remember, numbers in Spanish (up to thirty, **treinta**) are written as one word. But from thirty-one to ninety-nine, numbers are written as two words. It is fairly simple to form the rest of the numbers in Spanish. Memorize the numbers from 30 to 90 by tens, then add the word **y** (and) plus a number from 1 to 9; for example:

41 **cuarenta y uno**
51 **cincuenta y uno**
62 **sesenta y dos**
74 **setenta y cuatro**
85 **ochenta y cinco**
96 **noventa y seis**

Actividad

A

Read the following numbers aloud and place the correct numeral in the space provided.

1. setenta y uno _____ 2. cuarenta y siete _____

3. treinta y uno _____ 4. noventa y seis _____

5. ochenta y cuatro _____ 6. cincuenta y nueve _____

7. noventa y tres _____ 8. sesenta y dos _____

9. treinta y cinco _____ 10. setenta y uno _____

11. noventa y ocho _____ 12. ochenta y siete _____

Actividad

B

Match the list of Spanish numbers with the numerals. Write the matching numeral in the space provided.

1. ochenta _____   61

2. cuarenta y tres _____   57
   24
3. setenta y uno _____   35

4. veinticuatro _____   80
   16
5. cincuenta y siete _____   43

6. sesenta y uno _____   90
   71
7. treinta y cinco _____   84

8. ochenta y cuatro _____

9. dieciséis _____

10. noventa _____

Actividad

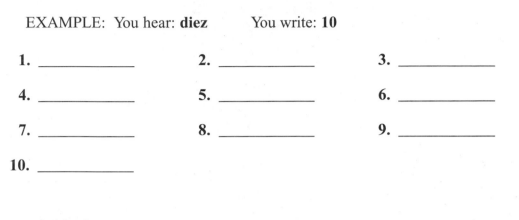

Your teacher will say a number in Spanish. Write down the numeral.

  EXAMPLE: You hear: **diez**   You write: **10**

1. _____   2. _____   3. _____

4. _____   5. _____   6. _____

7. _____   8. _____   9. _____

10. _____

Actividad

¿**Dónde está Pedro?** To find the answer, connect the dots by the numbers to create the picture that will give you the answer.

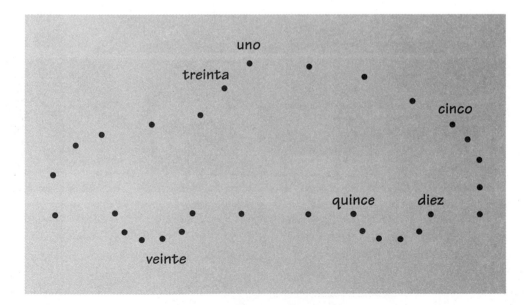

2

Here is a story about a very ambitious boy who works hard to get all the money he needs.

¡Necesito dinero!

Jaimito está loco por la música y decide comprar una grabadora. Pero tiene un problema. El precio de la grabadora es noventa y nueve dólares. Jaimito está muy triste. En el banco tiene sólo veintitrés dólares. ¿Qué puede hacer?

está loco por *is crazy for*
la grabadora *the cassette recorder*
¿Qué puede hacer? *What can he do?*

Jaimito tiene una buena idea: ¿por qué no trabajar para ganar el dinero necesario?

ganar *to earn*

Arregla un problema en el automóvil de la señora Ramírez por treinta dólares. Prepara la comida en casa y gana cuatro dólares por cada cena. Jaimito prepara cuatro cenas para la familia y cuida a los niños de la familia

arregla *to repair*
el automóvil *car*
prepara *prepares*
cada *each*
la cena *the dinner*

González cuando los padres van al cine. En dos semanas tiene dieciocho dólares más. Después arregla la puerta del garaje de la señora Pérez por treinta y cinco dólares.

cuidar *to take care of*
más *more*

Entonces Jaimito va a la tienda y compra la grabadora. Paga con su dinero y está muy contento porque ahora tiene su grabadora y todo su dinero también.

la tienda *store*
paga *pays*

Actividad

Tell how Jaimito earned his money by describing the pictures below.

1. _____

2. _____

3. _____

4. _____

Actividad

F

Work with a partner to get the arithmetic right. Write out all the numbers, basing your answers on Jaimito's story.

Jaimito tiene _____ dólares en el banco. La grabadora cuesta _____ dólares. Necesita _____ dólares. Jaimito gana _____ dólares con la señora Rámirez y gana _____ dólares en casa. Con los González gana _____ dólares. Y con la señora Pérez gana _____. Jaimito gana un total de _____ dólares. Si compra la grabadora y paga _____ dólares, todavía tiene _____ dólares en el banco, y también tiene su grabadora.

Actividad

G

Your Spanish teacher has dictated several arithmetic problems. Now see if you can solve the problems and write out the numbers in full.

1. diez + cuarenta	2. treinta + cincuenta	3. setenta + diez
_____	_____	_____
4. dieciséis − tres	5. veinte − catorce	6. cincuenta − cuarenta
_____	_____	_____
7. tres × nueve	8. diez × tres	9. dos × siete
_____	_____	_____

10.   sesenta
    ÷ tres
_____

11.   veinticuatro
    ÷ dos
_____

12.   treinta y cinco
    ÷ cinco
_____

Actividad

The Parents Association received some donations for its scholarship fund. Patricia has to rearrange the following list in numerical order, the largest donation first, the smallest last.

1. _____

2. _____

3. _____

4. _____

5. _____

6. _____

7. _____

8. _____

9. _____

10. _____

a. noventa y cinco dólares
b. trece dólares
c. sesenta dólares
d. quince dólares
e. cuarenta dólares
f. veintinueve dólares
g. treinta dólares
h. setenta y dos dólares
i. catorce dólares
j. cincuenta dólares

Actividad

Your friend Marcos is reading out the numbers in a Bingo game. He has to leave for a minute and asks you to take over. What are these numbers? Say them aloud in Spanish.

1. 12	**2.** 63	**3.** 51	**4.** 49	**5.** 14
6. 93	**7.** 78	**8.** 36	**9.** 15	**10.** 80
11. 24	**12.** 76	**13.** 19	**14.** 87	**15.** 99

Actividad

J

The way most people say phone numbers in Spanish is by dividing them in pairs. Read the following phone numbers according to the example.

EXAMPLE: 24-39-76   **veinticuatro, treinta y nueve, setenta y seis**

1. 21-53-49
2. 85-60-74
3. 91-23-86
4. 29-39-72
5. 58-46-33
6. 44-09-05

Actividad

K

How much money do you think you could make doing the following things? Write out the numbers in Spanish.

1. vender tus videos usados   _____ dólares

2. preparar la comida para la familia   _____ dólares

3. leer para una persona que no ve   _____ dólares

4. escribir una novela   _____ dólares

5. vender sodas frías o café caliente   _____ dólares

6. llevar personas viejas al médico   _____ dólares

7. trabajar en un garaje   _____ dólares

8. cuidar niños   _____ dólares

Conversación

¡Claro que no! *Of course not!*
llevar *to take*
quiero *I want*

Diálogo

Complete the following dialogue.

Información personal

Write out the numbers in Spanish.

1. the age of your oldest relative _____

2. the number of your house (in pairs) _____

3. your telephone number _____

4. the score on your last Spanish test   _____

5. the number of students in your Spanish class   _____

6. the number of books you have in your desk   _____

Vamos a conversar

You and your friend Paquita are discussing some ways of earning money.

PAQUITA:	Necesitamos dinero para la Navidad. ¿Qué vamos a hacer?
TÚ:	*(Tell her that we need to work.)*
PAQUITA:	¡Claro! Pero, ¿qué tipo de trabajo?
TÚ:	*(Say "take care of children.")*
PAQUITA:	¿Cuánto pagan por hora?
TÚ:	*(Tell her how much they pay per hour.)*
PAQUITA:	Bueno, está bien. ¿Y por qué no trabajar en una tienda?
TÚ:	*(Say "that's a good idea" and "we are going to earn a lot of money.")*

Escríbalo

Your cousin wants to spend some time with you and your family, but he needs to earn an allowance or some spending cash. Write a short note about the jobs he can do and how much money he could earn.

_____

_____

_____

_____

_____

IT'S A BARGAIN—
¡UNA GANGA!

In many public markets throughout the Spanish speaking world, you can (and are even expected to) bargain over the price of an item. But remember: in general, artisans are poor and get little money for their craft. Don't be too stingy; bargain only if you really want an item.

Usually the seller or vendor gives you a high price first. You counter by offering a lesser amount. Then both you and the seller discuss it until you agree on a price somewhere in between. For example:

BUYER: This is very pretty. How much is it?

SELLER: It's the only one I have. But I'll let you have it for 200 pesos.

BUYER: That's a lot. I only wanted to spend 100 pesos.

SELLER: Impossible. I'll be losing money. But, I'll give you a special price: 175 pesos.

BUYER: It's still a lot. I'll give you 125 pesos.

SELLER: All right, señor. I'll give it to you for 150 pesos. It's my last price.

BUYER: It's a deal!

Later, you'll probably see the exact same item somewhere else for half the price, but you'll still have fun in having bargained and gotten it for less than the price originally asked. Happy shopping and ¡**buena suerte!** (good luck!)

 ## Quick Quiz

1. The word for bargain in Spanish is _____.

2. In Spanish-speaking countries people usually bargain over the _____ of an item.

3. Usually, the seller or vendor gives a _____ price.

4. The buyer counters by offering a _____ price.

5. You think you got a bargain when you pay _____ than you were asked.

Let's Find Out More

1. Find out what crafts you can get in markets in Mexico, Guatemala, Peru, or the Southwest of the United States.

2. Compare the practice of bargaining with fixed prices.

3. Give examples of places where can you bargain for things in our cities.

Vocabulario

WORDS TO KNOW

arreglar *to repair*
cada *each*
la cena *dinner*
cien *one hundred*
cincuenta *fifty*
cuarenta *forty*
cuidar *to take care of*
entonces *then*
ganar *to earn; to win*
la grabadora *cassette recorder*

llevar *to take*
más *more*
noventa *ninety*
ochenta *eighty*
pagar *to pay*
preparar *to prepare*
sesenta *sixty*
setenta *seventy*
la tienda *store*
treinta y uno *thirty one*

EXPRESSIONS

¿Qué haces? *What are you doing?*
quiero *I want*

¡Claro que no! *Of course not!*
por hora *per hour*

Repaso IV
(Lecciones 14–17)

LECCIÓN 14

a. **Tener** is an irregular verb meaning *to have*. Remember all of its forms.

yo	tengo	nosotros / nosotras	tenemos
tú	tienes	Uds.	tienen
Ud. / él / ella	tiene	ellos / ellas	tienen

b. Remember the meanings of these special expressions with **tener**. They may be used with any subject representing a living creature.

tener calor	*to be warm*
tener frío	*to be cold*
tener hambre	*to be hungry*
tener sed	*to be thirsty*
tener miedo	*to be afraid*
tener sueño	*to be sleepy*
tener razón	*to be right*
no tener razón	*to be wrong*
tener... años	*to be . . . years old*

EXAMPLES: **Yo *tengo* calor.**   *I'm warm.*

Nosotros *tenemos* sed.   *We are thirsty.*

415

LECCIÓN 15

LOS DÍAS DE LA SEMANA

el lunes *Monday*	**el jueves** *Thursday*	**el domingo** *Sunday*
el martes *Tuesday*	**el viernes** *Friday*	
el miércoles *Wednesday*	**el sábado** *Saturday*	

LOS MESES DEL AÑO

enero *January*	**mayo** *May*	**septiembre** *September*
febrero *February*	**junio** *June*	**octubre** *October*
marzo *March*	**julio** *July*	**noviembre** *November*
abril *April*	**agosto** *August*	**diciembre** *December*

LAS ESTACIONES DEL AÑO

primavera *Spring*
verano *Summer*
otoño *Autumn, Fall*
invierno *Winter*

To express dates, begin with the day.

¿Qué día es hoy?   **Hoy es el trece de mayo.**
Es el primero de abril.
Hoy es jueves, trece de julio.

LECCIÓN 16

Possession or belonging is indicated by the words **de**, **del**, and **de la**.

El hermano *de* Gloria.
La casa *del* médico.
La silla *de la* profesora.

Possessive adjectives also express that something belongs to someone.

SINGULAR	PLURAL	ENGLISH MEANING
mi	**mis**	*my*
tu	**tus**	*your* (familiar)
su	**sus**	*his/her, your* (singular & plural), their
nuestro, -a	**nuestros, -as**	*our*

LECCIÓN 17

30	**treinta**	36	**treinta y seis**	60	**sesenta**
31	**treinta y uno**	37	**treinta y siete**	70	**setenta**
32	**treinta y dos**	38	**treinta y ocho**	80	**ochenta**
33	**treinta y tres**	39	**treinta y nueve**	90	**noventa**
34	**treinta y cuatro**	40	**cuarenta**	100	**cien**
35	**treinta y cinco**	50	**cincuenta**		

Actividad

A

Write the word that describes each picture. After filling in all the words, look at the vertical box to find a phrase every Spanish student loves to hear.

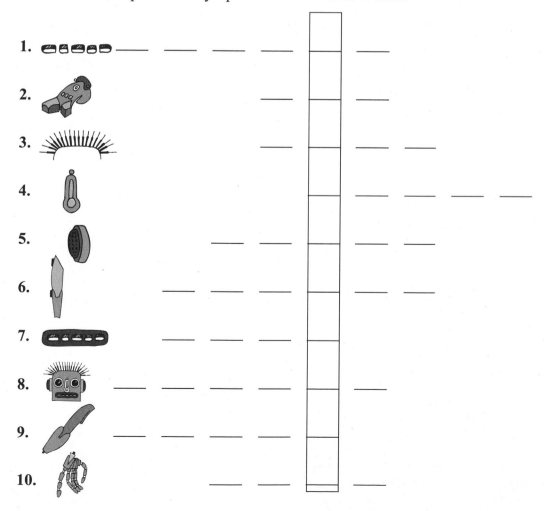

Actividad

B

Test how well a classmate has learned the numbers in Spanish. Take turns after five or six questions, choosing from the following.

1. ¿Cuál es el número de la casa donde vives?
2. ¿Cuál es tu número de teléfono? (OK to make it up if you don't want to give your number.)
3. ¿Cuántos años tienes?
4. ¿Cuántos años tienen tus padres o tus abuelos?
5. ¿Qué recibes normalmente en los exámenes de español?, ¿de inglés?, ¿de matemáticas?
6. ¿Cuánto cuesta una cena en tu restaurante favorito?
7. ¿Cuánto cuesta un boleto para el fútbol? ¿para un concierto? ¿para el cine?
8. ¿Qué temperatura hay hoy?
9. ¿Cuál es tu número de estudiante?

Actividad

C

Each of the following people has a problem. What is it?

1. _____   2. _____

3. _____

4. _____

5. _____

6. _____

Actividad

D

Complete the sentences with the appropriate form of the verb **tener.**

1. Paco _____ los pies grandes.

2. El niño _____ los ojos azules.

3. Alicia y su hermana _____ el pelo negro.

4. Yo _____ miedo.

5. Tú y yo _____ muchos amigos.

6. Tú no _____ razón ahora.

7. ¿_____ Ud. la hora, por favor?

8. ¿Cuántos dormitorios _____ tu casa?

Actividad

Crucigrama

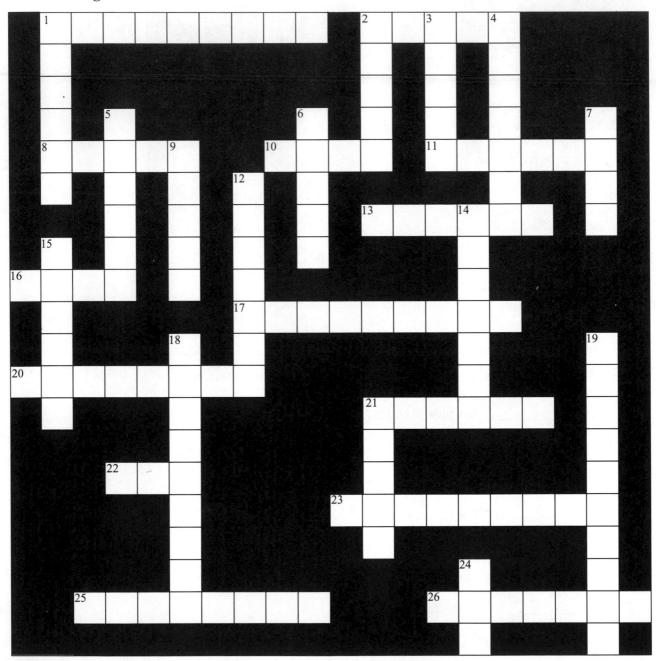

HORIZONTALES

1. Wednesday	**17.** November
2. July	**20.** Winter
8. January	**21.** August
10. May	**22.** Day
11. Saturday	**23.** December
13. Thursday	**25.** Season
16. But	**26.** February

VERTICALES

1. Tuesday	**12.** Sunday
2. June	**14.** Friday
3. Monday	**15.** Week
4. October	**18.** Spring
5. Summer	**19.** September
6. March	**21.** April
7. Hour	**24.** Month
9. Autumn	

Actividad

F

Look at the pictures and write out the dates they represent.

1. _____

2. _____

3. _____

4. _____

Actividad

Tell where are the different members of the family.

1. Los abuelos están en _____.

2. La mamá está en _____.

3. El papá está en _____.

4. Patitas (el gato) está en _____.

5. Lobo (el perro) está en _____.

6. Marisol está en _____.

7. Paco está en _____.

Actividad

Work with a partner. Ask each other, taking turns, where are the things listed below.

EXAMPLE: ¿Dónde está la cama?
Está en el dormitorio.

1. el sofá azul
2. la comida
3. la grabadora
4. el auto
5. las sillas

6. el perro
7. el reloj
8. las flores
9. el escritorio
10. el dinero

Actividad

This word puzzle contains 13 parts of the body and 9 things found in a house. Find those words and circle them. Search from left to right, right to left, upwards, downwards, or diagonally.

```
C  A  R  A  A  N  I  C  O  C
B  O  A  O  T  R  A  U  C  A
L  Á  M  P  A  R  A  G  A  M
A  N  R  E  I  P  B  O  C  A
P  I  E  L  D  R  T  Z  N  Z
M  A  N  O  S  O  A  A  B  E
O  R  E  J  A  A  R  T  O  B
D  Á  F  O  S  I  L  L  A  A
E  B  R  A  Z  O  E  A  R  C
D  O  R  M  I  T  O  R  I  O
```

Actividad

J

Tell at what time each of the following events takes place. Tell also if it is in the morning, afternoon, or evening.

EXAMPLE: el partido de fútbol: 4:00
El partido de fútbol es a las cuatro de la tarde.

1. la película en televisión: 6:35

_____

2. la clase de español: 8:55

_____

3. el programa para niños: 4:30

_____

4. el concierto en el teatro nuevo: 9:00

_____

5. la cena en casa de la abuela: 6:45

_____

Actividad

K

Indicate possession by adding the appropriate adjective.

EXAMPLE: el profesor y **sus** diccionarios

1. la madre y _____ hijos

2. tú y _____ amiga

3. los muchachos y _____ profesor

4. usted y _____ perros

5. Carlos y_____ hermano

6. la abuela y _____ flores

7. ellos y _____ clase de español

8. nosotras y _____ auto

9. nosotras y _____ bicicletas

10. nosotros y _____ grabadoras

Actividad

Can you read this story? Much of it is in picture form. Whenever you come to a picture, read it as if it were a Spanish word.

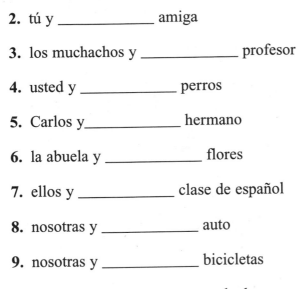

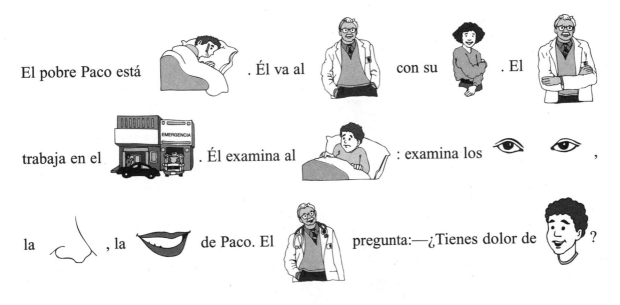

Paco dice: —Sí. El  dice: —Paco, estás enfermo. Necesitas estar

en una . No vas a ir a la .

Paco está . Él dice, —Me gusta la de español.

QUINTA
Parte

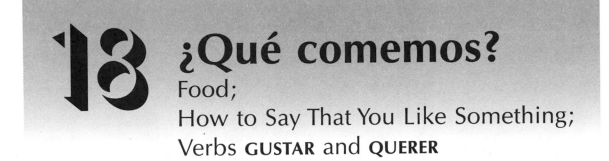

18 ¿Qué comemos?

Food;
How to Say That You Like Something;
Verbs **GUSTAR** and **QUERER**

If you ever visit a Spanish-speaking country, you will need to know the vocabulary related to food. Look at the pictures and figure out what the words mean.

el pan

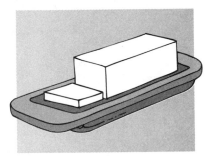

el queso

la mantequilla

el agua

el jugo de naranja

el pescado

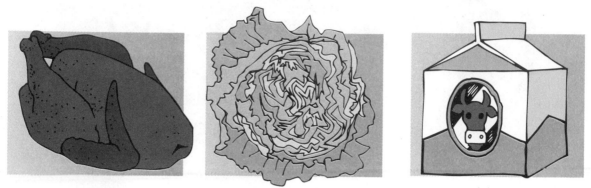

el pollo   **las legumbres**   **la leche**

la carne   **los vegetales**   **la sopa**

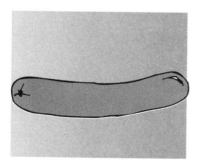
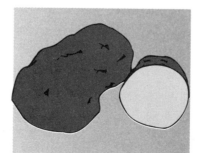

la salchicha,
el perro caliente   **las papas**   **la ensalada**

los huevos **los sandwiches** **el helado**

These are also important words to know.

el vaso **el plato**

And you can buy all these things here.

el supermercado

Actividad

A

One of your classmates is making a picture dictionary of foods. Help her match the words with the pictures.

la carne   el pan
la ensalada   el pescado
el helado   el queso
el jugo de naranja un vaso de leche

1. _____

2. _____

3. _____

4. _____

5. _____

6. _____

7. _____

8. _____

Actividad

Identify the following items in Spanish.

1. _____

2. _____

3. _____

4. _____

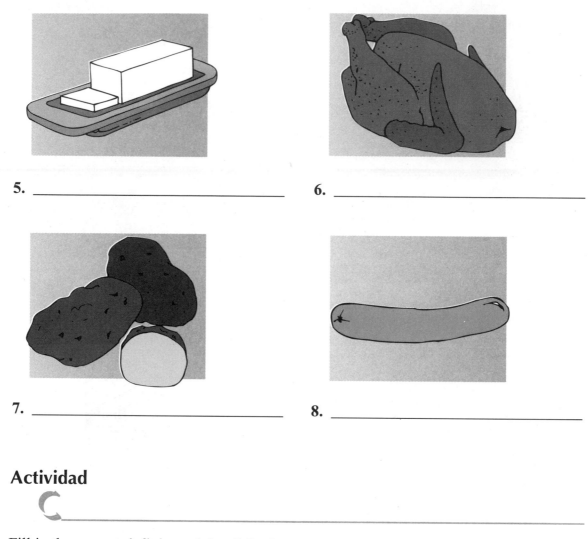

5. _____

6. _____

7. _____

8. _____

Actividad

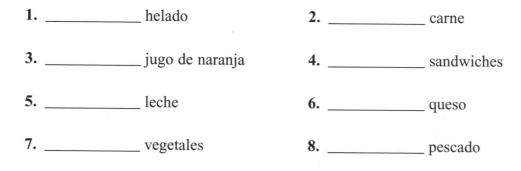

Fill in the correct definite article: **el**, **la**, **los**, or **las**.

1. _____ helado

2. _____ carne

3. _____ jugo de naranja

4. _____ sandwiches

5. _____ leche

6. _____ queso

7. _____ vegetales

8. _____ pescado

9. _____ agua

10. _____ papas

11. _____ mantequilla

12. _____ pollo

13. _____ ensalada

14. _____ frutas

15. _____ pan

16. _____ sopa

Actividad

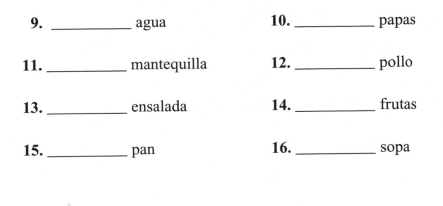

Now that you know the names of foods and beverages, classify the following items depending on whether you drink them (**beber**), or you eat them (**comer**).

agua
arroz
café
chocolate caliente

jugo de naranja
leche
papas

pescado
pollo
queso

PARA COMER

_____

_____

_____

_____

PARA BEBER

_____

_____

_____

_____

2 Look carefully at these sentences using forms of the verb **gustar** (to like).

Me *gusta* la leche.	Me *gustan* las frutas.
Me *gusta* el pollo.	Me *gustan* las legumbres.

How many things are referred to in each example in the left column? _____

How many things are referred to in the examples in the right column? _____

What do both **me gusta** and **me gustan** mean? _____

If you wrote "I like," you are correct. This is how it works.

Me gusta is followed by a noun in the SINGULAR:

Me gusta el libro.   *I like the book.*

Me gustan is followed by a noun in the PLURAL:

Me gustan los libros.   *I like the books.*

Let's put it another way: If what is liked is SINGULAR, use **gusta**. If what is liked is PLURAL, use **gustan**.

Actividad

E

What are some of the things you like? Complete the sentences with the correct forms of **gustar**.

1. Me _____ la carne.

2. Me _____ las salchichas.

3. Me _____ los jugos.

4. Me _____ el trabajo.

5. Me _____ la televisión.

6. Me _____ las papas fritas.

Now look at these sentences.

Me gusta *comer.*	*I like to eat.*
Me gusta *bailar.*	*I like to dance.*
Me gusta *estudiar.*	*I like to study.*

Note that **Me gusta** may also be followed by a verb in the INFINITIVE form.

Now that you know how to say *I like* (**me gusta** or **me gustan**), here are the other forms of *to like* in Spanish.

SINGULAR

Te gusta **la bicicleta.**   *You* (familiar) *like the bicycle.*

Le gusta **la bicicleta.**   { *You* (formal) *like the bicycle.*
                                   He / She likes the bicycle.

Nos gusta **la bicicleta.**   *We like the bicycle.*

Les gusta **la bicicleta.**   { *You* (plural) *like the bicycle.*
                                   They like the bicycle.

PLURAL

Te gustan **las bicicletas.**   *You* (familiar) *like the bicycles.*

Le gustan **las bicicletas.**   { *You* (formal) *like the bicycles.*
                                     He / She likes the bicycles.

Nos gustan **las bicicletas.**   *We like the bicycles.*

Les gustan **las bicicletas.**   { *You* (plural) *like the bicycles.*
                                      They like the bicycles.

Follow the same rule for all forms: Use **gusta** for the SINGULAR or an INFINITIVE; use **gustan** for the PLURAL.

CAUTION: with **gustar**, never use the subject pronouns **yo**, **tú**, **él**, **ella**, **Ud.**, **nosotros**, **Uds.**, **ellos**, and **ellas**. Instead, use **me**, **te**, and so on.

Actividad

F

The school newspaper is making a survey of the likes and dislikes of the student body. Answer the following questions.

1. ¿Qué te gusta ver en la televisión?

   _____

2. ¿Te gusta practicar fútbol o béisbol?

   _____

3. ¿Qué te gusta comer?

   _____

4. ¿Te gustan las películas de acción?

   _____

5. ¿Qué te gusta hacer los fines de semana?

   _____

6. ¿Qué clases te gustan más?

   _____

7. ¿Te gusta trabajar en casa?

_____

8. ¿Qué música te gusta escuchar?

_____

9. ¿Te gusta bailar?

_____

10. ¿Adónde te gusta ir en el verano?

_____

Actividad

G
_____

Pick some of the above questions (or make up your own) and interview a classmate. Then change roles and allow your partner to interview you.

3

What happens when you dislike something (or somebody else does)? Simply place the word **no** before the pronoun.

_No_ **me gusta la leche.**	_I don't like (the) milk._
_No_ **le gustan las legumbres.**	{ _He / She doesn't like vegetables._ _You_ (formal) _don't like the vegetables._

Asking a question is even simpler. Just use a rising pitch of voice when speaking and place question marks when writing.

¿Te gusta la música?   *Do you like (the) music?*
¿No te gustan los animales?   *Don't you like (the) animals?*

Actividad

Look at the pictures and write what the different people like.

EXAMPLE:

Le gusta la profesora.

1. _____

2. _____

3. _____

4. _____

5. _____

6. _____

7. _____

8. _____

9. _____

10. _____

Actividad

Change the sentences in Actividad H to the negative.

1. _____

2. _____

3. _____

4. _____

5. _____

6. _____

7. _____

8. _____

9. _____

10. _____

4 There is one more important verb to learn. Can you understand the following sentences using forms of **querer** (to want, to wish)?

Yo *quiero* una fruta.
Tú *quieres* un café.
Ud. *quiere* un vaso de agua.
Él *quiere* queso.
Ella *quiere* un vaso de leche.

Nosotros *queremos* helado de chocolate.
Nosotras *queremos* sopa.
Uds. *quieren* pastel.
Ellos *quieren* jugo.
Ellas *quieren* sodas.

As you can see, **querer** is somewhat irregular. The endings are regular, but an **i** is inserted in all forms except **nosotros**.

yo	quier*o*	*I want*
tú	quier*es*	*you want* (familiar)
Ud. ⎱ él ⎬ quier*e* ella ⎰		*you want* (formal) *he wants* *she wants*
nosotros ⎱ nosotras ⎰ quer*emos*		*we want*
Uds.	quier*en*	*you want* (plural)
ellos ⎱ ellas ⎰ quieren		*they want*

Actividad

Let's say what we want in Spanish. Complete each sentence with a form of the verb **querer** and the name of the object shown in the picture.

1. Tú _____ una _____.

2. Ella _____ _____.

3. Uds. _____ una docena de _____.

4. El niño _____ una _____.

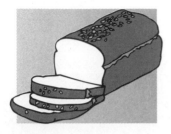

5. Nosotros _____ _____.

6. María _____ un _____ de vainilla.

7. Ellos _____ un _____ de _____.

8. Yo _____ mucho _____.

5

Now enjoy this conversation that takes place in a very special restaurant.

¿Qué desean comer Uds.?

EL CAMARERO:	Buenas tardes. ¿Qué desean Uds.?	**el camarero** *the waiter*

LA SEÑORA:	Para mí, una ensalada mixta de lechuga y tomate con huevos duros, y una soda. Me gustan la lechuga y los tomates.	**para mí** *for me*
		   mixta *mixed*
		 lechuga *lettuce*
		   el huevo duro *the hard-boiled egg*

EL CAMARERO:	Muy bien. ¿Y Ud., señor?	
EL SEÑOR:	Bueno, para mí arroz con pollo y un vaso de jugo de naranja.	**el arroz** *rice* **el vaso** *the glass*
EL CAMARERO:	Lo siento, señor, pero no tenemos arroz con pollo.	**lo siento** *I'm sorry*

EL SEÑOR: Entonces, una hamburguesa con queso.

EL CAMARERO: No hay hamburguesas, señor.

EL SEÑOR: Bueno, entonces, quiero un bistec con puré de papas.

el bistec *the steak*
el puré de papas *mashed potatoes*

EL CAMARERO: Lo siento otra vez, pero no tenemos bistec.

otra vez *again*

EL SEÑOR: ¡Caramba! ¿Qué pasa aquí? ¿Para qué pregunta? ¿Qué carne tiene?

LA SEÑORA: Ay, mi amor. Mira el menú. Es un restaurante vegetariano.

mi amor *my love, my dear*

Actividad

K

Answer the questions based on the restaurant conversation.

1. ¿Qué quiere la señora?

_____.

2. ¿Qué quiere el señor?

_____.

3. ¿Qué quiere beber el señor?

_____.

4. ¿Qué no tiene el restaurante?

_____.

5. ¿Qué tipo de restaurante es?

_____.

Actividad

L

Work with a partner. Take turns being the waiter/waitress or the customer ordering a full meal.

EXAMPLE: ¿Quiere Ud. ensalada de papas?
No, yo quiero papas fritas.

Conversación

el pastel *cake* **joven** *young man*
el bistec *steak* **por favor** *please*

Diálogo

Preguntas personales

1. Cuando tienes hambre, ¿qué te gusta comer?

_____

2. ¿Te gustan los vegetales? ¿Y las legumbres?

_____

3. ¿Te gustan las frutas?

_____

4. ¿Qué no te gusta comer?

_____

5. ¿Cómo te gustan las papas?

_____

Información personal

a. ¿Qué te gusta comer en el restaurante? Me gusta comer…

1. _____

2. _____

3. _____

4. _____

5. _____

b. ¿Qué te gusta hacer los fines de semana?

1. _____

2. _____

3. _____

4. _____

Las cinco diferencias

Every Sunday, the Soto family goes out for a buffet brunch. Today, however, there are five things missing in the restaurant. Can you find them?

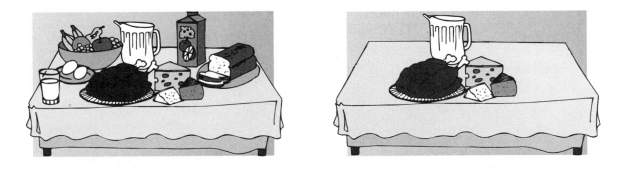

1. _____

2. _____

3. _____

4. _____

5. _____

Escríbalo

A friend from the Dominican Republic is considering spending a week in the U.S. Write her a short note giving her an idea of what you like to do for fun in your town.

_____

_____

_____

_____

_____

Vamos a conversar

You're sitting in a restaurant in Madrid. After you read the menu, the waiter comes to the table.

CAMARERO:	Buenas tardes. ¿Desea Ud. ordenar ahora?
TÚ:	*(Say yes and give your order.)*
CAMARERO:	¿Quiere una ensalada también?
TÚ:	*(Say yes and tell what kind.)*
CAMARERO:	Y para beber, ¿qué desea?
TÚ:	*(Tell him what you'd like to drink.)*
CAMARERO:	En un momento, joven.
TÚ:	*(Say good, that you are very hungry.)*

¿Sabías que...?

WHAT DO YOU EAT FOR BREAKFAST?

If you're like most Americans, a glass of orange juice, a bowl of cereal and milk, or a dish of scrambled eggs is probably what you'd have for breakfast.

In Spain, people eat very lightly in the morning. Many Spanish workers will have only a cup of coffee before going off to work. Those who do eat, don't eat much.

A typical Spanish breakfast consists only of **café con leche** (a cup of hot milk with some strong black coffee) and a **panecillo** (small roll) or **tostada** (buttered toast).

Sometimes Spaniards will have **churros**—thin doughnut-like fried dough sprinkled with powdered sugar long—and **chocolate**—thick hot chocolate. But if you really want to have a hearty meal in the morning, then you'll have to go to Mexico.

Have you ever heard of **huevos rancheros**? Here's how to make them: fry a couple of **tortillas** (thin cornmeal pancakes). Place one fried egg on each. Cover each **tortilla** and egg with hot, spicy ranchero sauce (tomato sauce, chopped onions and peppers, red chile powder). Serve with avocado slices, fried sausages and shredded cheese. Now, that's a breakfast!

 ## Quick Quiz

1. Most people in Spain eat a _____.

2. **Café con leche** consists of a cup of hot _____ with some strong _____.

3. A long thin doughnut in Spain is called a _____.

4. Mexican cornmeal pancakes are called _____.

5. Huevos rancheros are tortillas with fried _____ covered with hot sauce.

 ## Let's Find Out More

1. Compare American, Spanish and Mexican breakfasts.

2. Prepare a breakfast of **huevos rancheros** or of **chocolate con churros**. Share it with your classmates.

Vocabulario

WORDS TO KNOW

el arroz *rice*
el bistec *steak*
caliente *hot*
la camarera *waitress*
el camarero *waiter*
la carne *meat*
la ensalada *salad*
las frutas *fruit*
gustar (literally: *to be pleasing to*) *to like*
la hamburguesa *hamburger*
el huevo (duro) *(hard-boiled) egg*
el joven *young man*
el jugo (de naranja) *(orange) juice*
la leche *milk*
la lechuga *lettuce*
las legumbres *vegetables, greens*
la mantequilla *butter*

mixto(a) *mixed*
el pan *bread*
las papas *potatoes*
las papas fritas *French fries*
el pastel *cake, pastry*
el perro caliente *hot dog*
el pescado *fish*
el pollo *chicken*
el puré de papas *mashed potatoes*
querer *to wish, want*
el queso *cheese*
la salchicha *frank, sausage*
la sopa *soup*
el supermercado *supermarket*
el tomate *tomato*
el vaso *glass*
los vegetales *vegetables*

EXPRESSIONS

mi amor *my darling*
otra vez *again*
para mí *for me*

Articles of Clothing;
Colors;
ESTE and ESE

Can you guess the meaning of these words?

la tienda de ropa

el traje

el vestido

el sombrero

458

el abrigo

el suéter

la camisa

la blusa

la falda

la chaqueta

la corbata

los pantalones

los guantes

las medias/los calcetines

los zapatos

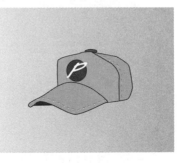

la gorra

Actividad

A

You've just gotten a summer job in a clothing store. The boss asks you to identify the mannequin's clothes to include them in the inventory. Can you do it?

LABELS

el abrigo	la falda	el sombrero	el traje
la blusa	las medias	el suéter	los calcetines
la camisa	los pantalones	el vestido	la gorra
la corbata	los guantes	los zapatos	

Actividad

Josefina and her husband Emilio are going on a short trip. Before packing, Josefina wants to make a list of all the clothing they're taking. Identify the article of clothing they will be taking on the trip. Start your sentences with **Van a llevar** (They will be taking).

1. _____

2. _____

3. _____

4. _____

5. _____

6. _____

7. _____

8. _____

9. _____

10. _____

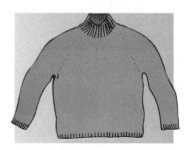

11. _____

12. _____

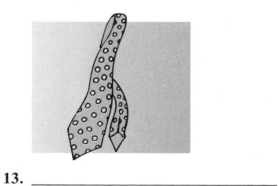

13. _____

14. _____

2

Now let's learn the colors in Spanish.

amarillo

negro

anaranjado

marrón

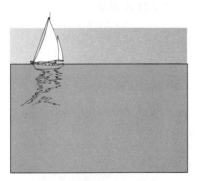

azul

rojo

blanco

rosado

gris

verde

Colors are also adjectives. As you learned in Lesson 9, adjectives agree in gender and number with the nouns they describe. Adjectives of color follow the same rules and they also come after the noun. Here are some examples.

MASCULINE SINGULAR	FEMININE SINGULAR
el automóvil rojo	**la casa roja**
el libro amarillo	**la pluma amarilla**

MASCULINE PLURAL	FEMININE PLURAL
los libros rojos	**las casas rojas**
los papeles azules	**las sillas azules**

If the name of the color ends in a consonant or **-e**, it does not change for the feminine.

MASCULINE SINGULAR	FEMININE SINGULAR
el lápiz verde	**la mesa verde**
el papel azul	**la silla azul**

Actividad

You're taking an inventory of the various articles of clothing you have in stock. Label the following items.

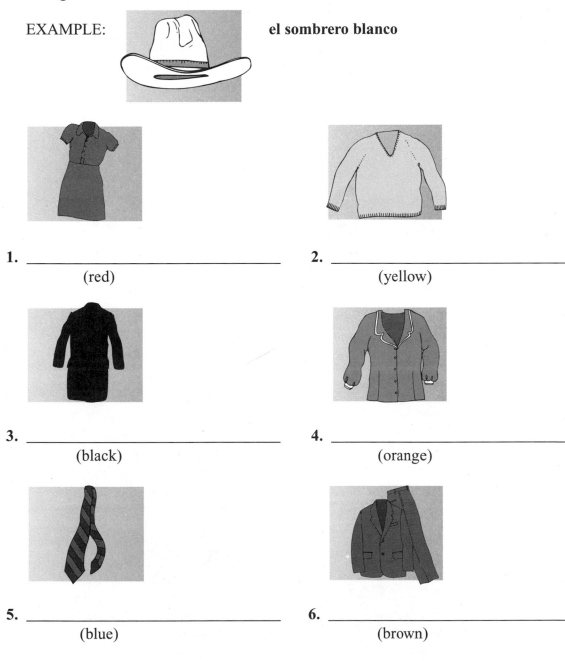

EXAMPLE: **el sombrero blanco**

1. _____
   (red)

2. _____
   (yellow)

3. _____
   (black)

4. _____
   (orange)

5. _____
   (blue)

6. _____
   (brown)

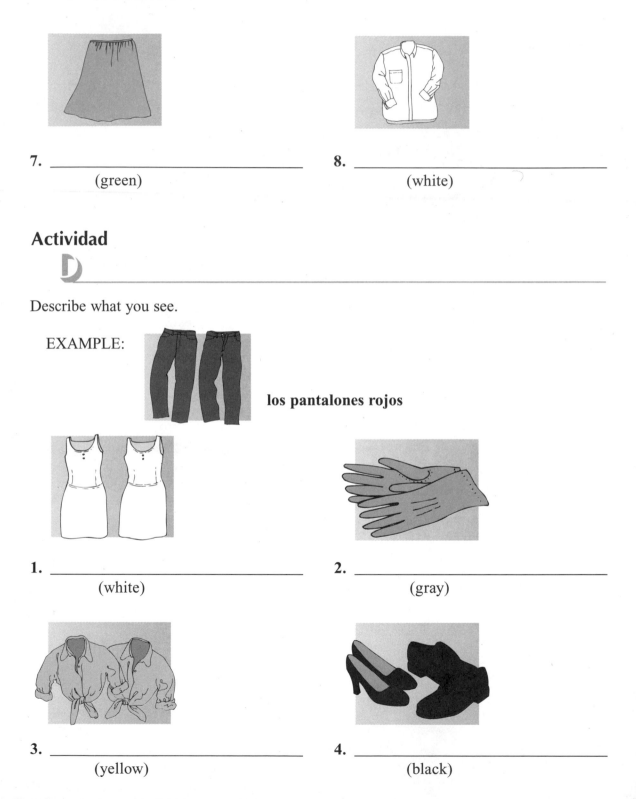

7. _____
(green)

8. _____
(white)

Actividad

D

Describe what you see.

EXAMPLE:

los pantalones rojos

1. _____
(white)

2. _____
(gray)

3. _____
(yellow)

4. _____
(black)

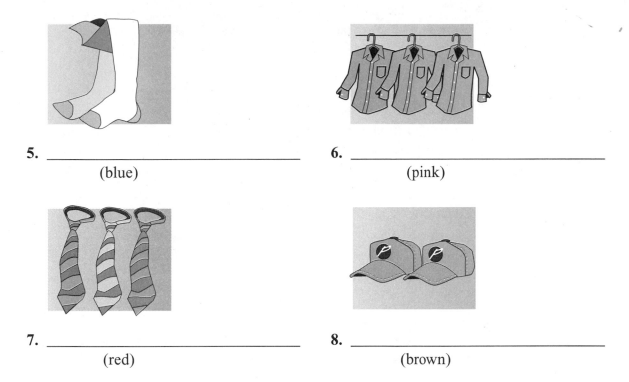

5. _____
(blue)

6. _____
(pink)

7. _____
(red)

8. _____
(brown)

3

Now read this story and see if you understand it. Then read it again with a partner, playing the roles of customer and salesperson.

Don Eugenio goes shopping for clothing. Are the clothes really for him?

Don Eugenio es un hombre grande y gordo. En una palabra, es enorme. Generalmente, tiene muchos problemas cuando compra su ropa porque necesita un tamaño extra-grande. Pero hoy entra en la tienda de ropa muy contento.

tamaño _size_

DON EUGENIO: Necesito mucha ropa nueva: dos o tres de cada artículo.

VENDEDOR: Muy bien, señor. Tenemos una buena selección. Aquí hay toda la ropa que Ud. necesita.

DON EUGENIO:	Primero, cuatro pares de pantalones: dos pares azules, un par gris y un par negro.	**tamaño** *size*
VENDEDOR:	¿De qué tamaño?	
DON EUGENIO:	Los pantalones medianos. Y también necesito una chaqueta azul y una verde y un traje negro.	
VENDEDOR:	¿De tamaño mediano también?	**mediano** *medium*
DON EUGENIO:	Sí. Y finalmente, cinco camisas blancas.	
VENDEDOR:	Perfecto. ¿Toda esta ropa es para su hijo?	
DON EUGENIO:	No, señor. Todo es para mí.	
VENDEDOR:	¿Para Ud.? Pero, ¿no es muy pequeño el tamaño mediano?	
DON EUGENIO:	Sí, yo sé. Pero estoy a dieta. Y con esta ropa nueva necesito perder peso.	**a dieta** *on a diet* **perder peso** *to lose weight*

Actividad

Read the following statements based on the story you just read. Write **Sí** if the statement is true. If it is false, correct it by changing the words in boldface.

1. Don Eugenio es un hombre **gordo y pequeño**. _____

2. Necesita un tamaño **mediano**. _____

3. Está **triste** cuando entra en la tienda. _____

4. No necesita **muchos** artículos de ropa. _____

5. Quiere dos pares de **pantalones**. _____

6. Desea comprar **cinco** camisas blancas. _____

7. La ropa es para **el hijo de don Eugenio**. _____

8. El tamaño es **pequeño** para él. _____

9. Don Eugenio está **a dieta**. _____

10. Él va a **perder** peso. _____

4 There is another kind of adjective that is used to point out things: **este** (this) and **ese** (that). Both **este** and **ese** reflect gender and number, like other adjectives. Notice that the masculine singular forms end in **-e** instead of **-o**.

Este sombrero es feo.	**Ese** sombrero es bonito.
Esta camisa es grande.	**Esa** camisa es pequeña.
Estos pantalones son negros.	**Esos** pantalones son marrones.
Estas blusas son blancas.	**Esas** blusas son rosadas.

Actividad

F

Point out the following people and things using **este**, **esta** (this) and **ese**, **esa** (that).

EXAMPLE:

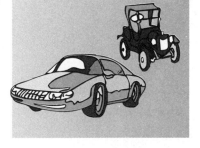

Este automóvil es nuevo.
Ese automóvil es viejo.

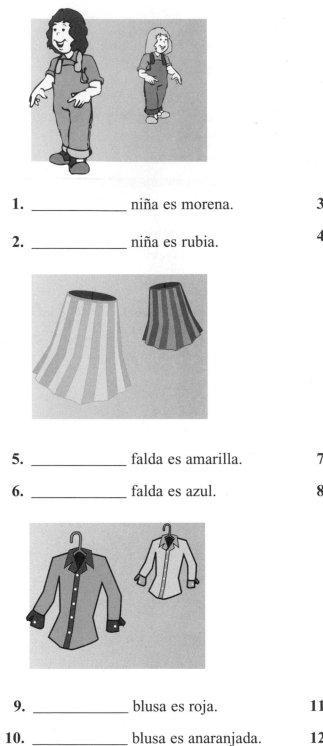

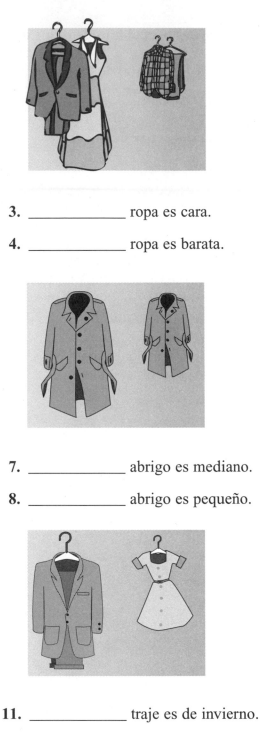

1. _____ niña es morena.

2. _____ niña es rubia.

3. _____ ropa es cara.

4. _____ ropa es barata.

5. _____ falda es amarilla.

6. _____ falda es azul.

7. _____ abrigo es mediano.

8. _____ abrigo es pequeño.

9. _____ blusa es roja.

10. _____ blusa es anaranjada.

11. _____ traje es de invierno.

12. _____ vestido es de verano.

Actividad

Point out the following articles of clothing using **estos**, **estas** (these) and **esos**, **esas** (those).

EXAMPLE:

Estos guantes son blancos.
Esos guantes son negros.

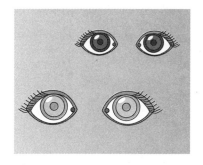

1. _____ zapatos son de Pepe.

3. _____ ojos son azules.

2. _____ zapatos son de María.

4. _____ ojos son marrones.

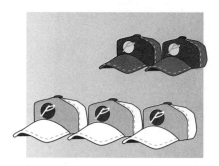

5. _____ gorras son amarillas.

7. _____ camisas son azules.

6. _____ gorras son negras.

8. _____ camisas son blancas.

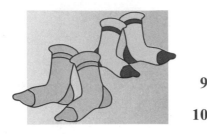

9. _____ calcetines son marrones.

10. _____ calcetines son grises.

Actividad

Jorge is going on a short trip and has just packed his suitcase. Can you name the articles he has put in it? Can you think of anything else he may need?

Actividad

Mariluz always loves to go window shopping. When she passed her favorite clothing store, the window looked different. Can you find the six things that were sold? List them below.

1. _____   2. _____

3. _____   4. _____

5. _____   6. _____

Conversación

buscar *to look for*   **el par** *the pair*
caro(a) *expensive*   **la fiesta de carnaval** *the costume party*

Diálogo

You are the first person in the dialog. Tell the salesman exactly what you are looking for.

Información personal

Mention or describe the color of five of your favorite pieces of clothing.

EXAMPLE: **Me gustan mis zapatos rojos.**

1. _____

2. _____

3. _____

4. _____

5. _____

Vamos a conversar

Next week you're going to an engagement party, so you go shopping for some really neat clothes.

VENDEDORA: Buenas tardes. ¿Qué desea?

TÚ: *(Tell her you are looking for a pair of gray pants.)*

VENDEDORA: Muy bien. ¿Quiere Ud. ver un suéter negro también?

TÚ: *(Say that you want a blue jacket, not very cheap.)*

VENDEDORA: ¿Necesita zapatos?

TÚ: *(Tell her you want a pair of brown shoes.)*

VENDEDORA: ¿Desea otra cosa?

TÚ: *(Tell her you also want a pair of gray socks.)*

LOS MARIACHIS—SERENADERS FOR HIRE

Would you like to sing a romantic song to someone of your dreams expressing your undying love? What's that you say? You can't carry a tune? No problem—if you're in Mexico. All you have to do is hire a mariachi band. Mariachis are strolling musicians who wear flashy costumes that make them look like dressed-up cowboys (which is what they are, since our cowboy image developed from the Spanish and Mexican cowboys).

Their outfits usually consist of huge sombreros, tight spangled pants, frilly shirts and cowboy boots. Each musical group can number from three to a dozen or more musicians and singers. Among the instruments, trumpets, guitars, and violins predominate. Mariachi music is the traditional music of Mexico. No Mexican home-party, wedding, public fiesta, or special occasion is complete without a mariachi band. Most groups know about a hundred songs, the majority of them sentimental and romantic.

In Mexico City, the mariachi groups gather in Garibaldi Square (**La Plaza Garibaldi**) playing and singing while waiting to be hired. Some are hired for parties. Others are hired by romantic husbands or boyfriends to serenade their wives or girlfriends, or often by tourists. Sometimes the hus-

band or boyfriend even sings along with the group. The most popular serenading hours are between 2 A.M. and 4 A.M. So, if you go to Mexico, don't be surprised if you're awakened early in the morning to the strains of sweet music outside your hotel window. It's probably some young man with a mariachi band serenading the love of his life, or celebrating his girlfriend's birthday!

Quick Quiz

1. Mariachis are strolling _____.

2. The typical mariachi costume is that of a _____.

3. Mariachi groups gather in Garibaldi Square waiting to be _____.

4. Mariachi musicians wear large _____.

5. Boyfriends hire mariachis to _____ their girlfriends.

Let's Find Out More

1. Find out more about the Mariachis, their instruments and the origin of their charro (Mexican cowboy) costumes.

2. Bring an example of Mariachi music to class.

3. Compare Mariachi music to country-western music in the U.S.

Vocabulario

WORDS TO KNOW

el abrigo *overcoat*
amarillo *yellow*
anaranjado *orange*
blanco *white*
la blusa *blouse*
buscar *to look for*
los calcetines *socks*
la camisa *shirt*
caro(a) *expensive*
la chaqueta *jacket*
el color *color*
la corbata *tie*
ese(a) *that*
esos(as) *those*
este(a) *this*
estos(as) *these*
la falda *skirt*
la gorra *cap*

gris *gray*
los guantes *gloves*
llevar *to wear, to take*
marrón *brown*
mediano *medium*
las medias *stockings*
los pantalones *pants*
el par *pair*
rojo *red*
la ropa *clothes*
rosado *pink*
el sombrero *hat*
el suéter *sweater*
tamaño *size*
el traje *suit*
verde *green*
el vestido *dress*
los zapatos *shoes*

EXPRESSIONS

estar a dieta *to be on a diet*
perder peso *to lose weight*
ir de compras *to go shopping*

20 ¿Qué tiempo hace hoy?

Weather Expressions;
Verbs **HACER** and **IR**

Let's learn to express the weather in Spanish. Study the pictures carefully.

Es primavera.
Hace buen tiempo.
Hace viento.

Es verano.
Hace calor.
Hace sol.

Es otoño.
Hace fresco.
Llueve.
Hace mal tiempo.

Es invierno.
Hace frío.
Nieva.

Actividad

A

Match the following expressions with the correct pictures.

Hace buen tiempo.   Hace viento.
Hace mal tiempo.   Hace sol.
Hace frío.   Nieva.
Hace calor.   Llueve.

1. _____

2. _____

3. _____

4. _____

5. _____

6. _____

7. _____

8. _____

Actividad

B

Look at the pictures and tell how is the weather.

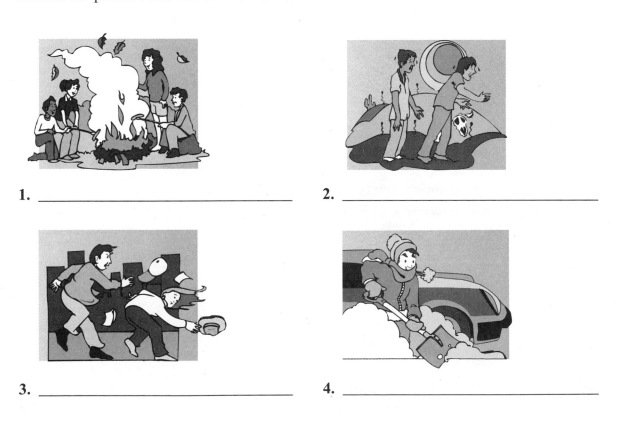

1. _____

2. _____

3. _____

4. _____

5. _____   6. _____

7. _____   8. _____

Actividad

Say in what kind of weather you do the following activities. There may be more than one answer possible, but use an answer only once.

EXAMPLE: Llevo abrigo, sombrero y guantes.
Es invierno.

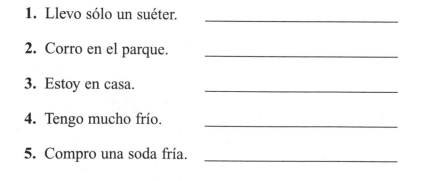

1. Llevo sólo un suéter.   _____

2. Corro en el parque.   _____

3. Estoy en casa.   _____

4. Tengo mucho frío.   _____

5. Compro una soda fría.   _____

6. Voy de vacaciones. _____

7. No salgo a caminar. _____

8. Hay muchas flores. _____

2

We all listen to the weathercasters to find out about the weather. But, are they always right? Read the story and you will know.

El meteorólogo maravilloso

¿Qué tiempo hace? ¿Hace calor o frío? ¿Hace buen tiempo o mal tiempo? Y para mañana, ¿qué tiempo tenemos? En Miami, para saber cómo va a estar el tiempo, todo el mundo escucha por radio a Mauricio Maltiempo, El Meteorólogo Maravilloso. Vamos a escuchar nosotros también.

el meteorólogo *weather person*
maravilloso *marvelous*

Buenas noches, señoras y señores. Aquí tenemos el último boletín. Después de una mañana con mucho viento, vamos a tener mucha nieve esta tarde. Va a hacer mucho frío hasta la noche. La temperatura ahora es de treinta grados. Después de la medianoche va a continuar el mal tiempo. (¡Ay, caramba! ¿Cómo es posible? Estamos en la cuidad de Miami y cuando miro por la ventana hace sol y hace buen tiempo. Este es el boletín oficial... de... ¡de Alaska!) Perdón, señoras y señores, aquí hay un error. Pero bueno, ¡nadie es perfecto! El boletín del tiempo para Miami es...

Actividad

D

Answer each sentence according to the story.

1. El Meteorólogo Maravilloso se llama _____.

2. Por la mañana hace mucho _____.

3. Por la tarde hay mucha _____.

4. Por la noche va a hacer _____.

5. Después de la medianoche no va a hacer _____.

6. Mauricio está en la _____ de Miami.

7. En Miami hace _____ tiempo ahora.

8. El último boletín del _____ es un error.

3   **Hacer** (*to make, to do*) has one irregular form in the present (**yo hago**), which you have already learned. Fill in the proper forms of **hacer** for each subject.

yo	_____	nosotros } nosotras	_____
tú	_____	Uds.	_____
Ud.	_____	ellos } ellas	_____
él } ella	_____		

Hacer is also used to express weather conditions.

Hace calor.	**Hace viento.**
Hace frío.	**Hace buen tiempo.**
Hace sol.	**Hace mal tiempo.**

Actividad

E

Can you match these descriptions with the right pictures?

Ellas hacen su trabajo.
Hace calor.
Hago una blusa.

Hacen una figura de nieve.
Hace buen tiempo.
Mamá hace un pastel.

1. _____

2. _____

3. _____

4. _____

5. _____

6. _____

Actividad

F

Answer the questions.

1. ¿Qué tiempo hace hoy?

_____

2. ¿Qué haces cuando hace calor?

_____

3. ¿Qué haces en el invierno?

_____

4. ¿A qué hora haces tus tareas?

_____

5. ¿En qué estación hacen bolas de nieve tus amigos y tú?

_____

Ask a classmate three of the above questions or (better still) make up one of your own, using the verb **hacer**. Then take turns and answer your classmate's questions.

EXAMPLE: **¿Qué _haces_ cuando _hace_ frío?**

4

Let's review the important verb **ir** (to go). Notice it's usually followed by **a**, **al**, or **a la**.

Yo *voy* a casa.

Tú *vas* al cine.

Él *va* al parque.

Ella *va* al teatro.

Ud. *va* al banco.

Uds. *van* a la tienda.

Nosotros *vamos* a la escuela.

Ellos *van* a la fiesta.

Ellas van a la pizarra.

The verb **ir** is important and also very irregular. Repeat the forms of ir and MEMORIZE them.

yo	**voy**	*I go, I am going*
tú	**vas**	*you go* (familiar), *you are going*
Ud.	**va**	*you go* (formal), *you are going*
él ⎫ **ella** ⎭	**va**	*he goes, he is going* *she goes, she is going*
nosotros ⎫ **nosotras** ⎭	**vamos**	*we go, we are going*
Uds.	**van**	*you go* (plural), *you are going*
ellos ⎫ **ellas** ⎭	**van**	*they go, they are going*

Notice that **ir** is also used to indicate intention or future action.

Mañana *vamos* a comprar una casa. *Tomorrow we are going to buy a house.*
***Voy a* estudiar el lunes.** *I'm going to study on Monday.*

Actividad

Where are these people going? Fill in the correct form of the verb **ir**.

1. Los muchachos _____.

2. Ellas _____.

3. Ud. _____.

4. Él _____.

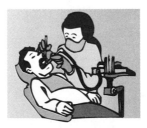

5. Yo _____.

6. María _____.

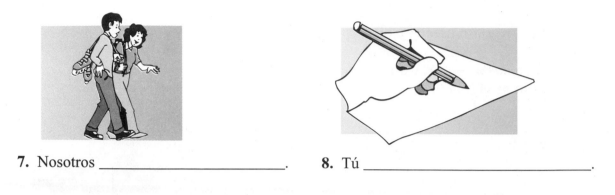

7. Nosotros _____.   **8.** Tú _____.

Actividad

H

Lupita is a busy teenager. She has written on her calendar all the things she will do in the coming week. Answer the questions about her schedule.

6 lunes	7 martes	8 miércoles	9 jueves	10 viernes	11 sábado
clases, lección de judo	clases, dentista	no hay clases, lección de judo	clases, examen de matemáticas	clases, examen de español	concierto de música mexicana
					12 domingo
					fiesta de cumpleaños de Juan

1. ¿Cuándo va Lupe al concierto?

_____

2. ¿Adónde va el domingo?

_____

3. ¿Por qué no va a la escuela el miércoles?

_____

4. ¿Qué días va a la escuela?

_____

5. ¿Va a la lección de música el lunes?

_____

6. ¿Qué día va al dentista?

_____

7. ¿Qué días va a tener un examen?

_____

8. ¿Va a tener un examen de matemáticas el viernes?

9. ¿Adónde va el miércoles?

_____

10. ¿Va al cine el sábado?

_____

Actividad

What is the question? Work with a partner taking turns at completing each exchange. You may use all the question words you know like **¿Qué?**, **¿Quién?**, **¿Quiénes?**, **¿Cuándo?**, and **¿Adónde?**

EXAMPLE: **Julia va al cine.**
¿Quién va al cine?

1. _____ Luis y Mónica van al teatro.

2. _____ Vamos a la tienda.

3. _____ Voy al parque con mis amigos.

4. _____ Ellas van a salir hoy.

5. _____ Va de vacaciones a Cancún.

6. _____ Cristina va a la cocina.

7. _____ Voy a terminar la actividad ahora.

Actividad

What are these people going to do? **¿Qué van a hacer?**

    EXAMPLE: (beber) Mario
        Mario va a beber una soda.

1. (comprar) Lucía

_____

2. (ganar) yo

_____

3. (comer) ellos

_____

4. (mirar) Juan y yo

_____

5. (abrir) la mamá

_____

6. (estar) yo

_____

Conversación

ir a esquiar *to go skiing*
patinar *to skate*
no sé... *I don't know how to . . .*

Diálogo

Play the role of the person in the first line of the following dialogue. Choose from the following list:

Tienes razón.

¿Te gusta el verano?

No hay problema. Yo soy un instructor muy bueno.

¿Qué tiempo hace hoy?

¿Entonces quieres ir a patinar?

¿Quieres ir a la playa?

Información personal

a. Your pen pal from Bolivia is going to be in your city for a year as an exchange student and he wants to know what the weather is like. Write him a note so he has an idea of the climate here.

1. en septiembre

_____

2. en noviembre

_____

3. en enero

_____

4. en abril

_____

5. en julio

_____

b. What do you like to do in different kinds of weather?

    EXAMPLE: ¿Qué te gusta hacer cuando nieva?
        Cuando nieva me gusta esquiar.

1. … cuando hace calor? _____

2. … cuando hace sol? _____

3. … cuando hace fresco? _____

4. … cuando hace mal tiempo?   _____

5. … cuando hace frío?   _____

Vamos a conversar

Your friend Wilfredo from Ponce, Puerto Rico, has never really experienced a cold winter. He wants to find out about it.

WILFREDO: ¿Qué tiempo hace en Nueva York en el invierno?

TÚ: *(Say it's very cold.)*

WILFREDO: ¿Qué hacen Uds. cuando nieva?

TÚ: *(Tell him some things you do.)*

WILFREDO: ¿Y cómo es el tiempo en el verano?

TÚ: *(Tell him it's hot in the summer.)*

WILFREDO: ¿Qué tiempo prefieres?

TÚ: *(Tell him your preference and why.)*

"*EL YUNQUE*" RAIN FOREST

When many of us think of a tropical rain forest, we think of a place like the Amazon jungle—that vast wilderness of millions of square miles extending into Brazil, Colombia, Ecuador, Peru and Bolivia. Most of us may never have the opportunity to explore a wilderness area of this magnitude. But does that mean we can never see a tropical rain forest? Not at all. On the island of Puerto Rico there is a lush inland rain forest called the Caribbean National Forest, more commonly known by its picturesque name: El Yunque (The Anvil).

Thanks to 200 inches of rainfall per year (more than NINETY-FIVE BILLION gallons!), this prehistoric forest is one of the most luxuriant in the world—28,000 acres of giant ferns, exotic trees, wild orchids, green vines, brilliantly colored parrots, and splashing mountain waterfalls.

Most of the wildlife that flourishes and is saved from destruction in this unique paradise is rare anywhere else. The Puerto Rican parrot, for example, is an extremely rare and endangered species. The fine for capturing one is $21,000! There are 240 different species of trees, all native to the area. There is even a Dwarf Forest where trees average only twelve feet in height. And, if you listen carefully, you might hear the charming call of the **coquí**. The **coquí** is a tiny one-inch tree frog. It lives only in Puerto Rico and sounds more like a bird than the usual frog species that "croak." Every evening, the coquí joins millions of his companions in their nightly chorus, as he clearly sings out his name: **co quí**, **co quí**.

El Yunque looks very much like an earthly paradise, provided you don't mind the rain!

Quick Quiz

1. The Caribbean National Forest (El Yunque) is located on the island of

   _____.

2. The forest has an area of about _____ thousand acres.

3. El Yunque receives an annual rainfall of _____ inches.

4. The fine for capturing a rare _____ is $21,000.

5. The coquí is one-inch _____ that lives only in Puerto Rico.

Let's Find Out More

1. What makes El Yunque unique and valuable?

2. Research the importance of rain forests in the survival of our planet. What resources are found in them?

3. Report on the causes of the destruction of these valuable resources. What are the consequences?

4. What are some suggestions for slowing and ultimately preventing this destruction?

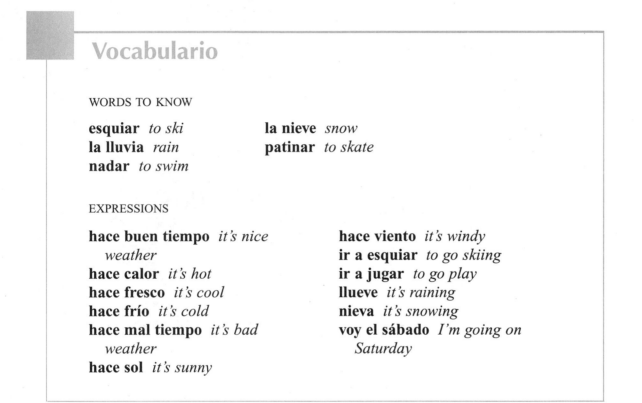

Vocabulario

WORDS TO KNOW

esquiar *to ski*
la lluvia *rain*
nadar *to swim*

la nieve *snow*
patinar *to skate*

EXPRESSIONS

hace buen tiempo *it's nice weather*
hace calor *it's hot*
hace fresco *it's cool*
hace frío *it's cold*
hace mal tiempo *it's bad weather*
hace sol *it's sunny*

hace viento *it's windy*
ir a esquiar *to go skiing*
ir a jugar *to go play*
llueve *it's raining*
nieva *it's snowing*
voy el sábado *I'm going on Saturday*

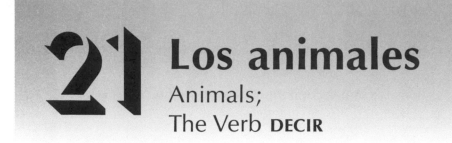

21 Los animales

Animals;
The Verb **DECIR**

Can you guess the meaning of these words?

el gato

el perro

el caballo

ls vaca

el cerdo

el león

el mono

el tigre

el elefante

la gallina

el pez

el pájaro

el ratón

el toro

Actividad

A

One of your classmates got a set of animal cards. Can you help him identify them in Spanish? Remember to use the correct definite article.

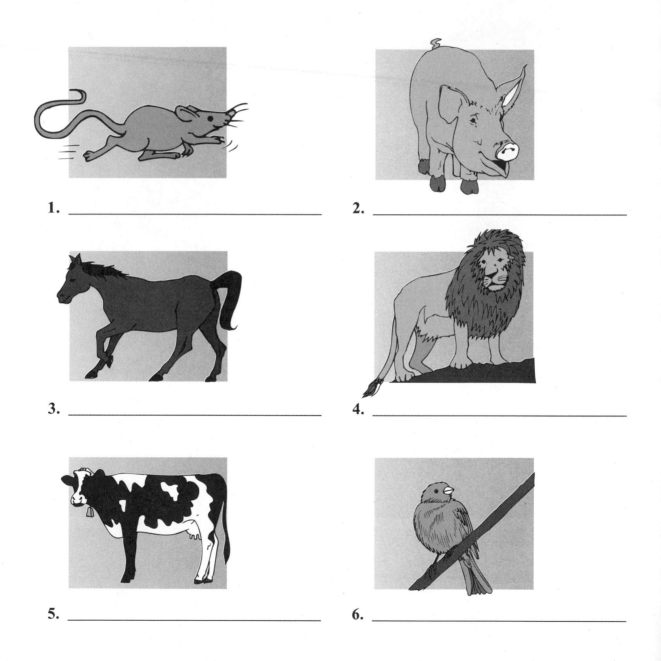

1. _____

2. _____

3. _____

4. _____

5. _____

6. _____

7. _____   8. _____

9. _____   10. _____

Actividad

B

All the animals have a home. List the animals in their proper settings.

1. _____

_____

2. _____

_____

3. _____

_____

_____

_____

_____

4. _____

_____

_____

_____

Actividad

C

Now that you know the Spanish names of some animals, let's see if you can match them with their descriptions. Write the matching letter in the space provided.

1. el perro _____ **2.** el mono _____

3. el gato _____ **4.** el tigre _____

5. la gallina _____ **6.** el cerdo _____

7. el elefante _____ **8.** el león _____

9. el pez _____ **10.** el toro _____

a. Yo soy cómico.
b. Soy de la familia de la vaca.
c. Soy el amigo del hombre.
d. Soy muy gordo.
e. Soy el de la jungla.
f. Soy de la familia del gato, pero grande y feroz.
g. Me gusta comer ratones.
h. Tengo una nariz grande.
i. Yo doy .
j. Vivo en el agua.

Actividad

D

Can you name all the animals on this farm? Start each sentence with **Yo veo** (I see).

1. _____

2. _____

3. _____

4. _____

5. _____

6. _____

Actividad

Find the hidden animals. There are 6 animals hidden in this picture. Find them and list them below.

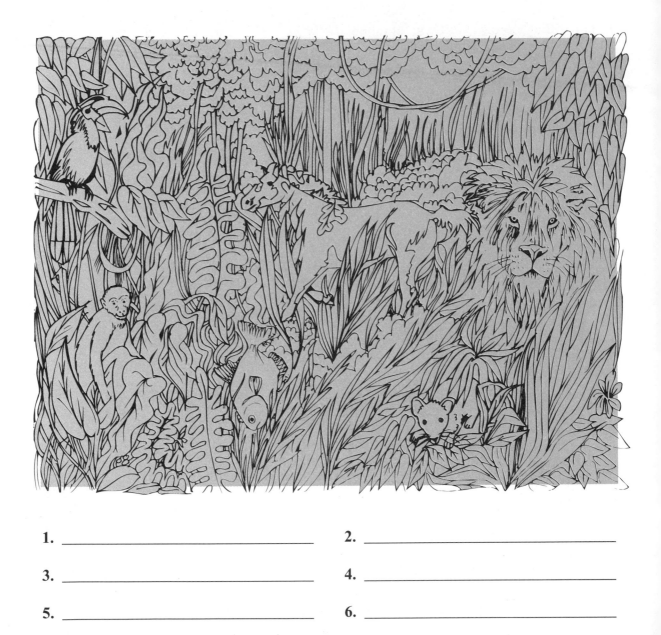

1. _____

2. _____

3. _____

4. _____

5. _____

6. _____

2 A class trip to the zoo should be a pleasant experience, right? Ms. Sanabria is having some second thoughts. Read all about it.

Al zoológico

Es el final del semestre y la señorita Sanabria decide llevar a su clase al parque zoológico, y de tarea van a escribir una composición. Ella quiere dar a los estudiantes, que viven en la ciudad, la experiencia de ver muchos animales.

el (parque) zoológico *zoo*
de tarea *for homework*
quiere dar *wants to give*

—Niños, ahora mismo van a ver muchos animales salvajes: leones, tigres, monos, pájaros y elefantes. También hay animales domésticos: caballos, vacas, cerdos, y gallinas. OK, hasta más tarde.

salvaje *wild*
doméstico *domestic*
hasta más tarde *see you later*

Media hora más tarde llega un guardia del parque. Está furioso, y dice:

llega *comes, arrives*
  el guardia *guard*

—Señorita, los muchachos de su clase quieren dar de comer a los animales salvajes. ¡Es muy peligroso!

dar de comer *to feed*
peligroso *dangerous*

—¡Ay, Dios mío! ¡Mis estudiantes!

¡Dios mío! *My God!*

—Señorita, sus estudiantes son los peligrosos. ¡Son peligrosos para mis animales!

los peligrosos *the dangerous ones*

Actividad

F

Did you understand the story? Here are some questions to test you.

1. ¿Qué parte del semestre es?
2. ¿Adónde va la clase de la señorita Sanabria?
3. ¿Cuáles son los animales salvajes que van a ver?

4. ¿Qué animales domésticos hay?

5. ¿Quién llega media hora más tarde?

6. ¿Qué quieren hacer los muchachos de la clase?

7. ¿Dice el guardia que los animales son peligrosos?

3 Here's our final verb: **decir** (to say, to tell). Let's practice it again.

yo	**digo**	*I say, I tell*
tú	**dices**	*you say, you tell* (familiar)
Ud.	**dice**	*you say, you tell* (formal)
él **ella** }	**dice**	*he says, he tells* *she says, she tells*
nosotros **nosotras** }	**decimos**	*we say, we tell*
Uds.	**dicen**	*you say, you tell* (plural)
ellos **ellas** }	**dicen**	*they say, they tell*

As you can see, the forms of **decir** do not follow the regular **-ir** verbs that you learned in Lesson 11. All except the **nosotros** form (**decimos**) are irregular and have to be memorized.

Actividad

G

People always have something to say. Complete their statements with the correct form of **decir**.

1. Yo siempre _____ «por favor» y «gracias».

2. ¿ _____ tú «buenos días» cuando llegas?

3. ¿Qué _____ ellos a sus amigos cuando van a casa?

4. Nosotros _____ que no queremos ver los animales.

5. ¿Por qué tú no _____ que no te gustan los animales?

Actividad

What is everyone saying? Match their sentences with the correct pictures.

El meteorólogo dice que va a llover mañana.
Ana María dice que tenemos mucho tiempo.
Digo que hoy es lunes.
Dicen que el examen es muy difícil.
¿Tú dices que tienes razón?
¿Qué decimos al profesor si no hacemos nuestras tareas?

1. _____

2. _____

3. _____

4. _____

5. _____

6. _____

Actividad

How do you say it in Spanish?

1. You say (**tú**) that the pig is intelligent.

_____

2. I say that he is not stupid.

_____

3. He says that he's dangerous.

_____

4. The girls say that they feed the horse.

_____

5. They say that the monkey is funny.

_____

6. Elena says that it's late.

_____

7. We say good-bye.

_____

Conversación

Ana is trying to convince her mother to go to the zoo.

Diálogo

Sonia wants her older brother Rafael to take her to the ice-skating rink.

Complete the dialogue choosing from the following phrases.

Sí, ¡vamos ahora mismo!   Vamos el jueves.
No. Y no hace mucho frío.   El tiempo está perfecto para patinar.
Si llueve no voy.   Claro, si salimos ahora.

Información personal

Describe the animal you would like to have and what it does in five sentences.

1. _____

2. _____

3. _____

4. _____

5. _____

Vamos a conversar

Your teacher is discussing a trip to the zoo with your class.

PROFESORA: ¿Desean Uds. ir al parque zoológico?
TÚ: *(Respond affirmatively.)*
PROFESORA: ¿Qué animales quieren ver?
TÚ: *(Name a few.)*
PROFESORA: ¿Cuándo quieren ir?
TÚ: *(Tell when.)*
PROFESORA: Está bien. ¡Entonces vamos!
TÚ: *(Express your feelings.)*

Escríbalo

Dogs and cats are our favorite pets. The local newspaper is having a contest to see which animal is more popular. Write a short entry (5 lines) in Spanish describing your feelings as to which animal makes the better pet.

_____

_____

_____

_____

THE LAND THAT TIME FORGOT

About 650 miles off the coast of Ecuador lie the thirteen Galápagos Islands. The islands are made of lava, since they are the tops of gigantic volcanoes, covering an area of almost 3,000 square miles. No large land mammals ever reached the islands; reptiles are the dominant species here as they were all over the earth millions of years ago.

Because of the isolation of the islands from the mainland of South America, the creatures here developed in a unique way. Also, there are creatures here that do not exist anywhere else on earth.

There are fourteen different species of giant turtles. Some of them weigh up to 550 pounds and can live 160 years. The Spanish word for the tortoises, **galápagos**, gave the islands their name. Most fantastic of all the thousands of lizards are the iguanas. Many of them grow to be four feet long!

Because the islands are so far away from the mainland and few people came here, the creatures did not develop fear of man. They approach people and swim with them instead of moving away.

The Ecuadorian government has set out to preserve these endangered species and established the Galápagos as a national park giving protection to all native mammals, reptiles, and birds. Currently, however, people are starting to migrate to the islands, which could eventually endanger the various species.

Quick Quiz

1. The Galápagos islands belong to _____.

2. Galápagos means _____ in Spanish.

3. Iguanas are giant _____.

4. Since the islands are so _____ very few people visited them.

5. All animals on the island are _____ by the government.

Let's Find Out More

1. Research the different creatures that live on the Galápagos Islands. Why is it important to preserve these islands?

2. Read about Charles Darwin and the voyage of the *Beagle*.

3. What is the much-discussed *The Origin of the Species* (1859) and how is it related to the Galápagos Islands?

Vocabulario

WORDS TO KNOW

el caballo *horse*
el cerdo *pig*
el elefante *elephant*
la gallina *hen*
el león *lion*
llegar *to arrive, to come*
el mono *monkey*
el (parque) zoológico *zoo*
el pájaro *bird*

el pez *fish*
peligroso(a) *dangerous*
el ratón *mouse*
salvaje *wild*
la tarea *homework*
el tigre *tiger*
el toro *bull*
la vaca *cow*

EXPRESSIONS

ahora mismo *right now*
dar de comer *to feed*
doy *I give*

quiere dar *wants to give*
de tarea *for homework*

Repaso V
(Lecciones 18-21)

a. Expressing "to like" in Spanish.

me gusta(n)	*I like*
te gusta(n)	*you like* (familiar)
le gusta(n)	$\begin{cases} you\ like\ (\text{formal}) \\ he\ likes \\ she\ \ likes \end{cases}$
nos gusta(n)	*we like*
les gusta(n)	$\begin{cases} you\ like\ (\text{plural}) \\ they\ like \end{cases}$

If the object that is liked is singular, use **gusta** for all persons. If more than one thing is liked, use **gustan**.

Me gusta el caballo.	*I like the horse.*
Me gustan los caballos.	*I like the horses.*
No me gustan los mosquitos.	*I don't like mosquitoes.*

b. The verb **querer** (to want) is irregular. MEMORIZE its forms.

yo	**quiero**	**nosotros** **nosotras** $\Big\}$ **queremos**
tú	**quieres**	

518

Ud.	quiere	Uds.	quieren

él
ella } quiere

ellos
ellas } quieren

LECCIÓN 19

a. Colors, like other adjectives, agree in gender and number with the nouns they describe.

el sombrero negr*o*	**los sombreros negr*os***
la blusa blanc*a*	**las blusas blanc*as***
el traje azul	**los trajes azul*es***
la camisa amarill*a*	**las camisas amarill*as***

Notice also that Spanish adjectives are placed after nouns.

la casa blanca   *the white house*

b. There are other adjectives that also agree in gender and number with the noun: **este** and **ese**.

***este* libro** *this book*	***esta* casa** *this house*
***estos* libros** *these books*	***estas* casas** *these houses*
***ese* libro** *that book*	***esa* casa** *that house*
***esos* libros** *those books*	***esas* casas** *those houses*

LECCIÓN 20

a. The verb **hacer** (to make, to do) is irregular. Remember all its forms.

yo	hago	nosotros / nosotras	hacemos
tú	haces		

Ud.	hace	Uds.	hacen

él
ella } hace

ellos
ellas } hacen

b. Hacer is used in weather expressions.

Hace (mucho) calor.	*It's (very) hot.*
Hace (mucho) frío.	*It's (very) cold.*
Hace fresco.	*It's cool.*
Hace (mucho) sol.	*It's (very) sunny.*
Hace (mucho) viento.	*It's very windy*
Hace buen tiempo.	*It's beautiful.*
Hace mal tiempo.	*It's bad (weather).*

Note also: **Llueve.** *It's raining.*

Nieva. *It's snowing.*

c. The verb **ir** (to go) is irregular. Remember all its forms.

yo	voy	nosotros nosotras	vamos
tú	vas		

Ud.	va	Uds.	van

él ella	va	ellos ellas	van

The verb **ir** is usually followed by **a la** when the place one is going to is feminine and **al** when it's masculine.

Luis *va a la* escuela.   **Yo *voy al* parque.**

This verb is also used to indicate future actions.

Mañana voy a correr.   *Tomorrow I'm going to run.*

Actividad

A

Isabel has just come back from grocery shopping and put the food in the refrigerator of her brand-new home. What did she buy?

¿Qué hay en el refrigerador?

LECCIÓN 21

The verb **decir** (to say, to tell) has irregular forms except for the **nosotros** form.

yo	digo	nosotros / nosotras	decimos
tú	dices		
Ud.	dice	Uds.	dicen
él / ella	dice	ellos / ellas	dicen

Actividad

B

In each group, circle the word that does not belong.

1. hamburguesa   bistec   salchicha   papel
2. arroz   helado   leche   queso
3. pescado   pan   pollo   policía
4. ensalada   azul   legumbres   vegetales

Actividad

Crucigrama

HORIZONTALES

1. (we) say
4. (we) want
6. trousers
9. suit
10. (they) go
11. you (fam. sing.)
12. opposite of *yes*

14. gray
15. Sunday
16. yes
17. greens
22. coat
23. fish (to eat)

VERTICALES

1. sports
2. movie theater
3. dress
4. cheese
5. supermarket
7. yellow
8. shirt

13. pink (masculine plural)
16. soup
18. cat
19. monkey
20. red
22. (he) goes

Actividad

Write the Spanish words under the pictures.

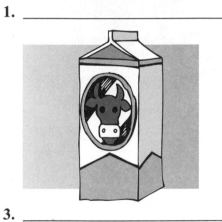

1. _____

2. _____

3. _____

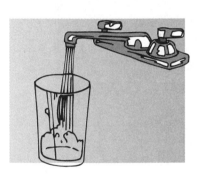

4. _____

5. _____

6. _____

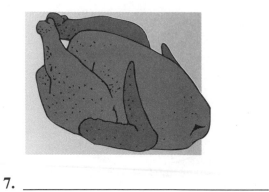

7. _____

8. _____

9. _____

10. _____

11. _____

12. _____

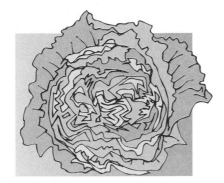

13. _____

14. _____

15. _____

16. _____

17. _____

18. _____

Actividad

E
_____

Say whether or not you like the following things.

EXAMPLES: papas fritas
No me gustan las papas fritas.

arroz con pollo
Me gusta el arroz con pollo.

1. carne con naranja
2. pollo con chocolate
3. arroz con leche
4. pan con papas
5. pescado con tomates
6. huevos con salchichas
7. leche con helado
8. perros calientes con mantequilla
9. puré de papas con carne

Actividad

F
_____

Say what colors the following things are. Make sure you use the appropriate forms of adjectives.

EXAMPLE: la rosa
La rosa es roja.

1. la ensalada
2. la pizarra
3. los papeles
4. el huevo
5. el dinero de papel
6. la noche
7. los ojos
8. los zapatos
9. el queso
10. los tomates

Actividad

Reynaldo and Rafael have taken out the Ríos twins Mirta and Mayra on a double date. Here's what they ordered. Which couple spent more? The answer may surprise you.

Reynaldo y Mayra $ _____

Rafael y Mirta $ _____

Actividad

H

¿**Qué lleva Mariluz a la fiesta?** To find out, identify the objects in the pictures and write the words in the blanks provided.

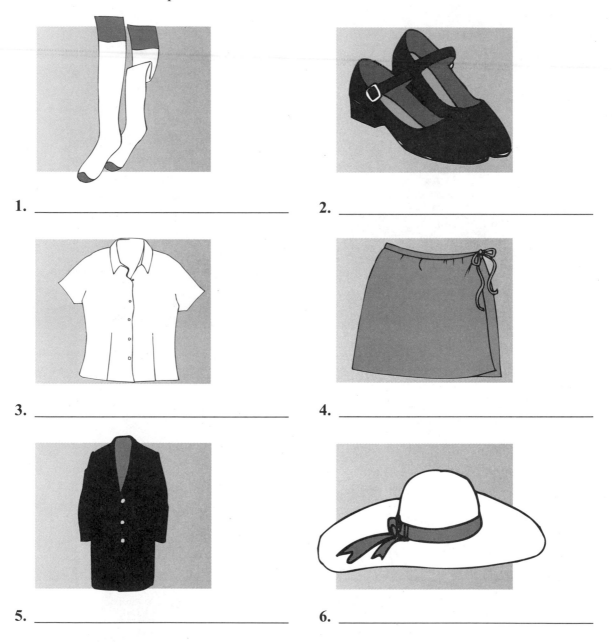

1. _____

2. _____

3. _____

4. _____

5. _____

6. _____

Actividad

Choose the appropriate verb form.

1. ¿Te (*gusta, gustan*) los caballos?
2. Yo no veo televisión cuando yo (*hago, hacen*) la tarea.
3. Elisa (*quiere, quieren*) tener tres gatos.
4. ¿Quién va a (*decir, digo*) la hora?
5. Roberto (*dice, dices*) que quiere bailar.
6. ¿Qué (*hace, hacen*) ellos? Nada.
7. Yo (*dice, digo*) que ellos son inteligentes.
8. ¿Qué (*dice, dices*) usted?
9. Ana María quiere (*va, ir*) de compras.

Actividad

Read this story. Much of it is in picture form. Whenever you come to a picture, read it as if it were a Spanish word.

Todos hablan del [sun/rain]. Siempre preguntan: ¿Qué [sun/rain] hace? En el, [winter] hace mucho [ice]. Llevamos [coat] y [gloves]. En la [spring] y en el otoño hace [wind] y llevamos una [jacket].

En el  hace mucho . No necesitamos mucha

No hay . Hace mucho . ¿Cuál es tu estación favorita?

¿Es la , el , el , o el ?

Vocabulario español-inglés

The Spanish-English Vocabulary is intended to be complete for the context of this book.

Nouns are listed in the singular. Regular feminine forms of nouns are indicated by (**-a**) or the ending that replaces the masculine ending: **abogado(-a)** or **alcalde(-esa)**. Irregular noun plurals are given in full: **voz** *f.* voice; (*pl.* **voces**). Regular feminine forms of adjectives are indicated by **-a**.

ABBREVIATIONS

adj.	adjective	*m. & f.*	masculine or feminine
f.	feminine	*pl.*	plural
inf.	infinitive	*sing.*	singular
m.	masculine		

A

a to, at; **a las (dos)** at (two) o'clock; **a casa** home
abierto open
abogado(-a) lawyer
abrigo *m.* coat
abril *m.* April
abrir to open
abuela *f.* grandmother
abuelo *m.* grandfather; **los abuelos** grandparents
aceptar to accept
actividad *f.* activity, exercise
actor *m.* actor
actriz *f.* actress
adiós good-bye
admirar admire

¿adónde? (to) where?; **¿adónde vas?** where are you going?
adorar to adore
aeropuerto *m.* airport
agosto *m.* August
agua *f.* **(el agua)** water
ahí there
ahora now; **ahora mismo** right now
alegre happy
alemán German (*f.* **alemana**)
algo something
alguna cosa something
almacén *m.* store, warehouse (*pl.* **almacenes**)
alto, -a tall
alumno(-a) pupil, student
allí there

amar to love
amarillo, -a yellow
ambulancia *f.* ambulance
americano, -a American
amigo(-a) friend
amor *m.* love; **mi amor** my love, dear
anaranjado, -a orange (color)
animal *m.* animal; **animal doméstico** pet
año *m.* year; **tener... años** to be . . . years old; **¿cuántos años tiene Ud.?, ¿cuántos años tienes?** how old are you?
apartamento *m.* apartment
aprender to learn
aquí here
árbol *m.* tree

arreglar to repair

arroz *m.* rice; **arroz con pollo** yellow rice with chicken

así so, in this way, thus; **así así** so so

atención *f.* attention

ausente absent

auto *m.* car

autobús *m.* bus

automóvil *m.* automobile

avenida *f.* avenue

avión *m.* airplane

¡ay! oh! (*expression of distress*)

ayudar to help

azul blue

B

bailar to dance

bajo, -a low; *prep.* under

banana *f.* banana

banco *m.* bank, bench

bandera *f.* flag

barato, -a cheap, inexpensive

barbero(-a) barber, hairdresser

beber to drink

béisbol *m.* baseball

bicicleta *f.* bicycle

bien well

biología *f.* biology

billete *m.* ticket

bistec *m.* steak

bizcocho *m.* biscuit, cake

blanco, -a white

blusa *f.* blouse

boca *f.* mouth

bolígrafo ballpoint pen

bolso *m.* purse, bag

bonito, -a pretty

bota *f.* boot

brazo *m.* arm

broma *f.* joke

bueno, -a good; all right, O.K.; **¡qué bueno!** how nice!

buscar to look for

buenos días good morning; **buenas tardes** good afternoon; **buenas noches** good night, **¡buena suerte!** good luck!

C

caballo *m.* horse

cabeza *f.* head

cada each

caer to fall (down)

café *m.* coffee; coffee house

calcetín *m.* sock

cálculo *m.* calculation; **hacer cálculos** to calculate; to do math

calendario *m.* calendar

caliente warm, hot

calor *m.* heat; **hacer calor** to be warm/hot (weather); **tener calor** to be (feel) warm/hot

calle *f.* street

cama *f.* bed

camarera *f.* waitress

camarero *m.* waiter

camello *m.* camel

camisa *f.* shirt

caminar to walk

campamento *m.* camp

campista *m. & f.* camper

cansado, -a tired

cantante *m. & f.* singer

cantar to sing

capaz capable; (*pl.* **capaces**)

cara *f.* face

caro, -a expensive

¡caramba! well!, goodness gracious!, gosh!

carne *f.* meat

carpintero(-a) carpenter

cartero(-a) letter carrier

casa *f.* house, home; **en casa** at home

catorce fourteen

celebrar to celebrate

cena *f.* supper, dinner

centavo *m.* cent, penny

cerdo *m.* pig

cereal *m.* cereal

cerrado closed

cesto *m.* basket

chaqueta *f.* jacket

chocolate *m.* chocolate

cien one hundred; **ciento uno** one hundred one

ciencia *f.* science; **cienca ficción** science fiction

cierto true; **¿no es cierto?** isn't it true?

cinco five

cincuenta fifty

cine *m.* movie theater; **ir al cine** to go to the movies

ciudad *f.* city

claro of course; **claro que no** of course not, no way

clase *f.* class; classroom; kind, type; **la clase de español** Spanish class; **no hay clases hoy** there's no school today; **muchas clases de** many kinds of; **¿qué clase de...?** what kind of . . . ?

cocina *f.* kitchen

colombiano, -a Colombian

color *m.* color

combatir to combat, to fight

comedor *m.* dining room

comer to eat

cómico, -a funny

comida *f.* meal; food

como as, like; **¿cómo?** how?; **¿cómo estás?, ¿cómo está Ud.?** how are you? **¿cómo se llama?, ¿cómo te llamas?** what is your name?

comprar to buy

comprender to understand

computadora *f.* computer

con with; **conmigo** with me;

contigo with you
concurso *m.* contest
confortable comfortable
consejero(-a) counselor
contar to count; **yo cuento** I count
contento, -a glad, happy
contestar to answer
conversación *f.* conversation
corbata *f.* necktie
correo *m.* post office
correr to run
costar to cost; **cuesta** it costs
creer to believe; **creo que no** I don't think so; **creo que sí** I think so
crucigrama *m.* crossword puzzle
cuaderno *m.* notebook
¿cuál(es)? which?, what?
cuando when; **¿cuándo?** when?
¿cuánto? how much?; **¿cuántos?** how many?; **¿cuánto cuesta?** how much does it cost?
cuarenta forty
cuarto *m.* room; **cuarto de baño** bathroom
cuarto fourth; quarter
cuatro four
cubano(-a) Cuban
cubrir to cover
cuerpo *m.* body
cuidar to look after
cultura *f.* culture
cumpleaños *m.* birthday

D

dar to give; **yo doy** I give; **dar de comer a** to feed
de of, from; **la hermana de María** María's sister; **de repente** all of a sudden
deber must, to have to

decidir to decide
decir to say, to tell
dedo *m.* finger
delicioso, -a delicious
dentista *m. & f.* dentist
deporte *m.* sport
derecho, -a right
descripción *f.* description
desear to wish, to want
descubrir to discover
después de after
destruir to destroy
día *m.* day; **buenos días** good morning; **día de fiesta** holiday; **todo el día** all day; **todos los días** every day
diálogo *m.* dialogue
diccionario *m.* dictionary
diciembre December
dictador(-a) dictator
diente *m.* teeth
diez ten
diferente different
difícil difficult, hard
dinero *m.* money
director(-ora) director; school principal
disco *m.* record
discoteca *f.* discotheque
disfraz *m.* costume; **la fiesta de disfraces** costume party
divertido, -a amusing
dividido por divided by
dividir to divide
doce twelve
docena *f.* dozen
doctor(-ora) doctor
dólar *m.* dollar
dolor *m.* pain, ache; **tener dolor de...** to have an . . . ache
domingo *m.* Sunday
¿dónde? where?
dormir to sleep
dormitorio *m.* bedroom
dos two

dragón *m.* dragon
durante during

E

edad *f.* age
ejercicio *m.* exercise
el the
él he *m.*
elefante *m.* elephant
elegante elegant, stylish
ella she *f.*
ellos(-as) they
enero *m.* January
enfermedad *f.* illness, sickness
enfermero(-a) nurse
enfermo, -a sick, ill
ensalada *f.* salad
entonces then; in that case
entrar (en) to enter; **entrar en la clase** to enter (come into) the class
entre among, between
entrevista *f.* interview
escribir to write
escritorio *m.* desk
escuchar to listen (to)
escolar: año escolar school year
escuela *f.* school
esa, ese, eso that; **por eso** for that
español(-ola) Spaniard; **español, -ola** Spanish
especial special
especialidad *f.* specialty
esquiar to ski
estación *f.* season; station
estar to be; **está bien** O.K., all right
este, esta this; **esta noche** tonight
estricto, -a strict
estudiante *m & f.* student
estudiar to study
estupendo, -a marvelous, terrific

estúpido, -a stupid
exacto, -a exact
exactamente exactly
examen *m.* examination, test;
  (*pl.* **exámenes**)
examinar to examine
excelente excellent
extraordinario, -a extraordinary

F

fabuloso, -a fabulous
fácil easy
falda *f.* skirt
falso, -a false
familia *f.* family
famoso, -a famous
fantástico, -a fantastic
farmacia *f.* pharmacy, drugstore
favor *m.* favor; **por favor** please
favorito, -a favorite
febrero *m.* February
fecha *f.* date
feliz happy; **¡feliz cumpleaños!**
  happy birthday!
feo, -a ugly
feroz ferocious, fierce;
  (*pl.* **feroces**)
fiesta *f.* party
fin *m.* end
finalmente finally
flaco, -a thin, skinny
flor *f.* flower
fotografía *f.* photograph
francés *m.* Frenchman, French
  language, (*f.* **francesa**
  Frenchwoman); **francés, -cesa**
  French
fresco, -a fresh; **hace fresco** it's
  cool/chilly (*weather*)
frío *m.* cold; **hacer frío** to be
  cold (*weather*); **tener frío** to
  be (feel) cold; **estar frío** to be
  cold (*liquids or objects*);
  frío, -a cold
fruta *f.* fruit

fuerte strong
fútbol *m.* soccer

G

gallina *f.* hen
ganar to win; to earn
garaje *m.* garage
garganta *f.* throat
gasolina *f.* gasoline, gas
gatito *m.* kitten
gato(a) *m.* cat
general *m.* general
generalmente in general
gigante *m.* giant
gordo, -a fat
gorra *f.* cap
gracias thanks, thank you;
muchas gracias thanks very
  much
grabadora *f.* cassette
  recorder/player
grande big, large, great
gripe *f.* flu
gris gray
gritar to cry out
guante *m.* glove
guapo, -a handsome,
  good-looking
gustar to please (someone):
  me gusta(n) I like
gusto pleasure: **el gusto es mío /
mucho gusto** it's my pleasure,
my pleasure

H

habitante *m.* inhabitant
hablar to speak, to talk
hacer to do, to make; **hace buen
tiempo** the weather is nice;
hace calor it's warm/hot; **hace
fresco** it's cool/chilly; **hace
frío** it's cold; **hace mal tiempo**
the weather is bad; **hacer sol**

it's sunny; **hace viento** it's
windy; **¿qué tiempo hace?**
how's the weather?
hambre *f.* hunger; **tener hambre**
  to be hungry
hamburguesa *f.* hamburger
hasta until; **hasta la vista,**
  see you (later); **hasta mañana**
  see you tomorrow; **hasta luego**
  so long
hay there is, there are; **no hay**
  there isn't, there aren't
helado *m.* ice cream; **helado de
vainilla** vanilla ice cream
hermana *f.* sister
hermano *m.* brother
hija *f.* daughter
hijo *m.* son; **los hijos** sons,
  son(s) and daughter(s)
historia *f.* history
hola hello, hi
hombre *m.* man
hora *f.* hour; **¿qué hora es?**
  what time is it?
hospital *m.* hospital
hotel *m.* hotel
hoy today
huevo *m.* egg; **huevos duros**
  hard-boiled eggs

I

idea *f.* idea
iglesia *f.* church
imaginación *f.* imagination
importar to matter
importante important
imposible impossible
independiente independent
información *f.* information
inglés *m.* Englishman, English
  language, (*f.* **inglesa**
  Englishwoman); **inglés, -esa**
  English
inmediatamente immediately
insecto *m.* insect

inteligente intelligent
interesante interesting
invierno *m.* winter
invitado, -a guest
invitar to invite
ir to go; **ir de compras** to go shopping
italiano *m.* Italian man, Italian language, (*f.* **italiana** Italian woman); **italiano, -a** Italian

J

jardín *f.* garden
joven *m. & f.* young person (*pl.* **jóvenes**)
jueves *m.* Thursday
jugar to play (*games*)
jugo *m.* juice; **jugo de naranja** orange juice
julio *m.* July
jungla *f.* jungle
junio *m.* June

L

la(s) the
laboratorio *m.* laboratory
lámpara *f.* lamp
lanzar to throw
lápiz *m.* pencil; (*pl.* **lápices**)
largo, -a long
lección *f.* lesson
leche *f.* milk
lechuga *f.* lettuce
leer to read
legumbre *f.* vegetable, green
lengua *f.* tongue, language
león *m.* lion
libro *m.* book
llamar to call; **¿cómo te llamas?, ¿cómo se llama Ud.?** what is your name?; **yo me llamo Susana** my name is Susana; **él se llama Pablo** his name is Pablo

llegar to arrive
llevar to wear
llover to rain; **llueve** it rains, it is raining
lluvia *f.* rain
loco (por) crazy (about)
lodo *m.* mud
lotería *f.* lottery
los the
lugar *m.* place
lunes *m.* Monday

M

madre *m.* mother; **¡madre mía!** my goodness!
magnífico, -a splendid, wonderful
mal, malo, -a bad
mamá *f.* mother, mom
mano *f.* hand
mantequilla *f.* butter
mañana tomorrow; **de la mañana** A.M., in the morning
marrón brown
martes *m.* Tuesday
marzo *m.* March
más more; **más de, más que** more than; **no puede... más** he/she can . . . no longer
matemática mathematics
mayo *m.* May
mecánico(-a) mechanic
medalla *f.* medal
media *f.* stocking, sock
mediano, -a medium
medianoche *f.* midnight
medicina *f.* medicine
médico(-a) doctor
medio half; **es la una y media** it is half past one (o'clock)
mediodía *m.* noon
menos minus
menú *m.* menu
mercado *m.* market
mes *m.* month
mesa *f.* table; desk

método *m.* method
mexicano(-a) Mexican person
mi(s) my
miedo *m.* fear; **tener miedo de** to be afraid of
miembro *m. & f.* member
miércoles *m.* Wednesday
mirar to look (at); **mirar la televisión** to watch television
mismo, -a the same
mixto, -a mixed
moderno, -a modern
mono *m.* monkey, ape
moreno, -a brunette, dark-skinned
mosquito *m.* mosquito
muchacha *f.* young woman
muchacho *m.* young man
mucho much, a great deal (of, a lot (of); **muchos** many; **tengo mucho calor** I'm very hot
mueca *f.* grimace; **hacer muecas** to make faces
mujer *f.* woman
mundo *m.* world; **todo el mundo** everybody
música *f.* music
muy very

N

nacionalidad *f.* nationality
nada nothing; **de nada** you're welcome
nadie nobody
naranja *f.* orange
nariz *f.* nose
naturalmente naturally
Navidad *f.* Christmas
necesario, -a necessary
necesitar to need
negro, -a black
nieva *f.* it is snowing, it snows
nieve *f.* snow; **la bola de nieve** snowball; **la figura de nieve** snowman

niño(-a) *f.* child
no no, not
noche *f.* night; **buenas noches** good evening; good night; **todas las noches** every night; **de la noche** P.M., in the evening, at night
nosotros(-as) we
noventa ninety
noviembre *m.* November
nuestro(-a) our
nueve nine
nuevo, -a new
número *m.* number; **número de teléfono** telephone number
nunca never

O

o or
octubre *m.* October
ochenta eighty
ocho eight
odiar to hate
oficina *f.* office
ojo *m.* eye; **ojos marrones** brown eyes
once eleven
orden *m.* order
ordinario ordinary
oreja *f.* ear
otoño *m.* autumn, fall
otro, -a, otros,-as other, another
otra vez again

P

paciente *m. & f.* patient
padre *m.* father; **padres** parents
pan *m.* bread
pantalones *m. pl.* pants, trousers
papá *m.* father, dad
papa *f.* potato; **papas fritas** French fries; **el puré de papas** mashed potatoes
papel *m.* paper

par *m.* pair
para for; to, in order to
parecer to resemble
parque *m.* park; **parque zoológico** zoo
parte *f.* part, section; **partes** piece (of) **por todas partes** everywhere
partido *m.* match
pasar to pass; to happen; **¿qué te pasa?** what's the matter with you?
pasear to go for a walk
pastel *m.* cake
pata *f.* paw
patinar ice skate; skate
pato *m.* duck
película *f.* film, movie
peligroso, -a dangerous
pelo *m.* hair
pensar (en) to think (of); **yo pienso** I think
pequeño, -a small
perder to lose
perfecto, -a perfect
periódico *m.* newspaper
pero but
perro(-a) dog
persona *f.* person
personal personal
personaje *m.* character (in a play)
pescado *m.* fish (after it's been caught)
peso *m.* weight
pez *m.* fish (alive in the water)
piano *m.* piano
pie *m.* foot
pierna *f.* leg
pizarra *f.* blackboard, chalkboard
plástico, -a plastic
plato *m.* plate, dish
playa *f.* beach
pluma *f.* pen
pobre poor
poco, -a little (in quantity); **un**

poco de agua a little water;
pocos few
poema *m.* poem
policía *m. & f.* police officer
pollo *m.* chicken
por by, through (in exchange); for; "times" (x); **dividido por** divided by; **por eso** for that reason; **¿por qué?** why? **por todas partes** throughout, everywhere; **por favor** please
porque because
postre *m.* dessert
portátil portable
practicar to practice
precio *m.* price; **a precios bajos** at low prices
preferir to prefer; **yo prefiero** I prefer
pregunta *f.* question
preguntar to ask
premio *m.* prize
preocupar to worry; **no te preocupes** don't worry
preparado, -a prepared
preparar to prepare
presidente(-a) president
primavera *f.* spring(time)
primer, primero, -a first
princesa *f.* princess
principal principal, main
probablemente probably
problema *m.* problem
profesor(-a) teacher, professor
programa *m.* program
proponer to propose
pueblo *m.* town
puerta *f.* door
pues well, then
puré de papas *m.* mashed potatoes

Q

que that, than; **más que** more than; **¿qué?** what?, which?;

¡qué trabajo! what a job!
querer to want
querido, -a dear
queso *m.* cheese
¿quién(es)? who?
quince fifteen
quinto, -a fifth

R

radio *m. & f.* radio
rápido fast, rapid; **rápidamente** fast, rapidly
ratón *m.* mouse
razón *f.* reason, right; **tener razón** to be right; **no tener razón** to be wrong
recibir to receive
regalo *m.* gift, present
regla *f.* ruler; rule
regular regular; so so
reloj *m.* clock, watch
repente sudden; **de repente** all of a sudden
reportero(-a) reporter
resfriado *m.* cold (illness); **tener un resfriado** to have a cold
responder to respond, to answer, to reply
responsabilidad *f.* responsibility
respuesta *f.* answer, response
restaurante *m.* restaurant
rico, -a rich
rojo, -a red
romántico, -a romantic
ropa *f.* clothes, clothing
rosa *f.* rose
rosado, -a rose (color), pink
rubio, -a blond
ruido *m.* noise
ruidoso, -a noisy

S

sábado *m.* Saturday
saber to know; to know how;

yo sé I know
sacar to pull out, to take out
sala *f.* living room
salchicha *f.* sausage, frankfurter
salir to leave, to go out; **yo salgo** I leave; **salir de la casa** to leave the house
sandwich *m.* sandwich
sección *f.* section
secretario(-a) *f.* secretary
sed *f.* thirst; **tener sed** to be thirsty
segundo, -a second
seis six
semana *f.* week
sentado, -a seated
sentir to feel; **lo siento** I'm sorry
señor *m.* Mr.; **señores** *m. pl.* Mr. and Mrs.; sir, madam
señora *f.* lady; Mrs.
señorita *f.* young lady; Miss
septiembre *m.* September
ser to be
serio, -a serious
sesenta sixty
setenta seventy
si if
sí yes
siempre always
siete seven
silla *f.* chair
simpático, -a nice
sin without
sobre on, on top of; about, regarding
soda *f.* soda
sofá *m.* sofa
socio(-a) associate
sol *m.* sun; **hace sol / hay sol** it's sunny
sólo, solamente only
sombrero *m.* hat
sopa *f.* soup
sorpresa *f.* surprise; **la fiesta de sorpresa** surprise party
su(s) your, his, her, their

sueño *m.* sleep; **tener sueño** to be sleepy
suerte *f.* luck; **¡buena suerte!** good luck!
suéter *m.* sweater
sufrir to suffer
sumar to add (up)
supermercado *m.* supermarket
supuesto: por supuesto of course

T

tablón (bulletin) board
también also, too
tamaño size
tan so
tarde late; **más tarde** later; **se hace tarde** it's getting late; **tarde** *f.* afternoon; **buenas tardes** good afternoon; **de la tarde**, P.M., in the afternoon
tarea *f.* task, homework, assignment; *(pl.)* homework *(all homework assignments for a given day)*
taxi *m.* taxi, cab
teatro *m.* theater
telefonista *m. & f.* telephone operator
televisión *f.*, **televisor** *m.* television; **mirar la televisión** to watch television
tener to have; **tener… años** to be . . . years old; **tener calor** to be (feel) warm/hot; **tener frío** to be (feel) cold; **tener hambre** to be hungry; **tener razón** to be right; **no tener razón** to be wrong; **tener sed** to be thirsty; **tener sueño** to be sleepy; **¿qué tienes?** what do you have?, what's a matter?
terminar to end, to finish
tenis *m.* tennis
tercero, -a third

tía *f.* aunt

tiempo *m.* time; weather; **¿qué tiempo hace?** how's the weather?

tienda *f.* store

tigre *m.* tiger

tímido, -a shy, timid

tiza chalk

todavía still

todo everything; **todos, -as** all (of them);
  todo el mundo everybody;
  todos los días every day;
  todos los años every year;
  por todas partes everywhere

tomar to take

tomate *m.* tomato

trabajar to work; **trabajar mucho** to work hard

trabajo *m.* work

traje *m.* suit; dress

transformar to transform

transporte *m.* transportation

trece thirteen

treinta thirty

tren *m.* train

tres three

triste sad

tropical tropical

tú you (familiar)

tu(s) your (familiar)

U

último, -a last

un(a) a, one; **uno** (number) one; **unos, -as** some, a few

usado, -a used

usar to use

usted (Ud.) you (*formal sing.*); **ustedes (Uds.)** you (pl. formal & familiar)

V

vaca *f.* cow

vacaciones *f.* pl. vacation

vainilla *f.* vanilla

¡vamos! (¡vámonos!) let's go

varios several

vaso *m.* (drinking) glass

vegetal *m.* vegetable, green

vegetariano, -a vegetarian

veinte twenty

vendaje *m.* bandage

vendedor(-ora) salesperson, seller

vender to sell

ventana *f.* window

ver to see; **yo veo** I see

verano *m.* summer(time)

verdad *f.* truth; **es verdad** it's true; **¿verdad?** isn't it so?

verde green

vestido *m.* dress

vez *f.* (*pl.* **veces**) time; **otra vez** again; **la segunda vez** the second time

viejo, -a old

viento *m.* wind; **hace viento** it's windy

viernes *m.* Friday

visitar to visit

vivir to live

vocabulario *m.* vocabulary

Y

y and; plus

yo I

Z

zapatería *f.* shoe store; shoemaker's shop

zapato *m.* shoe

zoológico *m.* zoo

Vocabulario inglés-español

A

a(n) un, una
about de, sobre
absent ausente
accept: to accept aceptar
activity actividad *f.*
actor actor *m.*
actress actriz *f.*
add (up): to add up sumar
adore: to adore adorar
afraid: to be afraid tener miedo
after después de
afternoon tarde *f.*; **good afternoon** buenas tardes
again otra vez
age edad *f.*
airplane avión *m.*
airport aeropuerto *m.*
all todo; **(all of them)** todos, todas
also también
always siempre
ambulance ambulancia *f.*
American americano(-a)
among entre
amusing divertido, -a
and y
animal animal *m.*
answer respuesta *f.*; **to answer** contestar, responder
apartment apartamento *m.*
April abril *m.*
arm brazo *m.*
arrive: to arrive llegar
ask: to ask preguntar

associate socio(-a)
at a; **at home** en casa; **at one o'clock** a la una; **at two o'clock** a las dos; **at what time?** ¿a qué hora?
attention atención *f.*
August agosto *m.*
aunt tía *f.*
automobile automóvil *m.*
autumn otoño *m.*
avenue avenida *f.*

B

baby nene *m.*, nena *f.*, bebé *m. & f.*
bad mal, malo, -a
bag bolsa *m.*
banana banana *f.*
bandage vendaje *m.*
bank banco *m.*
barber barbero(-a)
bathroom (cuarto de) baño *m.*
be: to be ser, estar; **to be cold** estar frío; **to be (feel) cold** tener frío; (*weather*) hacer frío; **to be warm** estar caliente; **(to feel warm)** tener calor; (*weather*) hacer calor; **to be hungry** tener hambre; **to be thirsty** tener sed; **to be . . . years old** tener... años; **I am ten years old** tengo diez años
beach playa *f.*
because porque

bed cama *f.*
bedroom dormitorio *m.*
bench banco *m.*
between entre
bicycle bicicleta *f.*
big grande
biology biología *f.*
birthday cumpleaños *m.*
biscuit bizcocho *m.*
black negro, -a
blackboard pizarra *f.*
blond rubio, -a
blouse blusa *f.*
blue azul
body cuerpo *m.*
book libro *m.*
boot bota *f.*
boy muchacho *m.*
bread pan *m.*
brother hermano *m.*; **brother(s) and sister(s)** los hermanos
brown marrón; **brown eyes** los ojos marrones
bus autobús *m.*
but pero
buy: to buy comprar

C

cab taxi *m.*
cake pastel *m.* bizcocho
calculate: to calculate hacer cálculos, calcular
calculation cálculo *m.*
calendar calendario *m.*

call: to call llamar
camel camello *m.*
camp campamento *m.*
camper campista *m. & f.*
cap gorra *f.*
capable capaz
car auto *m.*, coche *m.*
carpenter carpintero(-a)
cassette player grabadora *f.*
cat gato *m.*
celebrate: to celebrate celebrar
cereal cereal *m.*
cent centavo *m.*
chair silla *f.*
character (in play) personaje *m.*
cheese queso *m.*
chicken pollo *m.*
child niño(-a) **children** los niños
chilly: it is chilly hace frío
chocolate chocolate *m.*,
  chocolate ice cream helado de
  chocolate
Christmas Navidad *f.*
church iglesia *f.*
city ciudad *f.*
class clase *f.*; **in class** en la clase
clock reloj *m.*
clothes, clothing ropa *f.*
coat abrigo *m.*
coffee café *m.*
cold frío; **to be cold** estar frío;
  to feel cold tener frío; (*weather*)
  hacer frío; **to have a cold**
  tener un resfriado
Colombian colombiano(-a)
color color *m.*
comfortable confortable
computer computadora *f.*
contest concurso *m.*
conversation conversación *f.*
cool fresco; **it's cool** (*weather*)
  hace fresco
cost precio m., **it costs** cuesta
costume disfraz *m.*, **costume**
  party la fiesta de disfraces

counselor consejero *m.*
count: to count contar; **I count**
  yo cuento
course: of course por supuesto
cover: to cover cubrir
cow vaca *f.*
crazy loco, -a
crossword puzzle crucigrama *m.*
cry: to cry out gritar
Cuban cubano(-a)
culture cultura *f.*

D

dance: to dance bailar; **dance**
  baile *m.*
dark: dark-skinned moreno, -a
date fecha *f.*
daughter hija *f.*
day día *m.*
dear querido, -a
December diciembre *m.*
decide: to decide decidir
delicious delicioso, -a
dentist dentista *m. & f.*
description descripción *f.*
desk mesa *f.*
dessert postre *m.*
destroy: to destroy destruir
dialogue diálogo *m.*
dictator dictador(-a)
dictionary diccionario *m.*
different diferente
difficult difícil
dining room comedor *m.*
disco discoteca *f.*
dish plato *m.*
divide: to divide dividir; **divided**
  by dividido por
do: to do hacer; **to do the**
  homework hacer la(s) tarea(s)
doctor doctor(-ora); médico(-a)
dog perro(-a)
dollar dólar *m.*
door puerta *f.*

dozen docena *f.*
dragon dragón *m.*
dress vestido *m.*;
drink bebida *f.*; **to drink** beber
drugstore farmacia *f.*
duck pato *m.*
during durante

E

ear oreja *f.*
earache dolor de oído *m.*
earn: to earn ganar
easy fácil
eat: to eat comer
egg huevo *m.*; **hard-boiled eggs**
  huevos duros
eight ocho
eighteen dieciocho
eighty ochenta
elegant elegante
elephant elefante *m.*
eleven once
end fin *m.*; **to end** terminar
English inglés *m.*,(*f.* inglesa)
enter: to enter entrar
everybody todo el mundo
everything todo
exactly exactamente, ¡exacto!
examination examen *m.*
examine: to examine examinar
excellent excelente
exercise ejercicio *m.*
extraordinary extraordinario, -a
eye ojo *m.*

F

fabulous fabuloso, -a
face cara f.; **to make faces** hacer
  muecas
fall otoño *m.*, **to fall (down)** caer
false falso, -a
family familia *f.*
famous famoso, -a

fantastic fantástico, -a
fast rápidamente, rápido, -a
father padre *m.*
favorite favorito, -a
February febrero *m.*
ferocious feroz
fifteen quince
fifth quinto
fifty cincuenta
fight: to fight combatir
finally finalmente
finger dedo *m.*
first primer, primero, -a
fish pescado *m.*; pez *m. (live one)*
five cinco
flag bandera *f.*
flower flor *f.*
food comida *f.*
foot pie *m.*
forty cuarenta
four cuatro
fourteen catorce
fourth cuarto
French francés *m., (f.* francesa)
French fries papas fritas
Friday viernes *m.*
friend amigo(-a)
from de
fruit fruta *f.*
funny cómico(-a)

G

garage garaje *m.*
garden jardín *m.*
gasoline gasolina *f.*
general general *m.*; **in general** generalmente
German alemán *m.; (f.* alemana)
giant gigante *m.*
gift regalo *m.*
girl muchacha *f.*
give dar; **I give** yo doy
glass vaso *m.*; **glass of milk** vaso de leche

go: to go ir; **to go in** entrar a; **to be going to (do something)** ir a + *inf.:* **I'm going to read** voy a leer
good bueno; **good morning** buenos días; **good afternoon** buenas tardes; **good evening, good night** buenas noches
good-bye adiós
grandfather abuelo *m.*
grandmother abuela *f.*
grandparents los abuelos
gray gris
green verde

H

hair pelo *m.*
half medio, -a; **half past one** la una y media
hamburger hamburguesa *f.*
hand mano *f.*
handsome guapo, -a
happy contento, -a, alegre; **to be happy** estar contento, -a, estar alegre
hard difícil; **to work hard** trabajar mucho
hat sombrero *m.*
hate: to hate odiar
have tener
he él *m.*
head cabeza *f.*
hello hola
help: to help ayudar
hen gallina *f.*
her su(s)
here aquí
his su(s)
history historia *f.*
holiday día de fiesta *m., (pl.* los días de fiesta)
home: to be (at) home estar en casa; **to go home** ir a casa
homework tarea *f.*

horrible horrible
horse caballo *m.*
hospital hospital *m.*
hot caliente; **to be hot** estar caliente; **to feel hot** tener mucho calor; (**weather**) hacer mucho calor
hotel hotel *m.*
house casa *f.*
how? ¿cómo?; **how are you?** ¿cómo está Ud.?, ¿cómo estás?; **how much?** ¿cuánto?; **how many?** ¿cuántos?
hundred cien; **a hundred dollars** cien dólares; **one hundred fifty dollars** ciento cincuenta dólares
hungry: to be hungry tener hambre

I

I yo
idea idea *f.*
ice cream helado *m.*
if si
illness enfermedad *f.*
important importante
impossible imposible
in en
independent independiente
information información *f.*
inhabitant habitante *m.*
insect insecto *m.*
intelligent inteligente
interesting interesante
invite: to invite invitar
it (*subject*) él, ella
Italian italiano(-a)

J

jacket chaqueta *f.*
January enero *m.*
juice jugo *m.*; **orange juice** jugo

de naranja
July julio *m.*
jungle jungla *f.*
June junio *m.*

K

kitchen cocina *f.*
kitten gatito(-a)
know: to know saber; **I know** yo sé; **to know how to (do something)** saber + *inf.*; **she knows how to sing** ella sabe cantar

L

laboratory laboratorio *m.*
lady señora *f.*
lamp lámpara *f.*
language lengua *f.*
large grande
last último, -a
late tarde; **it's getting late** se hace tarde
lawyer abogado(-a)
learn: to learn aprender
leave salir; **I leave** yo salgo; **to leave school** salir de la escuela
leg pierna *f.*
lesson lección *f.*
letter carta *f.*; **letter carrier** cartero(-a)
like: to like gustar; **I like the book** me gusta el libro; **do you like the photos?** ¿te gustan los fotos?
lion león *m.*
listen: to listen escuchar
little (in size) pequeño; **(in quantity)** poco
live: to live vivir
living room sala *f.*
long largo, -a; **he can ... no longer** no puede... más
look: to look at mirar; **to look**

after cuidar; **to look for** buscar
lot: a lot (of) mucho, -a; **lots of** muchos, -as
lottery lotería *f.*
love amor *m.*; **to love** amar

M

mailcarrier cartero(-a)
main principal
man hombre *m.*
many muchos, -as
March marzo *m.*
market mercado *m.*
marvelous estupendo, -a; maravilloso, -a
mashed potatoes el puré de papas
match partido *m.*
mathematics matemáticas *f. pl.*; **to do math** calcular
matter: it doesn't matter no importa
May mayo *m.*
meal comida *f.*
meat carne *f.*
mechanic mecánico(-a)
medal medalla *f.*
medicine medicina *f.*
member miembro *m. & f.*
menu menú *m.*
method método *m.*
Mexican mexicano(-a)
midnight medianoche *f.*
milk leche *f.*
minus menos
Miss señorita *f.*
mixed mixto, -a
modern moderno, -a
mom mamá *f.*
Monday lunes *m.*
money dinero *m.*
monkey mono *m.*
month mes *m.*
more más

morning mañana *f.*; **good morning** buenos días
mosquito mosquito *m.*
mother madre *f.*, mamá *f.*
mouth boca *f.*
movie película *f.*
movies cine *m.*; **to go to the movies** ir al cine
Mr. señor *m.*
Mrs. señora *f.*
music música *f.*
must deber
my mi(s)

N

name nombre *m.*; **what's your name?** ¿cómo te llamas? (*familiar*); ¿cómo se llama Ud.?; (*formal*) **my name is María** me llamo María; **what's his (her) name?** ¿cómo se llama él (ella)?; **his (her) name is ...** él (ella) se llama... ; **their names are ...** se llaman...
nationality nacionalidad *f.*
natural natural; **naturally** naturalmente
necessary necesario, -a
necktie corbata *f.*
need: to need necesitar
never nunca
new nuevo, -a
newspaper periódico *m.*
nice bueno, -a; (**person**) amable, simpático, -a
night noche *f.*; **good night** buenas noches
nine nueve
nineteen diecinueve
ninety noventa
no, not no
noisy ruidoso, -a
noon mediodía *m.*

nose nariz *f.*
notebook cuaderno *m.*
nothing nada
November noviembre *m.*
now ahora
number número *m.*; **telephone number** número de teléfono
nurse enfermero(-a)

O

o'clock: at one o'clock a la una; **at two o'clock (three o'clock,** etc.) a las dos (las tres, etc.)
October octubre *m.*
of de; **of course** claro; **of course not** claro que no
office oficina *f.*
old viejo, -a; **how old are you?** ¿cuántos años tiene Ud.?, ¿cuántos años tienes? **I am fifteen years old** (yo) tengo quince años
on en, sobre
one uno, -a
one hundred cien
only sólo, solamente
open: to open abrir; **the door is open** la puerta está abierta
or o
orange naranja *f.*; (*color*) anaranjado, -a; **orange juice** jugo de naranja *m.*
order orden *m.*
ordinary ordinario, -a
original original
other otro,-a, otros, -as
our nuestro, -a, nuestros, -as

P

pain dolor *m.*
pair par *m.*
pants pantalones *m. pl.*
paper papel *m.*

parents padres *m. pl.*
park parque *m.*
party fiesta *f.*
pass pasar
patient paciente *m. & f.*
paw pata *f.*
pen pluma *f.*
pencil lápiz *m.* (*pl.* lápices)
penny centavo *m.*
perfect perfecto, -a
person persona f.
personal personal
pet animal doméstico m.
pharmacy farmacia *f.*
photograph fotografía *f.*
piano piano *m.*
pig cerdo *m.*
place lugar *m.*
plastic plástico, -a
plate plato *m.*
play: to play jugar
please por favor
plus y
poem poema *m.*
police policía *f.*; **police officer** policía *m. & f.*
poor pobre
popular popular
portable portátil
post office correo *m.*
potato papa *f.*; **French fries** papas fritas; **mashed potatoes** el puré de papas
practice práctica *f.*; **to practice** practicar
prefer: to prefer preferir; **I prefer** yo prefiero
prepare: to prepare preparar; **prepared** preparado, -a
present regalo *m.*
president presidente(-enta)
pretty bonito, -a
price precio *m.*
princess princesa *f.*
principal (*school*) director(-ora)

prize premio *m.*
probably probablemente
problem problema *m.*
program programa *m.*

Q

quarter: a quarter past one la una y cuarto
question pregunta *f.*; **to ask a question** hacer una pregunta

R

radio radio *m. & f.*
rain lluvia *f.*; **to rain** llover; **it's raining, it rains** llueve
read: to read leer
receive: to receive recibir
record disco *m.*
red rojo, -a
repair: to repair arreglar
reporter reportero(-a)
resemble: to resemble parecer; **it resembles** parece
responsibility responsabilidad f.
restaurant restaurante f.
rice arroz *m.*
rich rico, -a
right derecho, -a; **to be right** tener razón
romantic romántico, -a
rose rosa *f.*; rosado, -a (*color*)
rule regla *f.*
ruler regla *f.*
run: to run correr

S

sad triste
salad ensalada *f.*
salesperson vendedor(-a)
sandwich sandwich *m.*
Saturday sábado *m.*
sausage salchicha *f.*

say: to say decir
school escuela *f.*; **in school** en la escuela; **school year** año escolar; **there's no school today** no hay clases hoy
science ciencia *f.*; **science fiction** ciencia ficción *f.*
season estación *f.*
seated sentado, -a
second segundo, -a
secretary secretario(-a)
section sección *f.*, parte *f.*
see: to see ver; **I'll be seeing you / see you later** hasta la vista, hasta luego; **see you tomorrow** hasta mañana
sell: to sell vender
September septiembre *m.*
serious serio, -a
seven siete
seventeen diecisiete
seventy setenta
several varios(-as)
she ella *f.*
shirt camisa *f.*
shoe zapato *m.*; **shoe store** zapatería *f.*
shy tímido, -a
sick enfermo, -a
sing: to sing cantar
sister hermana *f.*
six seis
sixteen dieciséis
sixty sesenta
ski: to ski esquiar
skinny flaco, -a
skirt falda *f.*
sleep: to sleep dormir; **sleepy: to be sleepy** tener sueño
small pequeño, -a
snow nieve *f.*; **it snows, it's snowing** nieva
snowball bola de nieve *f.*
snowman figura de nieve *f.*
so tan, así; **so so** así así, regular

soccer fútbol *m.*
sock calcetín *m.*, media *f.*
soda soda *f.*
sofa sofá *m.*
some unos, -as
something algo, alguna cosa
son hijo; **sons or son(s) and daughter(s)** los hijos
sorry: I'm sorry lo siento
soup sopa *f.*
Spaniard español(-a)
Spanish español(-ola)
speak: to speak hablar
special especial
splendid magnífico, -a
sport deporte *m.*
spring primavera *f.*
station estación *f.*
steak bistec *m.*
still todavía
stocking media *f.*
store tienda *f.*, almacén *m.* (*pl.* almacenes)
street calle *f.*
strict estricto, -a
strong fuerte
student alumno(-a)
study: to study estudiar
stupid estúpido, -a
suffer: to suffer sufrir
suit traje *m.*
summer verano *m.*
sun sol *m.*
Sunday domingo *m.*
sunny: it's sunny hace sol, hay sol
superior superior
supermarket supermercado *m.*
supper cena *f.*
sweater suéter *m.*

table mesa *f.*
take: to take tomar

talk: to talk hablar
taxi taxi *m.*
teacher profesor(-ora)
telephone teléfono *m.*; **telephone operator** telefonista *m. & f.*
television la televisión *f.*; **to watch television** mirar la televisión
tell: to tell decir
ten diez
tennis tenis *m.*
terrible terrible
terrific estupendo, -a
test examen *m.*
thanks, thank you gracias; **thanks very much** muchas gracias
the el, la, los, las
theater teatro *m.*
their su(s)
then entonces
there allí; **there is, there are** hay
they ellos(-as)
thin flaco, -a
thing cosa *f.*
think (of) pensar (en); **I think** yo pienso
thirsty: to be thirsty tener sed
third tercero, -a
thirteen trece
thirty treinta
this este(a)
three tres
throat garganta *f.*
through por
throw: to throw lanzar
Thursday jueves *m.*
ticket billete *m.*
tiger tigre *m.*
time vez *f.* (*pl.* veces); (*clocktime*) hora *f.*; **at what time?** ¿a qué hora?; **what time is it?** ¿qué hora es?
times (X) por
tired cansado, -a; **to be tired**

estar cansado
to: a; **in order to** para
today hoy
tomato tomate *m.*
tomorrow mañana
tongue lengua *f.*, lenguaje *m.*
town pueblo *m.*
train tren *m.*
transform: to transform
 transformar
transportation transporte *m.*
tree árbol *m.*
tropical tropical
true cierto; **it's true** es verdad,
 es cierto
truth verdad *f.*
Tuesday martes *m.*
twelve doce
twenty veinte
two dos

U

ugly feo, -a
understand: to understand
 comprender
until hasta
use: to use; usar; **used** usado, -a

V

vacation vacaciones *f. pl.*
vanilla vainilla *f.;* **vanilla ice
 cream** helado de vainilla
vegetable legumbre *f.;* vegetal *m.*
vegetarian vegetariano, -a
very muy; **the water is very
 warm** el agua está muy
 caliente; **I am very warm** (yo)

tengo much calor; **it's very
 warm today** hoy hace mucho
 calor
visit: to visit visitar
vocabulary vocabulario *m.*

W

walk: to walk ir a pie, andar;
 to take a walk pasear
want: to want desear, querer
warm caliente; **to be warm** estar
 caliente; **(to feel warm)** tener
 calor; **(warm weather)** hacer
 calor
watch: to watch mirar;
 (*timepiece*) reloj *m.*
water agua *f.* (el agua)
we nosotros(-as)
wear: to wear llevar
weather tiempo *m.;* **how's the
 weather?** ¿qué tiempo hace?;
 the weather is bad hace mal
 tiempo; **the weather is nice**
 hace buen tiempo
Wednesday miércoles *m.*
week semana *f.*
welcome: you are welcome
 de nada
well bien
what? ¿qué?; **at what time?** ¿a
 qué hora?; **what's your
 name?** ¿cómo te llamas?,
 ¿cómo se llama Ud.?
when cuando; **when?** ¿cuándo?
 where donde; **where?**
 ¿dónde?; **where to?** ¿adónde?;
 where are you going?
 ¿adónde vas?, ¿adónde va Ud.?

which ¿cuál(es)?
white blanco, -a
who que; **who?** ¿quién?, ¿quiénes?
why? ¿por qué?
win: to win ganar
wind viento *m.*
window ventana *f.*
windy: it is windy hace viento
winter invierno *m.*
wish: to wish desear, querer
with con; **with me** conmigo;
 with you contigo (*familiar*)
woman mujer *f.*
wonderful magnífico, -a
work trabajo *m.;* **to work**
 trabajar; **to work hard** trabajar
 mucho
world mundo *m.*
worry preocupar; **don't worry**
 no te preocupes
write: to write escribir
wrong mal, malo, -a; **to be
 wrong** no tener razón

Y

year año *m.*
yellow amarillo, -a
yes sí
you tú, usted (Ud.), ustedes
 (Uds.)
young joven (*pl.* jóvenes); **young
 lady** señorita *f.*
your tu(s), su(s)

Z

zoo (parque) zoológico *m.*

Grammatical Index

Topical Index